Encounters
WITH
Mermaids

"One of the world's foremost experts on the water element shares his profound knowledge and personal experiences pertaining to this mystical realm. Overflowing with vivid descriptions of undine evocations, insightful meditations for accessing the wisdom of water, and profound reflections on the watery depths of the human psyche, this book will provide readers with a new appreciation for this element as well as clear guidance for beginning their own journey of exploration. Written by an adept magician after decades of research, this is the definitive book on the spirituality of water.

VIRGIL, CHRISTIAN MAGICIAN AND AUTHOR OF
THE COVERT SIDE OF INITIATION AND
THE ELEMENTAL EQUILIBRIUM

"William Mistele excavates the deep mysteries of the sea and the treasures in ancient myths through brilliant use of poetry and prose. As a prominent bard of his time, Mistele makes the energy of magical beings accessible to the layperson, while providing deep insights into practical uses of elemental energy that all practitioners of magic will want to know."

ELYRRIA SWANN, AUTHOR OF
HOW TO BECOME A MERMAID

"A beautiful, lyrical work of great depth that inspires and teaches."

PHILIP CARR-GOMM, AUTHOR OF
THE GIFT OF THE NIGHT

"William Mistele defies conventional labels; you might call him an alchemist or even a Hermeticist, but his true essence is that of a 'modern-day bard.' Unlike traditional bards who weave tales of fantasy, Mistele, much like James Cameron, transports you into a world that is both fantastical and rooted in reality, enriched with science and history. With more than 30 years dedicated to honing his craft, Mistele is akin to an aquanaut exploring the depths of the water element. Few possess his unique ability to blend magic with bard-like storytelling. His work is a must-read for those seeking to understand the profound connections and wonders found within these invisible realms."

DANIEL O'HARA, AUTHOR OF
BUDDHA FIELDS FOR ADDICTIONS,
TANTRIC GOLF, AND *KRISHNA'S KINGDOM*

"William Mistele has unique insight to the world of elementals, having studied it seriously his whole life."

RICHARD GROSSINGER, AUTHOR OF
BOTTOMING OUT THE UNIVERSE

ENCOUNTERS
WITH
MERMAIDS

Lessons from the Realm
of the Water Elementals

A Sacred Planet Book

WILLIAM R. MISTELE

Destiny Books
Rochester, Vermont

Destiny Books
One Park Street
Rochester, Vermont 05767
www.DestinyBooks.com

Destiny Books is a division of Inner Traditions International

Sacred Planet Books are curated by Richard Grossinger, Inner Traditions editorial board member and cofounder and former publisher of North Atlantic Books. The Sacred Planet collection, published under the umbrella of the Inner Traditions family of imprints, includes works on the themes of consciousness, cosmology, alternative medicine, dreams, climate, permaculture, alchemy, shamanic studies, oracles, astrology, crystals, hyperobjects, locutions, and subtle bodies.

Originally published in 2010 by North Atlantic Books under the title *Undines: Lessons from the Realm of the Water Spirits*

Cataloging-in-Publication Data for this title is available from the Library of Congress

ISBN 978-1-64411-742-2 (print)
ISBN 978-1-64411-743-9 (ebook)

Printed and bound in the United States by Lake Book Manufacturing, LLC

10 9 8 7 6 5 4 3 2 1

Text design and layout by Kenleigh Manseau
This book was typeset in Garamond Premier Pro with Mason Sans OT, Mason Serif OT, and Krete used as display typefaces

To send correspondence to the author of this book, mail a first-class letter to the author c/o Inner Traditions • Bear & Company, One Park Street, Rochester, VT 05767, and we will forward the communication, or contact the author directly at **williammistele@yahoo.com**.

Contents

◎

PART III

Connecting to the Undine Realms

◎

◎

Acknowledgments

I would like to express my gratitude to the Czech magician Franz Bardon for the marvelous system of magical training that he presents in his first book, *Initiation into Hermetics*. Without Bardon's guidance, most of my interactions with nature spirits would have been haphazard and without clarity. The sylphs, undines, gnomes, and salamanders mentioned in this work are briefly introduced by Bardon in his second book, *The Practice of Magical Evocation*.

What I have found most enjoyable about Bardon's training system is its level of challenge. Bardon offers a path that is as precise and powerful for the inner world of imagination and spirit as are science and technology in the outer world of industry, research, and development. But the truth is that the outer and the inner worlds are not separate. We live equally within both, and the two are present in every decision we make.

I will leave it to the reader to determine in what light to view my stories. I will be happy if my dialogues with nature spirits provide entertainment, enjoyment, and delight. I have always loved creative writing that imbues the ordinary world with magic and wonder. This is in line with mythologist Joseph Campbell's thesis that the first task of any religion or mythology is to turn everyday life into a spiritual training ground by reminding us that life is awesome, wonderful, and mysterious.

On the other hand, it would be unfair if I fail to caution readers about the dangers of contacting nature spirits without first undertaking a serious training. In accordance with his goals of offering to mankind a complete introduction to the spiritual universe, Bardon has revealed the names and sigils of the most powerful nature spirits on our planet. These nature spirits are very ancient and possess great magical knowledge. It is my desire to share the beauty and the wonder of these beings who offer us so many gifts of wisdom and love.

Thanks also to Emilie Uyehara, a Wiccan priestess who channeled Istiphul for a poem and granted me a longer session, and to Ronda Voorhees, with whom I conducted interviews that were the basis for the story "A Modern Undine."

Preface to the Second Edition

When I first wrote this book, I had only met a few individuals who were willing to describe their interactions with nature spirits. In addition, it was extremely difficult to persuade people to share their experiences. On the other hand, several mermaid queens offered me the opportunity to meet women who had mermaid souls (incarnated mermaids). (See appendix A.)

To make sense of this suggestion from the mermaid realm, I carefully interviewed at least fifty women who appeared to be incarnated mermaids along with several men who were incarnated mermen. Consequently, I can add to this book a section on incarnated mermaids in appendix A, which also contains an essay called "Traits of Mermaid Women." These women present an entirely new personality profile never described before in world literature.

But you do not have to be psychic and read the aura of such individuals to discover who they are. You can quite simply ask people, "Can you tell me about your relationship to the ocean?" And they give answers such as, "When I am in the ocean, I feel I am in the arms of my mother," "I feel like I am home," "Once I am in the ocean, I never want to leave," or "I feel one with the ocean." But you do not need me to do this for you. You can ask individuals the above question for yourself.

Some of these incarnated women have their own internet blogs and teach classes. To say the least, this book on mermaids keeps on giving, producing new insights and areas of research. I have also added a short meditation on the water element that anyone can do. The exercise is straightforward, works with your body sensations, and yet you can practice it for a lifetime as you explore its various applications. This exercise is titled "A Simple Meditation on Water" and presented in chapter 3 after the section, "The Franz Bardon Training System."

Preface to the First Edition

The natural world abounds with elemental beings composed of water, air, earth, and fire. Undines are nature spirits composed of the water element. It has not been easy to describe the undines in this book. In thirty years of magical practice, I have met perhaps ten individuals who interact on some level with these beings. Not only are undines poorly represented in literature, religion, and folktales, but direct experience with them is quite rare as well.

If we turn to religion, it is only in a few instances that we find any discussion of nature spirits. Interaction with these beings, even in nature religions such as among Wiccans and Druids, often occurs only indirectly or at a distance. There are Sufi masters and Hindu yogis whose religions have historical references to these beings. But again you will be hard-pressed to find a Sufi master or a swami who can say, "Oh yes, last Tuesday I spent some time with a salamander as I was learning to control fire" or "A sylph instructed me on how to change the course of a hurricane."

As a result, I have turned to art. I present entertaining stories and dialogues rather than discussing rituals and employing esoteric diagrams and symbols. If I can entertain, then at least on this level I am communicating something. Life is magical. Our sense of awe and wonder constantly reminds us of the primacy of perception, the delight of mutually shared empathy, and the power of intuition. There are kingdoms that have yet to be explored within the depths of our feelings.

I suspect there remain a few problems on earth that can only be solved through magic or high levels of applied spiritual power. In my mind, such problems include replacing war with peace and limiting the use of weapons of mass destruction. It is these issues involving survival and establishing justice that motivate me. The undines offer gifts that contribute to these ends—developing a direct, heart-to-heart connection to anyone else on earth and taking one's deepest desires and transforming them in ways that are both satisfying and fulfilling.

PART I

Nature Spirits in Our World

1

THE FIVE ELEMENTS AND THEIR ELEMENTALS

This book focuses on undines. These are nature spirits that legend tells us dwell within the element of water. Following the Western tradition, there are a total of five elements—four of nature and one of spirit. I begin with the fifth element of akasha before moving on to water and the other elements.

AKASHIC ELEMENT

Akasha refers to the fifth element in nature alongside earth, air, fire, and water that supervises, enriches, and perfects life. It offers opportunities and maintains the other four elements. It also refers to a plane or level of consciousness, as in the physical, etheric, astral, mental, and spiritual or akashic planes. In both examples, it is formless and timeless; it is a state of awareness penetrating through space and time without restriction.

Although scientific questions may arise concerning the notion of an "ether," akasha as used in this book is primarily a physical sensation. You can approximate this sensation by imagining that your body is emitting a dark violet light that penetrates through space and time. And then imagine that you are this vast space. The idea is that with sufficient training, anything anywhere in time or space that you concentrate on can be perceived as being immediately in front of you.

Here is one way of working with this element. Imagine that the inside of your body is empty except for a dark, ultraviolet light. The sensation of this light, its vibration, is that it penetrates through space and time.

Next imagine that this light is being emitted from all the pores of your body and is filling a vast, empty void around you with its vibration. Then you become the light you are emitting in your awareness. Without referring to your body or a central point, you become the vast void penetrating through space and time.

The akashic plane is not dependent on form to sustain its power or existence. We can also speak of akasha as it operates in and through each of these denser, form-defined planes.

I discuss five planes in this book: the physical, relating to the body and the physical world; the etheric, relating to health and vitality; the astral, relating to the world of feelings, dreams, and inner visions; the mental, relating to the realm of thoughts and the processes of thinking, analyzing, and clarity of mind; and the akashic, relating to a timeless and spaceless state of awareness or corresponding to pure spirit.

Spiritual or divine ideals are often associated with the akashic plane or akashic body. In terms of the water element, we might encounter universal experiences or ideals such as cosmic or all-embracing love. On this level, we learn to feel one with all beings and also to develop an inner peace in which we feel one with the universe.

Akasha is represented in the physical body in the blood and reproductive system, such as in the sexual fluids. Akasha is an awareness that is able to penetrate into the physical being of the body—the bones, blood, and muscles. It is the operating system seen in the metabolism that regulates organic life. In nature, akasha is extremely intense and commanding in that it penetrates and exercises control over the physical being of earth, air, fire, and water.

Akasha in the etheric body maintains vitality, life-force, and health. On this level, akasha is nurturing and flowing like water;

it is balancing and circulating like air; it is metabolizing and heat-sustaining like fire; and it is solid and enduring like earth. It is all of these at once.

The astral refers to our emotional capacity to respond. The astral animates things. It has great sensitivity and empathic receptivity. The astral plane surrounds and penetrates the physical world. Sometimes referred to as the "other side" or the "world beyond," the astral plane pertains to the realm of the soul. As feeling and soul are to the body, the astral plane is to the material world. Undines, as well as many other conscious entities, exist on the astral plane. Sometimes we enter this realm in our dreams. Some individuals who are naturally sensitive or clairvoyant can perceive the astral plane directly. Akasha here is the ability to take a feeling and make it positive or negative, strong or weak. Akasha can even take one emotion and change it into its opposite or back again. Akasha has this power of command over dreams, desires, and feelings.

Akasha sees the desire and the outcome, the intention and the result of that intention. It is the ability to feel alive, to live life to its fullest in every moment of time. This ability is within us should we but seek it and claim it as our own. It is found at the edge of our five senses and in the feelings that flow through us in every moment.

The purpose of the mental body is to oversee a plan of action from conception to completion. Throughout the entire process it ensures that the focus is clear and that momentum and motivation are sustained. It focuses its attention on its priorities. It sees that the job gets done.

If you have a good conscience and akasha is active within you on the mental plane, you will notice when something is missing or when things do not feel right. And then you will add or invent something new to bring about balance and progress.

I have already discussed the four elements in terms of the akashic body. For water, you feel an inner connection to all beings. It is water on a divine level. You feel within and a part of others' lives from beginning to end.

With earth, you seek and perform work that enriches the world. Many already do this. With the divine intent of akasha, you seek to do work that will endure in value and enrich life through the ages.

With air, you learn to see, and you seek to know free of bias, ideology, selfishness, or personal interest. You see life with the clarity of a divine being that has attained transcendence and who celebrates the ability to act out of joy and freedom.

With fire, you gain access to unlimited energy, will, and power, which you are free to use to fulfill a purpose on earth.

What is the fifth element within one's body on this plane of existence? It ensures the balance of the four elements on the lower planes.

The future is imagination. You have to dream it if you wish to make it happen and experience it. Akasha reveals the deeper purposes of life. In a nutshell, akasha asks, what are your innermost dreams? What do you envision that would make life complete? Let us then put in place whatever is required so that what you seek can happen. The task of akasha is to make the world new.

In summary, akasha reveals the purpose you seek to fulfill. On the mental plane, one then asks, what is your plan of action for pursuing this purpose? On the astral plane, the question becomes, what kind of sensitivity or emotional involvement will you need in order to persevere in this endeavor and bring it to life? For the physical plane, the question is, what is the result you seek in specific and concrete terms, and how will you stabilize this so it endures and continues to be of value through time? Each element has its own contribution to this process. Akasha oversees and intervenes when necessary to ensure that everything keeps working.

THE WATER ELEMENT

In the physical body, it is possible to sense the fluids of the body in blood, tears, urine, and so on. In nature, we have the waters of the earth in their many expressions.

The etheric body is vitality, life-force, and the energy that is produced by the physical body, but it is subtler. It is what you use when you do some physical action. The etheric body is primarily sensed as physical sensations as opposed to astral feelings. If you imagine the inside of your physical body being filled with cool water, you may experience a sense of letting go, of flowing, of the body purifying itself. I often feel like I am floating in a tide pool totally relaxed and experiencing complete release from tension.

The astral body is the ability to feel, to be receptive and responsive. It is the ability to feel alive through being sensitive and emotionally connected, animated in and through our interactions with our surroundings and other people. It is dreamlike at times and sensitive to images and the specifics of the situations we enter. If you imagine the inside of your astral body empty and filled with cool water, you may experience feelings such as peace, serenity, contentment, well-being, and a sense of oneness with all things.

The mental body is the realm of ideas, concepts, analytic thinking, investigations, questions, and answers. It is also the clarity of mind that can take in or hold in its gaze many things at once without having to form an opinion. In the mental body, water produces a stillness of mind. The mind is mirrorlike, reflective, and receptive. There is a sense of being able to see through time. The undine Isaphil has this quality on a very powerful level.

The akashic body is timeless and spaceless. It has no need of form to express its consciousness. It is the realm of spirit that creates from nothing according to the purposes it ordains or that it finds within its heart or at the core of its being. On this level, water gives a sense of nourishing all life, of being within and a part of all living beings. The water inspires and seeks to lead all beings to perfection.

THE EARTH ELEMENT

The earth element is seen in the density and weight of the body. It is the muscles and the bones. We can easily sense these things. In nature, we have rocks, mountains, trees, minerals, and everything physical about the earth.

Again, sense the physical body empty inside and imagine it filled this time with dense weight. It is not so much a substance as it is with water. Instead it is a feeling of solid mass and gravity—that is, it is heavy. The result is that you feel rock solid. Your strength is not in acting in and on the external world. It is in your inner cohesion; your strength is the way you hold yourself together. You endure through time regardless of the changes in the world around you.

The earth element in the astral body produces the feelings of being stable, steadfast, and persevering. There is a sense of inner silence. This stability is being able to last until your goal is achieved. You are focused 100 percent on what you need to do as you build the foundation for your next move.

In the mental body, the earth element is being organized. You fit things together. You design and work at a project. If it is possible, you build so that what you make will outlast time.

The earth element in akasha takes the other three elements—air, fire, and water—and weaves and binds them together, uniting the best in each so that life is enriched. From the point of view of the earth element, if something is of value, then in some way it will manifest in physical form in order to show itself.

THE AIR ELEMENT

The air element is seen in the breath, in breathing, in feeling balanced as you walk and at ease as you talk. It is impossible to miss the sensation of air moving inside your chest as you breathe in and then let it go again.

In nature, we have the winds, the weather, the atmosphere, and the biosphere. Air is everywhere—in the sea and even in rocks and trees.

In the etheric body, the air element, the opposite of earth, is the sensation of being weightless. It is a sense of floating free of all gravity.

In the astral body, the element of air is playful and outrageously cheerful and joyous. Even if the air element is oversensitive, its sensitivity makes for great artistic achievement. In an instant it can pass into rapture—that is, it gets carried away with what it perceives or dreams.

In the mental body, the element of air is vast, open, and clear like the sky. It is detached and, like a mirror, it neither clings to nor flees the desirable or the fearful. It is this clarity that produces wisdom and understanding.

In the akashic body, the air element senses the vibration of the universe. It attunes itself to a great harmony embracing all things. It knows the deep purposes and meanings of life.

THE FIRE ELEMENT

Fire in the body is felt in the metabolism—food and air transformed into heat and energy. Think about hot flashes, adrenaline rushes, and breaking into a sweat—fire in the body as heat is quite evident. And then there is the sensation of power rising up and seizing control of the body, ready to perform feats of endurance and accomplishment. That is fire, instinctual and primordial, awakening and focused through our wills.

In nature, we have the sun above. We have captured the power of fire to work, shape, and transform matter. We still use stored energy from past geologic ages to power our cars. We are turning to solar energy but soon will have the nuclear fusion that runs the stars. But in a simple way, if you recall, wood and coal kept the house warm at night and cooked our food in our cabins on the frontier or in our city dwellings. Coal, oil, gas, and fission still produce the electricity that runs your laptop or the light over your head. Yet nature knows also the forest fire, the volcano, the hot springs, and the desert.

If you visualize the body as being empty inside, you can imagine it is then filled with the sensation of heat. This heat sensation leads to a feeling of pressure, of an expanding, even explosive force. It is power ready to be unleashed.

Dominant individuals, such people with an alpha personality, always have this vibration about them. Whether positive or negative, they communicate and transmit to others their abundance of etheric energy. Like a powerful electric wire, they keep what is around them aligned to their purposes and goals. This energy can produce a charismatic, inspiring, and dynamic leader. You will notice that all great leaders seem to carefully contain and control great power that they hold in reserve within them.

With this energy, you like to work. You like to do things that impact upon and change the world. It is the nature of fire—it likes to seize and control, if not transform, what is around it.

In the astral body, the fire element produces familiar emotions—courage, daring, boldness, and enthusiasm. Electricity causes a lightbulb to light up a room. Heat in the astral body causes feelings to become animated and bright so that they seek expression—the desire to feel fully alive. It is exciting, exhilarating, and invigorating. Fire in the astral body is passion.

Fire knows it is alive within the moment because it is totally ready to seize upon whatever opportunities are available to it to express, confirm, and expand itself. When completely positive, it expands its emotions out and through everyone around itself to make them feel fully alive as well.

In the mental body, fire produces a plan of action. Fire on this level likes to expand its will and power and considers how and what it must do to accomplish this. Fire as will immediately sets up boundaries to claim what it controls and to defend what it owns. It takes hold. It sustains itself by ensuring that its needs are satisfied. Fire on this level asks, what can we do right now to solve this problem? This is not so much an intellectual concept. It is willpower that is dynamic, effective, and commanding in such a way as to produce results.

You have to keep in mind the quality or nature of heat and fire. It is not possessive or controlling for its own sake, though we often meet people who do precisely those things. As an energy, fire comes from a more primordial place than does thinking. It asks, what do I need to do, to have, or to control so that the life that burns within me remains fully alive and bright? From the point of view of fire, if this question is not answered, then the greatest and the best things in life will never happen.

In the akashic body, the fire element is far more expansive than what we perhaps will ever encounter in our personal lives. It is a divine level of awareness. From this vantage point, the question is, what level of will and power must an individual have access to so that the deeper purposes of life may be fulfilled on earth.

Some prophets in the Old Testament had this energy, such as Elijah. Doubtless General Patton had this fire in his akashic body when he was leading his troops during the Battle of the Bulge in World War II. Perhaps General Eisenhower needed it during the invasion of Europe on D-day. George Washington was certainly being asked by akasha to embody this fire during the War of Independence.

On this level, fire is very expansive. It says, "This is what needs to be done, what I envision for the future. It shall be so because I possess the energy and will to make it happen."

In summary, if you have the power of fire, you are able to use it to make things happen. If you use it with the wisdom of air, what you do is harmonious. If you use it with the love of water, what you do is healing, nurturing, and inspiring to others. If you combine it with the solidity of earth, what you make endures. And if you use power in all these ways and add in the purposes of akasha, then what you make endures, inspires, heals, and transforms others through all ages of the world.

THE ELEMENTAL BEINGS: SYLPHS, GNOMES, AND SALAMANDERS

Fairy tales often involve characters such as elves, trolls, goblins, dwarves, dragons, and giants along with some form of magic. As such, the stories do not reflect reality as we know it. Instead, they are folktales and part of oral traditions belonging to specific locales and ethnic traditions. It would seem that children more easily than adults understand the enchantment these stories offer.

A fairy tale is usually classified as fiction. It may, however, involve legends or historical events. Generally a fairy tale takes place "once upon a time" rather than in reference to a particular historical date. To be sure, I make fun of this notion by giving specific times, dates, and real-world locations for my interactions with the undines.

On the other hand, some say that for a fairy tale to work, the author must treat it as if it is real. I do this also. I seek to gather into one place a record of anyone on earth who has experience with undines. I am after the evidence. All the same, it goes without saying that most people would consider my writings to be fiction and fantasy. So I also try to write in a way that is entertaining. Let us say that I treat "imaginary" beings as if they are real just to see what follows.

However, if we wish to modernize this literary genre so that it relates to our world, we might want to upgrade our fairies. After all, our scientists study the entire planet. Why not have fairies whose range of magical power interacts with the entire biosphere? Thus we might want a sylph who knows more than any meteorologist about weather and the atmosphere. We would want his opinion on global warming and the possible onset of an ice age. We might like to hear from a salamander who controls the eruption of super volcanoes. What would such a salamander tell us about the increasing number of earthquakes under Yellowstone National Park? How about a gnome who can heal any disease? Does he have anything to say about delaying the onset of aging?

We can treat fairies then, as intelligent beings who are masters of the energies underlying nature. In this way, we also upgrade our imagination. We keep our sense of wonder as well as our critical thinking in line with the political and moral choices we need to make concerning our survival as a race.

But from my point of view as a psychic with a clairsentient ability that has no historical precedent, I notice that many politicians and businesspeople already employ telepathy and magical empathy. Consciously or not, they use their abilities to further their careers and to retain power. For me, enchantment is as active in our world as it ever was in any prior time. Similarly, those who are psychic like me can easily perceive these elemental beings who exist just slightly outside the range of normal perception.

The four undine queens I describe in this book are among the most powerful undines on earth. In a similar manner, there are other nature spirits belonging to the elements of air, earth, and fire. The sylphs are composed of air, the gnomes of earth, and the salamanders of fire.

These beings who reside within the four elements embody states of awareness and capabilities that, though perhaps strange and mysterious to us, are nevertheless inherent in human nature. Here is a brief synopsis of the psychological and spiritual qualities of the four elemental beings.

The element of water is something very easy to relate to as a human being. In water are love and sharing—the experience of life giving birth to life and of flowing in and through another. In water is the absolute destruction of loneliness, separation, and isolation. For the undines, each moment is a magnetic sea containing the dreams and the taste of ecstasy—each moment arises from and resonates with the love sustaining all life on earth.

In the air element are found clarity of mind and the attainment of freedom. The air element is so vast and expansive, so encompassing, that those who are illuminated by its wisdom vanquish all confusion and overcome all attachment. The beings who reside in the sky, the sylphs, enter each moment seeking to attain and to abide in complete harmony.

In the earth element—through comprehending shape, weight, density, and the molecular vibration of minerals and elements—is the wisdom that banishes depression, sadness, and sorrow. The most powerful gnomes who dwell within the earth perceive time not only in terms of centuries and geologic ages. Their perception penetrates also into the processes through which matter is formed and through which it dissolves.

For gnomes, rocks and mountains do not possess solid and firm edges. Rather, their boundaries and shapes are fluid and liquid. For gnomes, anything in physical existence is constantly transforming—solidifying and dissolving again. In each moment matter and emptiness are flowing through each other like water being poured into water. And if you listen carefully with your heart, you can discover that each moment contains a wonderful silence and a stillness in which you can hear the stars singing. The elements of nature that we perceive as solid were born in the furnaces of stars and have passed through the emptiness of space.

In the fire element, by contrast, is an exuberant power. The beings who reside in fire, the salamanders, seize each moment with zeal in order to dissolve the obstacles blocking their path to fulfillment. Such fiery will destroys all fear and apprehension. For the salamanders, each moment presents the opportunity to purify, strengthen, and expand the power of will.

The salamanders exist within a realm of fire, and those uncomfortable with the sensations of intense heat or the imagery of vast lakes of flames may do well to avoid these beings. But power is a divine virtue even though religions often choose to avoid exploring it as a spiritual path. The salamanders are enchanted with the magic within fire to heal, to fuse, to refine, to integrate, to transform, and to electrify according to their individual inclinations.

Questions salamanders sometimes explore are, what is the one fire that burns without consuming and that integrates within itself all other kinds of fire? What is the highest light that exists, and what is the state of mind—the intensity of heat and will—from which it arises? What is the nature of sovereignty and absolute power—the ability to command that arises from being one with what it would control?

I am not going to recommend that people run out and begin evoking or meditating with elemental beings unless they are sufficiently prepared. When I write about elementals, I am always discussing human nature—what elementals are, all their powers and modes of perception, exist within us as latent abilities that we can develop. And the elemental beings, or the etheric and astral energies over which they preside, are the connecting link between the realm of mind and that of the physical world. To make our ideals real—to embody them in our lives—we do well to learn all we can from the elementals' way of perceiving and the energies that flow through their wills.

Traditionally, sylphs, undines, gnomes, and salamanders are composed of one element. The "little folk" or nature spirits referred to in folk traditions come in a vast variety of forms. The undines mentioned in this book represent the greatest masters of the magic of water. Rather than belonging to an earlier, naive age of the world, they guard spiritual realizations that the human race has not yet attained.

2

Undines

The word *mermaid* is from the Old English *mere* for sea and *mægden* for woman. The words *mermaid* and *undine* (from the Latin root *unda*, which means "wave") both refer to water spirits. In folklore, a mermaid might be encountered on a beach or by a sailor at sea. The word *undine* is used by individuals such as Paracelsus or Franz Bardon to refer to a mermaid that appears before them through evocation or through force of magic. Mermen are the male versions of undines.

Undines are part of oral traditions, historical literature, and mythology. They go by various names: water sprites, water spirits, water nymphs, nixies, naiads, ondines, and so on. Undines are sometimes considered to be half fish in their lower extremities and half woman in the upper; this image comes to mind especially when undines are called mermaids. In other legends, it is said that if an undine wishes to assume human form, she can enter the body of a woman at the moment of death. Restoring the body to health, the undine then lives out the rest of her days in the appearance of a human woman. In this case, she can marry a man. In some of these stories, if the man is unfaithful to her, they both die. At death, the undine returns to her own domain within the ocean.

The undines described in this book are not half fish and half woman. They are not attached to any well, lake, river, or ocean. No religion, race, or ethnic group has an affiliation with them. They do not belong to mythology or to the past. They do not need to be protected or sentimentalized. They are neither inferior nor fragile. They are not an endangered species.

They are in the form of beautiful women and are masters of the magic of water and magnetism. They embody and guard treasures of empathy, sensuality, and love that the human race has yet to discover. In this regard, they are our teachers.

THE WONDERS AND DANGERS OF FAIRY REALMS

Collectors of folktales such as W. B. Yeats in Ireland or the Brothers Grimm in Germany did not have to worry about any dangerous side effects for their readers. But they did have to worry about being accused of promoting superstition or of being enamored with occult mysticism. As a consequence, they went out of their way to remain academically detached. They presented their stories as carefully recorded collections of folktales and children's stories that were intended to enrich language, art, and literature.

Still, if someone recounts for us a story about a nature spirit, how are we to take it? Are they making it up? Perhaps they are dreaming it or, like some elderly people, confusing fact with fiction.

In his introduction to *Fairy and Folk Tales of Ireland,* W. B. Yeats says that in his collection of tales he has "tried to make it representative . . . of every kind of Irish folk-faith" while avoiding any kind of rational interpretation. Yeats goes on to quote a response Socrates made in the *Phaedrus* when asked about the tale in which "Boreas is said to have carried off Orithyia from the banks of the Ilissus. . . . I beseech you to tell me, Socrates, do you believe this tale?" In response, Socrates reviews the various legends relating to this story and the various interpretations of it. He points out that for those who believe this allegory, there is the further problem of having to continue on to ponder an entire array of similar monsters that are utterly inconceivable. Socrates then says, "Now, I have certainly not time for such inquiries. Shall I tell you why?

I must first know myself, as the Delphi inscription says; to be curious about that which is not my business, while I am still in ignorance of my own self, would be ridiculous. . . . I want to know not about this, but about myself."*

It is ironic for Yeats to make this reference. Yeats, like William Blake as well, was a registered and active member of a Druidic order. In quoting Socrates on fairies, Yeats is hiding the fact that he had performed rituals that attempted to interact with these beings. And as for Socrates, I think he was asking the wrong question. The only way to know the self is through encounters with others and with the world around us. For me, a better question is, what is it to be fully alive? Socrates never sat in the forest and became the rock, the tree, the stream, the wolf, and the deer in his mind. Enjoying his own eloquence and the delight of confounding others with his questions, Socrates did not explore the boundaries of sensory perception.

Humor me for a few moments and consider the possibility that undines lurk just outside of the normal range of human perception. If we gather all of our sensory experiences with lakes, rivers, and seas, we can begin to taste the awareness that undines possess. Water certainly embodies sensual release. Water invites us to let go, to flow, and to be enfolded by nurturing tenderness.

Did you ever float on a raft down the Little Colorado and feel as if time has begun to vanish? Ever float just at the edge of breaking waves and felt your feelings opening to the vastness of the sea? Ever float in a mountain pool and just let go into primal being as the first rays of dawn reach down into those watery depths? Have you ever experienced the clouds descending to the ground with drops of rain running down the bark of trees, poised on the tips of leaves, shivering, quivering, and then slipping into streams? In any one of these examples, you may have sensed a dreamlike serenity, a thrilling wildness, and a playful exuberance.

*Yeats, *Fairy and Folk Tales of Ireland,* introduction.

The gate to the realm of undines opens to us precisely at this point where sensual perception and feeling amplify each other. Nature grants us a chance to step outside of our social identities. Nature revives and renews us by taking us beyond ourselves into a timeless dimension where past, present, and future intermingle to reveal awe, wonder, and delight.

Moments of uninhibited sensuality and extended perception are a part of almost everyone's experience. But undines would take us further. Every undine in this book attempts to enchant through her heightened levels of empathy and magnetic attraction and through her mesmeric sensuality, all of which presents an entire spectrum of new ecstasies.

Why should this be a problem?

When going beyond the normal modes of perception, there is always a danger of disorientation. As in some of the stories I present, no matter how talented an individual is, a person can become obsessed and seemingly possessed—for example, experiencing exhilaration and ecstasy one moment and then depression and an acute sense of isolation after returning to everyday life in the next.

Consider that we are connecting to beings from an evolutionary path distinct from the sciences and wisdom traditions of human civilization. For example, elemental beings do not have human ethics. If you receive a gift for Christmas, you assume that the giver of the gift has your best interest and well-being in mind. But a gift from an elemental being may be a dangerous gift of pure power.

I was meditating one time with a partner who said an elemental being had given her an amulet to wear—something purely of a psychic nature and not material. She found that she started hallucinating at odd times during the day when she had it on. It turns out that the amulet empowered the woman to cross over to the Otherworld—to the astral plane, where the nature spirit exists.

Being pulled into the astral plane is an astonishing experience—especially if it happens when you are driving your car or shopping in a store! When you enter the astral plane of elemental beings, it is like entering a dream in the mind of a creature from a different evolution. There are no references to anything pertaining to your culture or civilization.

The elemental does not worry if his or her gift is going to present you with complications or side effects. The elemental's intent is solely to offer you an opportunity to experience its mode of existence. A gift of power is given out of respect. And no matter how beautiful or loving an undine may be, in their realm all interaction is based on power. Attraction and love are expressions of the magnetic properties of water, and with this magnetism they are grand masters.

Also, the elemental beings I describe are well acquainted with human beings. I am not the first person to talk to them. Some of the elementals in this book have formed extremely close ties with magicians. They have become companions and learned from each other. This has been beneficial for some individuals, but for others the connection to the fairy realm has been their undoing.

Some of the undines also claim to guard treasures of spirit and hidden destinies that world teachers have not yet revealed to mankind. Some elementals have incarnated as human beings. Even in the twentieth century, there are reports of this happening. This usually occurs because the elemental has temporarily taken a human lover.

When I talk with elementals, they may tell me about their relations with mages, poets, and sages from historical and forgotten civilizations. A bard is a poet who has trained extensively in meditation. In the Celtic tradition, a bard trains seven years in complete darkness. A bardic magician is someone who both creates poetry and performs magic. I consider myself a bardic magician. When it comes to cultural myths and legends, it is sometimes difficult to trace the sources of the stories handed down through the generations. It may be that a poet or bard cannot help but embellish and add entirely new chapters to ancient sagas in order to convey a message to his or her own time. It is probably wise, then, to take with a grain of salt the stories elementals tell. The astral plane is perhaps even more prone to exaggeration and to the excesses of imagination than is our own world.

Keep in mind that elemental beings are invisible except to clairvoyants. They do not eat food or drink water as do we; the energy sustaining them is altogether different. And they are not subject to human morality—they existed for millions of years before human religions began. When these elemental beings think, they do not use the lexical items in our dictionaries—neither the sounds nor the units of meaning they use relate to Indo-European or any other human language. When a "thought" is placed into your mind by an elemental, it is your experience that becomes the vehicle for translating that thought into something familiar that you understand. If you rush to label your sensory perceptions or take for granted your connection to elementals, you lose the depth and the beauty of what is being shared.

And though the life-span of elementals is a matter of speculation, it is fair to say that many live for countless ages and some have been around for millions of years. So when you enter the domain of elemental beings, you have to create your own reference points. Science, history, culture, and the works of mankind—these beings do not need any of this in order to flourish or to practice their arts.

A relationship with another person often takes a lot of work. Working with elemental beings also takes effort, patience, and contemplation if you are going to get anything out of it. As in any kind of relationship, there are times when you have to put aside your expectations if you are going to hear what is being said or make the most of the opportunities that arise.

Once you form a connection, an undine can show up unexpectedly, obtrusively, and without being called. These are the queens and the masters of their element. Unless you possess a mastery of the water element equal to their own, they can follow their own rules. The rituals and authority in human spiritual traditions are no more than a curiosity and minor hurdle for them to leap over.

They do not speak in human language. Instead, their communication is body to body, feelings to feelings, and mental imagery to mental imagery. This is intimate and at times absolutely overpowering.

Some of your experiences with these beings will be outside of anything described in literature by any mystic, poet, or philosopher. The undines act according to principles of psychology that the human race will not discover for hundreds of years.

Through extended interaction you can begin to see as they see, feel as they feel, and engage the natural world from their perspective. But your new perceptions are, nonetheless, outside the normal operating range of other human beings. It takes a huge effort to make sense of what you experience, and it is even more difficult to share your experiences with others.

And unless you immediately write down what you experience with an undine, everything that happened may vanish from your mind within a few minutes. Why? You have 200,000 years of neurological programming that makes you a human being. Undines have millions of years of uniting with nature. Joining these two perspectives and ways of being may not be as easy as it seems.

All the same, in reading through this book, a reader might ask, what is the point of this? What is the purpose?

What is not taught in our civilization is the essence of the feminine—the accepting grace, the healing power, and the all-embracing love within magnetic and attractive energy. The magnetic fluid, the essence of the feminine, is so receptive, so giving, so empty, so free of ego and of identifying with any form that it is able to contain within itself the soul of any being so as to shelter, transform, inspire, and make something completely new of it. This feminine power has no limitations or restrictions placed upon it.

This energy that exists within nature and that undines have mastered can be reproduced within us. This energy is cool, contracting, soothing, and attractive. It is nurturing and supportive. It shelters and protects. Instead of being intense, commanding, and explosive as is the masculine, it is rhythmic and gentle. In psychological terms, it is empathic, sensitive, and responsive. It draws together, bonds, joins, and unites. It accepts and affirms. In spiritual terms, it reaches toward an all-encompassing, all-embracing love.

If our society had the undines' knowledge, our empathy would be vastly expanded. Inner kingdoms of feeling would be revealed. Our receptivity and sensitivity to impressions and our intuitive abilities would be exponentially increased. In practical terms, this would mean we would have the ability to understand why others feel as they do—anyone anywhere on earth. We would be able to perceive and also to interact with their souls directly from within. Love, then, would not just be a moral imperative or a theological ideal. It would not just be an attraction that makes you feel good or bonds you with another. Love would be the power to hold and to contain anyone else's life, soul, or will within our hearts so as to heal, bring to completion, and transform from within.

We all know about weapons of war. Love, however, creates peace. It is greater than the desire to control, to dominate, or to destroy. It is more powerful. This is because the empathy I describe is more accurate, precise, and penetrating with awareness than is any form of knowledge we currently possess.

If you can understand others from within, then you can understand what motivates them, what drives them, what instincts are active, and every aspect of the power they hold in their hands. No general, dictator, warlord, politician, intelligence organization, corporation, or military industrial complex would be safe if it wished to abuse its power.

In the final analysis, it is love that takes responsibility for the world. It is love that is qualified to oversee the unfolding of history. It is love that has the power and authority to establish justice. It is love that sees the future. And it is love that offers us our greatest chance to be fully alive and to discover the best that life holds.

As I state in the dialogues, beings such as the queens of the undines have been created and imbued with wisdom and beauty commensurate with the destiny the human race is meant to achieve. Their knowledge awaits our discovery. They are an opportunity waiting to be seized.

As one undine queen said to me, "All that I am in my being you have the power to create in yourself as well." Whether we choose to learn from their love or not, it is our destiny as a race to embody their abilities within us. I have journeyed into the realm of the undines in order to share their treasures with the world.

ORDINARY AND MAGICAL EMPATHY

There are many definitions of empathy. Throughout this book, I have considered empathy as the ability to feel what others feel. This does not mean you are in the same emotional state or frame of mind as the other person. However, at a minimum it means you can sense what the other is going through by imagining how you would react in the same circumstances.

The television talk show host Larry King often used questions that established empathy with his listeners. He would begin with a statement of fact and then follow with a question. For example, "You mentioned that this is a new job assignment for you in a field in which you have no previous experience. I am guessing that you had moments of doubt about your abilities the first few months?"

And then, even though the other person was on TV with millions of people watching, the guest would say something like, "No one has ever asked me about this. Yes. It was a terrible struggle until the second year." Larry just got someone he never met before to disclose something personal that they had never shared with anyone else. Empathy, even as a linguistic tool, is very powerful.

MAGICALLY INDUCED EMPATHY

We can simulate to some extent an aspect of undine empathy by adding imagination to several listening skills. Let us begin with active listening. In active listening, we do two things. We paraphrase the content—the ideas—of what a person has said. And separately we describe the feeling with which the other person expresses what is said.

People are often unaware of their own emotions as they talk. They may not realize they are angry or sad, enthusiastic or worried. By asking or describing what they are feeling, we give other people a chance to clarify for themselves what they feel.

Active listening is a form of feedback. You do not have to be accurate, only close. People look in the mirror. They may be surprised with how good they look or how bad. But until they look, they do not have that feedback. You are giving another a chance to look at himself more closely and make up his own mind about how he feels.

Part of active listening involves noticing incongruities—the difference between what a person is saying and the feelings expressed though body language (facial expression, gestures, intonation, and even word choice). Incongruity is one way in which words and feelings may not be in sync.

An individual says, "It did not bother me," but his face darkens, his eyes turn hard, his voice changes pitch, and his muscles tighten. That is an incongruity between what is said and what appears in the body. In a case like this, you can simply point out the changes in body language.

Another example, "As you talked about her, you started speaking slower and with a quieter voice than how you were talking before. Your feelings seemed to take more time to process." Or, "You say you love him, but you also mentioned some terrible things he did to you. But I did not see you express any anger. Are those feelings there too?"

I explained to one woman briefly a scale of physical reactions and also emotions relating to anger. I asked, "On a scale of one to ten, how angry were you at him?" It seemed that in her body language and word choices she was expressing anger at around a five when the events suggested it might have been much stronger. She said that on a scale of one to ten her anger was a twelve. Her response to my question gave us both a clearer picture.

For a magical level of empathy, we might use active listening for ten or fifteen minutes with a person. We listen. The other talks. Now we add to this a basic technique sometimes used in psychology. You imagine you are the other person. You imagine you are inside of the other's body. You imagine that you use their body language and voice.

You think the other's thoughts, possess the other's memories, and feel the other's feelings.

You continue exploring the other person's self-image until you notice a specific, concrete, and physical sensation in your body that arises in response to imagining you are the other person. When you get this sensation of being the other person, focus on it. Allow it to tell you something new. What is it like for you? Is there an image or symbol that you could use to express it? Does it tell you something about what the other person is like or about the inner flow of the other's life?

Getting physical sensations in this manner gives a direct body-to-body and heart-to-heart connection to the other person. For a brief period or longer you are now connected to this person in a way that no one else in the world is. You have an inner connection that is more fundamental than conversation or social interactions. If you try this, you might be able to notice an almost instant change in the body language of both yourself and the other person. There is greater rapport. People usually think that this level of rapport should happen naturally, and they rarely bother to make it happen.

Again, undines automatically produce these physical sensations indicating an inner connection. When we practice magical empathy, we are striving to sense the connection, but undines go much further. They add feelings of bliss and ecstasy to a degree that we rarely experience in life. For undines, water itself conveys these enchantments.

An undine's magnetic aura passes through anyone near to her or through anyone she focuses on. The magnetic fields of force in her aura automatically sense the other's deepest desires and dreams. They also sense the ways in which the other person might be fulfilled.

In this sense, an undine's empathy goes beyond feeling another person's feelings or even feeling compassion. It is a way of foreseeing the future. Or, more accurately, undines see the way an individual might become whole and complete. To feel what is at the core of another person's being is also to have a vision of what he or she can become. This is not precisely a prophetic function. The future depends on the individual's and others' choices. The undine may not see when something will happen as much as what will inevitably happen.

At the same time, empathy for an undine does not stop with insight or knowledge. It takes the individual into that vision and grants a taste—a powerful emotional affirmation that one's deepest dreams can be fulfilled. The undine takes you directly into the dream as if the dream is real right now.

We do not often experience this in our daily lives, so it might be a little hard to imagine. However, we sometimes notice something similar occurring in the moment of falling in love. I have mentioned this before. A lover will say, "I never felt fully alive until I met you. I can't imagine living my life without you. My life was blurred and confused until I met you; now everything is clear."

In other words, love makes people feel alive. Lovers, however, are usually focused one on one. Romantic love involves bonding with one other person. For an undine, love is not possessive in this way. Love is a property of water. The ecstasy and bliss that water contains are not derived from a connection to one person. It is in the rivers, the lakes, and the seas. This love encompasses the planet. Undines do not have an ego the way we do.

Though we might find it difficult to sense another person's deepest desires and dreams, we are already familiar with the idea of blessing another person. In some churches, the service ends with a blessing as in "May the blessing of God be upon you; may his peace abide with you; may his presence illuminate your lives now and forever more."

Now then, take the idea of a blessing and customize it for a specific individual. Visualize someone right now so you see the other in front of you. Now imagine this individual feeling whole and complete. Whatever is missing is now present. Desires are satisfied, purposes accomplished, and dreams fulfilled. It is a feeling, a thought, and a picture. You can put all three together as you imagine blessing the other person in this way. And it is the act of *daring*—you accept the person as he or she is, and you also dream what the person can be. For undines, to dare in this way is a property of water. It is the way of nature.

You could say the queens of the undines, as masters of water, automatically bless anyone they meet. It is a function of the magnetism in their auras. They empower others to feel alive and to fulfill their dreams.

But note that you have to be careful with empathy. Empathy seems like it is responding rather than acting. If you feel what another feels, then this implies you are passively sensing the other person. If we consider empathy as being more closely aligned with the feminine, with nurturing, then we might then think that femininity is weak. It would seem that masculinity, by contrast, takes charge and changes things.

This would be a great mistake.

Empathy can control just as easily as it can receive. It can recreate in itself what another feels, and it can implant new feelings in another person. This is perfectly clear in my dialogues with undines. Simply communicating with them is to experience wonder and profound states of love. It is not for nothing that even traditional literature refers to their abilities to enchant and cast spells.

Our own psychologists notice something similar. If you establish a subliminal bond with another person and then change your feelings, the other person tends to change also without even knowing that this is happening. In doing active listening, then, you do not want to be overly sympathetic or signal to the other that you have a strong reaction to what the other person has experienced. You do not want to define others' feelings for them by indicating that your feelings are already perfectly clear about what has happened.

Salesmen are constantly employing empathic techniques. They act like your best friend to establish trust so they can sell you something. They employ all sorts of nonverbal cues to accomplish this.

I met a real empath not long ago. She turned her immense powers of psychic sensitivity on me. It was in her tone of voice, her eyes, and her face. She conveyed in an instant that she understood who I was and what I was seeking to accomplish. I could tell that she sensed what was in me, but she did not really care. The water principle senses that the same life is flowing in and through all of us. And yet, though some people are highly sensitive in perceiving the life within others, they seek to strengthen themselves at the expense of others.

3
THE FRANZ BARDON APPROACH

COSMIC LANGUAGE

This language is composed of twenty-seven "letters" in the Hermetic tradition of Franz Bardon. Individually and in combination, these letters constitute words of power. They represent the building blocks from which matter, energy, life, time, and space are constructed. The Hebrew Kabbalah is a historically based but limited version of the cosmic language. Other religions and masters throughout history have also had access to the cosmic language.

The cosmic language represents the powers and qualities by which angels and deities engage in the act of creation. As such, the cosmic language predates the birth of mankind on earth. It is not and has never been the exclusive possession of any group of individuals.

In this book, I employ two-letter combinations that constitute words of power. The E-M and E-J formulas are specifically useful for connecting to undines because they embody the very ideals and ecstasies that undines cherish. For one presentation of the cosmic language, see *The Key to the True Kabbalah* by Franz Bardon.

The sounds spoken in the cosmic language have absolutely no meaning in themselves. Rather, specific sounds are combined with a color and a physical sensation through concentration. To be effective, the cosmic language must be understood intellectually and then empowered by imbuing it with energy created out of the magician's will and imagination.

THE FUNDAMENTAL ENERGIES

The fundamental energies are electric fluid and magnetic fluid.

Electric Fluid

The electric fluid is the essence of the masculine spirit. It is similar to but not as material as actual electricity in nature. In brief, the electric fluid is hot, burning, expansive, dynamic, intense, powerful, and explosive in sensation. It has the capacity to produce great light. In psychological terms, it is commanding, full of faith and conviction. It reaches for sovereign power in search of absolute control. It annihilates and destroys obstacles that stand in its way. In more spiritual terms, it seeks to manifest its vision using all the previous qualities—with certainty, with dynamic will and expansive power, and with implacable dedication and electrifying conviction.

We could say that independence, strength, courage, conviction, faith, will, determination, dedication, self-reliance, self-mastery, uprightness, clarity, order, adaptability, practicality, planning, productivity, excitement, exhilaration, creativity, and vision are qualities that are present when the electrical fluid is operating successfully.

There have been a lot of complaints about the abuses of masculine energy in our world. Indeed, the electric fluid can be very destructive. It can be a burning and consuming power that acts to dominate the wills of others. It tortures and torments, hazes and subjugates. It absorbs others' wills into itself. It utilizes every means possible to corrupt, divide, undermine, and enslave others to its purposes. In this negative version of the electrical fluid, the light is there, but it lacks purity and clarity; the vision is distorted and twisted. The faith and conviction are there, but they are often expressed in a degraded form such as through arrogance and self-righteousness.

But in either the positive or negative forms, the electric fluid is willing to put itself at complete risk to accomplish its mission and manifest its vision. In its most positive form, the electric fluid embodies the will of a creator, who stands amid a void and creates from nothing according to the vision found within their heart. And then the creator puts forth the energy required and oversees the process until the vision manifests on earth.

Magnetic Fluid

The magnetic fluid is the essence of the feminine spirit. Analogous to magnetism in nature, it is cool, cold, and contracting. It is attractive, soothing, and calming. It is receptive in that it is utterly empty of form and completely open—able to receive and contain anything in itself and preserve, nurture, and animate it with life.

In psychological terms, it is empathic, sensitive, and responsive. It draws together, bonds, joins, and unites. It accepts and affirms. In spiritual terms, it reaches toward an all-encompassing, all-embracing love. We could say that peace, repose, calmness, happiness, contentment, serenity, tranquility, well-being, delight, kindness, gentleness, affection, empathy, tenderness, sensuality, pleasure, bliss, ecstasy, compassion, and love are qualities that are present when the magnetic fluid is operating successfully.

What are the negative aspects of the magnetic fluid, of the feminine spirit in its dark aspects? In brief, the negative aspect of the magnetic fluid is that it absorbs and contains without releasing or giving birth. It shelters without enabling growth. Instead of healing, it poisons. Instead of nurturing, it denies. The negative paralyzes, seduces, wastes, and numbs consciousness. It induces insanity—that is, it destroys consciousness with guilt, shame, fear, terror, illusions, delusions, obsessions, fascinations, depressions, nightmares, and false visions.

In the I Ching, the Great Yin, mother, or magnetic fluid offers an individual continuous support that nurtures and serves to integrate the inner self of the individual throughout his or her entire course in life. The negative magnetic fluid, by contrast, acts to undermine, dissolve, and reabsorb into itself the inner life of the individual throughout his or her entire life.

But whether positive or negative, whether life-giving or life-destroying, the magnetic fluid is the guardian that reveals the deepest feelings and mysteries within the depths of the self.

As I have mentioned many times, in the past our world may not have been ready to endure the beauty of the undines and still develop rationality and science. I have not encountered anything negative in my experience with the undines described in this book. But beauty itself can be terrifying, and love can demand more than we can imagine. It is wise to be prepared when encountering the mysteries of beauty and love that the undine queens possess. Their very presence is magic beyond the knowledge of mankind.

USING A MEDIUM

In his books, Franz Bardon makes references to people using mediums for various purposes. In the Bible, King Saul has the witch of Endor channel the departed prophet Samuel. The deceased prophet appears and answers the king's questions, accurately predicting the king's future.

There are various interpretations of this story depending on the assumptions made by the authors. Though I mention this example, the channeling I discuss here relates to living spirits and not those who are deceased. (It is interesting to note that using a medium is forbidden in the Bible, but all biblical prophets were mediums channeling Yahweh.)

Some of the difficulties involving channeling also apply to telepathy: the nature spirit does not use any human language to think. It existed before religions appeared on earth. It is not bound by human ethics or morality. It dwells in a realm of pure power even if the expression of that power is love and empathy. And it perceives and acts outside of the symbols, rituals, and activities of human civilization.

Basically, to channel is to find a midpoint or areas of experience shared in common between the nature spirit and the human being. When I do telepathy, the spirit and I have the same vibration in each of our minds. I sense through that vibration how the spirit thinks and perceives, and the spirit uses my experiences and my understanding of life to express its wisdom and insight.

The test of channeling or telepathy is the extent to which it generates new insight and understanding. The goal is to experience something a little further beyond the familiar boundaries in which you feel or perceive. If you go too far beyond the familiar, you may end up with something that has no application and no meaning in our world.

I like to write poems based on my meditations with spirits because the poetic imagery helps me capture perceptions that are far outside of my daily life. As mentioned, I consider myself a bardic magician—one who both creates poetry and performs magic. But in a sense, we are all mediums. As the undine suggests, part of our brain or being is water. If we just focus in and through that aspect of ourselves, we see the world and can dream it in a completely new way. The voice of the undine is our own voice when we feel and dream through the element of water that is in us.

BEYOND THE PHYSICAL BODY

It can be helpful to describe human nature in terms of physical/etheric, astral, and mental bodies. We all know what it is to be healthy. We not only get through the day. We accept challenges and engage in various activities such as exercise, martial arts, hard work, and sports; through training, the athlete learns to focus on the physical body. They work to increase the amount of available energy so that they can perform at their highest level.

In a similar way, we can develop what we can call our astral body. We can fine-tune our emotions so that we shape them and even create the feelings and moods we choose. And of course, with our minds we can detach, step back, analyze, and review our actions, thoughts, and plans. What follows is a brief description of how our physical/etheric, astral, and mental bodies operate.

Etheric Body: The etheric body is similar in shape to the physical body. The metabolic and biochemical activities of the physical body produce a subtle field of energy that relates directly to health and vitality. Systems such as acupuncture or practices such as pranayama focus primarily on the etheric body. They seek to balance and increase the quantity and quality of the life-force or vitality in the physical body. In the examples of pranayama and acupuncture, they do this by adding imagination to breath or interacting with points in the body where the etheric and physical are closely aligned.

Astral Body: The astral body is in the shape of the physical body but is made of a subtler substance. The astral body pertains to the realm of the soul, to feelings and emotions. It is receptive, responsive, and impressionable. It gives a sense of being connected to and appreciative of others. It is this sensitivity to the present moment, our immediate environment, and our sensory perceptions that enables us to feel fully alive.

Mental body: The mental body is in the form of the physical body but is more refined or subtler than the astral body. It relates to ideas, thinking, and analyzing. Unlike the astral body, with its sensitivity and response to concrete images and situations, the mental body works with abstractions. We size up situations and solve problems with our minds. The mental body is rooted in concentration and attention. We choose when and how we focus our attention. Forming plans, setting priorities, and determining time frames and means for fulfilling our purposes are mental-plane activities.

THE FRANZ BARDON TRAINING SYSTEM

The following summarizes the principles and exercises of Franz Bardon's training system as presented in his books *Initiation into Hermetics, The Practice of Magical Evocation,* and *The Key to the True Kabbalah.*

Make your mind empty of thoughts so it is reflective like a mirror, receptive like the ocean, empty like a void, open like the sky, intense like air the moment before lightning strikes, serene like moonlight, fragile and responsive to suggestion like a dream, and solid and enduring like a mountain.

Within this empty mind free of thoughts and disturbances, focus your attention on something—a problem, your life path, an elemental being, or a spirit—or imagine what you wish to become or to accomplish.

Add to this a little technique. Techniques are endless in variety. You can visualize a picture, a sigil,* or an image or symbol of a god or goddess. You can meditate on a prayer or a chant. You can use incense, music, or a tone. You can do a path working or mental wandering, construct a magic circle or perform a ritual, gaze upon a crystal ball, speak a word of power, or some other activity. Techniques, methods, and procedures are employed to sense and to amplify impressions.

Finally, through direct experience and careful analysis, you interpret your impressions. You translate them into words and call it telepathy, into visual images and call it clairvoyance, into sensations and feelings and call it clairsentience, into all three while connecting to a spirit and call it an evocation, into new information and call it knowl-

---

*A sigil is a magical diagram. If drawn in a magical manner (i.e., using great concentration), it places an individual in direct contact with the spirit associated with the sigil. Another way of putting it is that a sigil is like a spiritual phone number—it puts you in contact with a spirit through telepathy or by using a high level of empathy. In this book, a sigil, or magical diagram, is occasionally used, but it is visualized rather than inscribed on something material, such as a silver plate. The sigils of the spirits mentioned in this book are found in Franz Bardon's book *The Practice of Magical Evocation.*

edge, into a spiritual realization and call it wisdom, into light and freedom and call it enlightenment, and so on. Impressions received from outside yourself can also be internalized so you embody their qualities and energy.

This same procedure can also be expressed in a more active manner typical of magic. All methods and techniques for changing oneself or the world boil down to a simple formula: you concentrate on what is desired as if it is real right now in this moment. You add an appropriate kind of energy to your picture, feeling, or thought so it has some power independent of your mind and can move with enthusiasm toward its objective on any or all planes. And you also take into consideration and comprehend every force, situation, resistance, and obstacle that blocks your vision from becoming reality. This last element ensures that your course of action is forged from wisdom and results in harmony.

For example, in chapter 3 of Bardon's *Initiation into Hermetics,* you practice imagining the elements of fire, water, air, or earth around yourself as if you are immersed within a boundless sphere of a single element. What is it, for example, to imagine you have within and around yourself a vast expanse of the earth element? This is the same as learning to think, feel, and perceive as a gnome.

Your mind attunes to that one element and learns to amplify, condense, and transform it. After a similar training with water, it is not so difficult to form connections and interact in a creative manner with undines. If you spent time concentrating on water in nature—lakes, rivers, and seas—you would be undergoing the training of an undine magician. And so it is with fire, earth, and air.

You can also use colors instead of the elements. If you imagine yourself within a boundless expanse of emerald-green light, then you are learning to think, feel, and perceive as a spirit of Libra or Taurus in the earthzone or a spirit from the sphere of Venus. The colors, then, can be used for probing the qualities, powers, and consciousness of the beings within the spheres regardless of whether you make connections to them or not.

In the end, when you can concentrate effectively, your thoughts increase in their power. They gain an autonomous influence similar to electricity or magnetism in nature. Everything else is attracted to and becomes aligned with them. The four planes cooperate with them. It is like akasha—obstacles dissolve in their presence. Something completely new and without precedent is introduced into the world, yet it feels so natural it seems like it was always meant to be.

In summary, Bardon asks his students to concentrate on their five senses to an extent not known in our world; he asks for a psychological balance that is beyond the practices of modern psychology; and he asks for a level of health and vitality stronger than what is possessed by the great martial artists on earth. Put these three together, and you have an authentic magical practice.

What exists in the external world can be understood as energy and experience that one can also master individually. What exists within oneself can be amplified and intensified until it changes the external world. Self-transformation, self-mastery, self-empowerment, and integration—aligning oneself with the forces, the laws, and the harmony of the universe—are at the heart of the process from beginning to end.

● A Simple Meditation on Water ●

Recall that blood is slightly less than 80 percent water. Focus on your feet. Imagine that water instead of blood is flowing through them. Some people will be able to feel the actual sensation, but it is sufficient to imagine flowing water moving through your feet. Flowing water is cool, yielding, receptive, purifying, adaptable, receiving energy into itself, storing it, and then releasing it.

Along with the physical sensations of flowing water, there are also feelings that arise in the practice. Water is relaxing, soothing, nurturing, healing, and renewing. It is calming, serene, and refreshing. It enables us to feel fully alive.

We begin, then, focusing on the sensations of water flowing through our feet. We then extend this flowing sensation through the lower legs and gradually upward through the rest of our body. Or you can begin with the feet and then imagine water flowing through your entire body.

Later on, you may feel a connection between the flowing water in your body and images of water in nature such as a mountain waterfall, a stream, a river, a lake, an ocean bay, and the sea. In addition, you can use your imagination to drop the temperature of water so it moves from feeling cool to very cold. Colder water heightens receptivity and healing capacity due to being able to absorb more heat quicker. And, as the meditation develops, you may notice you can heal things like headaches and dissolve tension in yourself as well as in other people.

In the beginning, then, there is nothing mystical about this exercise. The meditation takes place in your body and these are your own physical sensations. However, depending on your temperament and experience, you may prefer to work with other elements such as air or earth prior to working with water. For more on the elements, see my book *The Four Elements*. And for descriptions of the other elemental beings, see my book *Mermaids, Sylphs, Gnomes, and Salamanders*.

ALTERNATIVE TYPES OF PERCEPTION

Through training or natural ability, some individuals possess enhanced levels of perception. There is physical touch. There is also clairsentience where you can "touch" the auras or subtle, nonmaterial vibrations of people, plants, animals, or spirits, or you can perceive the history of physical objects.

Similarly, we see the physical world. We can also learn to see spiritual worlds, the past, or future, or pure energy fields. This is clairvoyance. We can hear sounds and words. We can also "hear" and communicate thoughts directly mind to mind. This is telepathy. What follows are more detailed explanations.

Telepathy: Telepathy extends the sense of hearing so as to perceive thoughts and impressions from sources that are not detectable as auditory signals. Some individuals actually hear frequencies of sounds that are outside of normal perception. A blind person may demonstrate that they can locate objects by the way echoes are reflected through the space around them. Another person can detect the low-resonance frequencies preceding an earthquake. This "hearing" is not telepathy but rather a very high level of acoustic sensitivity.

Telepathy simply picks up the activity occurring in the mind of another person or spirit. Since the two minds are different, what is transmitted through telepathy will always depend on the state of maturity and experience of those involved. From the point of view of this book, in the instant you think of something, your brain has already established an electronic connection to it. Telepathy is simply a matter of learning to make these very faint impressions conscious.

Clair-feeling or clairsentience: This is the ability to extend the sense of touch or feeling beyond what is physically present. This includes feeling what others feel as well as sensing the auras or the energies that compose the life in any being, whether in physical or spiritual form.

With clairsentience, it is often the case that a specific part of an individual's body is unusually sensitive. The neck, hands, chest, stomach, or thighs, for example, have extrasensory perceptions. People say the hair on their neck stands up when someone behind them is staring at them. Or another person may get a twinge in the stomach when something does not feel right. An individual may feel heat on their face upon entering a room that has a strange feeling.

There are a number of ways in which I am clairsentient. I can feel energy with my mind, my eyes, and my body on the outside or inside. I am unusually sensitive with my hands. I can feel the energy, vibrations, or auras of any person or of any spiritual being. There is no limitation on my ability other than having to figure out the meaning of what I am sensing. When attempting to explain the descriptions I give of nature spirits, particularly as to whether they are fanciful or fabricated, you might consider that the specific clairsentience I possess has never existed before in history.

Clairvoyance: This is the ability to use the sense of sight to perceive things of a nonmaterial nature. This may include auras, spirits, things not physically present, and also the past and future.

PART II

Meetings with Undines

4

DIALOGUES WITH ISTIPHUL

There was an ancient king known as Solomon who sat on an ivory throne. He was known throughout the world for his immense wealth and profound wisdom. And Solomon had 700 wives and 300 concubines.

But Solomon's thousand women were not as beautiful and did not bear such treasures of spirit from distant realms as those with whom I meditate. You may decide for yourself who has been more inspired by the opposite gender and who greets with greater welcome the mystery of love—the king when he wrote the Song of Solomon or I when I dialogue with the queen of the undines.

Have you heard this tale or even one song of Istiphul, queen of the undines? No? Then let us begin! Istiphul is perhaps the most beautiful creature on this planet. If it were possible, her beauty would rival what sages and poets describe as the goddess Dawn from Hindu mythology— the first feminine form born of Creation. Istiphul is that spirit of the sea whose touch more than bliss bestows and whose eyes know secrets no sailor on earth will ever discover by sailing the seven seas.

In the past, bards neither sang of Istiphul nor mentioned her name aloud—mankind was deemed too weak to endure such beauty. But my voice is not bound by the laws governing former bards. And where they would have kept Istiphul for themselves, I am more generous: I speak aloud and offer my songs to the entire world.

How did I happen to meet such a creature of wonder, so hidden and unknown? Whenever I gaze at the sea, I feel her presence. Her fragrance is in the wind; her voice is in the sound of the breaking waves. Her touch is in the spray and drops of water running down my skin.

To speak with her, to call her forth, is just a matter of opening your senses to the presence of the sea and following your feelings back to their source. But this is not to say that such an encounter is without risk. When I first spoke with Istiphul decades ago, I entered that place of soul some of us know well but cannot define—in quiet moments an uninvited feeling may accost us, an indescribable sadness fall upon us. This sadness is perhaps an echo, a reverberation from feeling separated, but we do not know precisely from what. And the instant I saw Istiphul, I said to myself—

I will never meet a woman who is this beautiful.

This thought was like a lightning bolt hurled through an empty void within my soul, a void her face had just revealed. It spoke of an unnamed loss—a tension with no release.

And though many others would have fled, thinking this knowledge too forbidden to behold, I stayed and faced it. Emptiness gripped my soul, and I tasted every bit of the sorrow that lingers in us from being so distant from nature.

But looking back two decades later, I think I was wrong about the beauty of women compared to the pure enchantment concealed within nature—for one of life's greatest secrets is that she is full of surprises. And though I have kept Istiphul's existence secret for many years, I am now free to sing of her beauty so that mankind might be informed of the power of love hidden within the depths of the sea.

Ah, Istiphul! She is the essence of feminine companionship. When I first touched her aura with my hand, I realized I had just met a woman who could and would willingly create out of her inner being and femininity the perfect counterpart to all of my desires. She even perceives unknown needs I have not yet discovered within myself. My dreams, what I have sought, what I have lost—she comes weaving a spell of love that harmonizes all that I am. The deepest place within me that I cannot find—she lives there already, shining with beauty that radiates and flows freely throughout my soul.

But Istiphul is not a fantasy. And it is not that she molds her identity to fit my imagination. She does not behave like many mortal women who out of insecurity create something fake to please their mate, surrendering their own will and life in the bargain, as collateral. Rather, she is a master of what magicians* call the magnetic fluid: the feminine counterpart to the electric, masculine energy in the universe. Together, these two elements are a part of every creative act, whether it be conception, the moment of inspiration in art, or the birth of the universe. When the magnetic and electric fluids are acting together, Fate (the laws of the universe) comes forth to bargain and accept them as payment for the changes we wish to make in reality—so great is their value and their influence.

With magical empathy, Istiphul senses my whole being and uses her beauty to make me feel complete. She creates a space of love where two souls may find each other and unite as one. Her great gift and mastery are nothing other than the knowledge that all those on earth who have found true love practice and celebrate.

A SECRET LONGING OF THE KINGS OF THE EARTH

Istiphul is the one whom the kings of the world have longed to have as their consort. But their bards, wise men, sages, priests, Druids, and

---

*As opposed to a stage magician, a magician or mage in the context of this book seeks self-transformation to bring body, soul, mind, and spirit into alignment with the laws of the universe. In this endeavor, they strive to develop to an equal extent their will, intellect, feelings, and consciousness. In some traditions, a magician might choose to utilize various ritual implements to aid their concentration. These include pentagrams, hexagrams, sigils, talismans, magic mirrors, magic circles, robes, magic belts, a wand, incense, and lanterns.

Brahmans, at least those who knew of her, would not disclose her name or reveal her existence—due to selfishness, yes, but there is more. They were strangely silent as if something they could not even bring into their consciousness bound them, forbidding even one song to be written or spoken lest human evolution take a different turn from what has been ordained or veer from a course that moves within acceptable boundaries.

And so it has been that some bards have had a distinct advantage in living their lives with an unknown zest, a passion and abandon kings do not possess. But sensing that this happiness is a real possibility, the kings of old made it against the law to interfere with the work of bards; they were waiting to hear songs such as this that it might lighten their woes and replace the darkness in their souls with songs of mirth and rapture blended.

I tell you that if Helen of Troy had been as beautiful as Istiphul, it would not have been just the Greeks and Trojans but the entire world at war over the right to kiss her lips. And Lancelot, our knight in shining armor, would have overcome his obsession with Guinevere, though not many knights would have been left to quest for the Holy Grail if they had known the name Istiphul. And forget not that Merlin, too, met his match in Niniane, who made a fool of him and trapped him under a rock. Yet Niniane was but a mortal woman and could not compare to Istiphul.

Henry VIII would not have embraced Protestant Christianity; nor would he have pursued so many wives seeking an heir if there had been a John Dee to show the king Istiphul in his magic mirror. No, the king would have lost his interest in posterity with distractions this ripe. For that matter, if Gauguin or Michelangelo had met Istiphul, their faces would have turned white, their hands shaking, and their heartbeats arrhythmic. But their eyes would not have strayed for an instant. They would have stood for two days without pausing until they had captured her face on their canvases.

Even Hegel and Marx would have had second thoughts. They would have added a new twist to the march of the dialectic. They would have insisted that there is a place where both the Geist that unfolds history and the human soul must go in order to be rejuvenated. Kierkegaard, too, would have renounced despair and angst had Istiphul's touch traced lightning through his bones. His "fear and trembling" would have had an entirely different meaning—on this I speak from experience! In fact, if William Blake had seen Istiphul as more than a blur in the distance, his visions would have rivaled those of the prophet Isaiah and the apostle John.

The sages whose songs originated the Vedas and Upanishads did not know of Istiphul—barely an echo of her is heard anywhere in the world's mythologies. For if they had known her, the poets of India would not have been so fanciful in populating the celestial realms with such a glittering array of deities. No! They would have been more empirical and stuck closer to nature as they fashioned images—their mystical dreams would have been more concrete and filled with the sounds of waves, wind, rain, and the seas.

And that other child of India, the Buddha—his gentle, enigmatic, and transcendental smile would have been kinder, its compassion more convincing, had the artists of India sculpted statues of Istiphul from marble and ivory. The Tibetans say that the Buddha already knew of Istiphul. The Buddha once changed his form into that of Kalachakra at the request of King Suchandra, who was from Shambhala. At that time, the Buddha included Istiphul as one of the 720 entities within the mandala of planetary liberation, though she is known there by another name, and her beauty is not seen as clearly as it is within my poetry.

My exploration of the four elements on earth would not be complete if I did not speak of Istiphul. And though until now no bard was free to speak her name aloud and reveal her beauty to the world, neither seal nor secret may bind or limit my voice—you see, my patron, Divine Providence, has so ordered it.

A FEW HISTORICAL TALES TO
SCARE OFF THE FAINT OF HEART

It is like this: often the songs of gods and goddesses arise from our dreams and the lips of priests, poets, and mystics. But this is not the case with Istiphul. She is not a goddess, but an intelligence dwelling within nature, and she existed before the human race was born. In fact, many magicians have met their fates at the hands of her beauty and charms.

Poor Donovan

Take, for example, poor Donovan, who possessed second sight and could spy into the mysteries of fairy realms. He was a little too adventurous for his own good with those eyes of his. He once walked the shores of Ireland, not far from Dublin. Donovan knew well the charms and the cold call of the sea, for his father was a fisherman, though, oddly enough, some say he had noble blood in his veins.

At night Donovan could hear the songs in the stars, and they shone even brighter for him than they did for van Gogh. He could see the inner essence of whatever he gazed upon. The ocean waves and their spray continuously called for him to dance and play in a place of pure delight.

Though Donovan had no formal magical training, he did not need to use a familiar or a conjured spirit to gain a woman. He could hold the image of a maiden's face in his mind's eye for five hours. As he concentrated, the maiden would walk fifteen miles to his house to spend the night with him even if she was a virgin—such was his telepathic power of suggestion and the nature of his erotic imagination.

One night Donovan dreamed of Istiphul, who dwells under the sea. He saw her dancing naked, and from that moment it was more than wonder and curiosity that motivated him. He wanted to know her charms. He wanted to taste her beauty, though his conscience informed him that he could neither stare her down, nor bind her with his voice, nor hold her with his mind's might.

One day, agitated and unable to bear the torment of his desires any longer, Donovan sent his mind into the sea. The power of his intuition was such that he could already feel Istiphul's touch. And so he was not surprised when an emerald path of light lit up as he wandered in search of Istiphul beneath the waves.

Donovan went directly to Istiphul's palace. She greeted him at the gate and invited him in. For as "the sea refuses no river," Istiphul refuses none who wish to know the mysteries of love. Her charms, like the beauty of nature, are for all to taste. Her embrace is for all to receive—her magic is like sunlight, moonlight, starlight, dawn, and twilight. Who would conspire to bind or confine beauty such as this? Who would blind our eyes and deny such wondrous gifts because they do not fall within the boundaries of human morality?

What general has ever refused to stock their arsenal with a weapon because it gave them an unfair advantage over the enemy? What scientist has ever refused to probe a secret of nature because some things are best left unknown? What poet has ever said, "These poems I write should be locked away, perhaps burnt someday, because they are too beautiful to behold"?

I do not think Donovan's infatuation was unnatural or his quest excessive. Instead, I would say this: Donovan did not adequately prepare himself. He did not honor the mystery he sought to embrace. He did not create a sacred space where he and the undine queen could meet on equal terms. He did not hold in his heart that wisdom every true magician knows—when to guard the boundaries of the world and when to dissolve them for the sake of love.

This is what happened: Istiphul's touch and embrace were so compelling, so mind-altering, that poor Donovan forgot there was a Donovan left without a mind back on the shore not far from Dublin. To wit, Donovan forgot to return to his body.

So strong can be the power of desire that breath, heartbeat, and the hunger of the flesh are not enough to stay the quest for gratification. This was such an example. Young Donovan's body fell into a coma. Without a soul, the body did not last very long, only a day or so. It soon grew cold, and the heart forgot how to beat—there was no sign that Donovan's soul would ever return.

So let us say for the sake of argument, if you wish for an explanation, that Donovan's soul was out of its element. When the season of desire had passed, his soul sought again the shore of life and found another body in which to be born. This was a boy child who, when he grew to be a man, found work far from the sea.

A desert would not be dry enough for his liking! He did not wish to hear any reminder of that terrible, heart-wrenching longing and soul-shattering call of the ocean. Hidden in waves and even in the taste of salt was that specter of beauty with which the sea called, "Come, Donovan, I will be your lover again; come far from land and be with me under the sea—ride your dreams to me, young Donovan."

However, it was not Istiphul who called but only his own memory and unfortunate obsession. The man was haunted by the choice of another too faint to recall, who unwisely sought to have intercourse with an unfathomable beauty, a beauty wisely hidden in the mysterious depths of the sea.

Ahmed the Wizard

There are a great many tales I could tell about Istiphul. But the ones relayed here pertain directly to issues that must be addressed if I am to reveal Istiphul to the world. Consider this story about Ahmed the Wizard.

Ahmed, with the power of Merlin, could summon Istiphul and keep her with him. But Ahmed did not realize that when it comes to the intricacies of magic and the heart, the issues are seldom those of the subtle nuances of servitude and domination, of mastery over nature, or of Mars over Eros. When dealing with Istiphul, the issues are altogether different.

Ahmed was a giant man. He had a thick neck and dark eyes with an uncanny, penetrating gaze. He had a lion's roar for a laugh. And though Ahmed was jovial most of the time, when he was not, he sometimes had a fiendish look on his face. An insatiable hunger was devouring him from inside.

But what was his hunger for? For knowledge? For mysterious ways to gain power? For some dark mystery hidden beyond the stars? Who could ever really say for sure? After all, as everyone knew back in that age, magicians and wizards are of mixed blood. Their bloodlines include those of dragons or salamanders, devils or angels, creatures known or unknown, or celestial beings galore.

Of course, I am not arguing for the existence of angels or demons. I wish only to point out that at times we experience hungers and desires that are stronger than we are and that defy our attempts to understand them. But there are always a few individuals who will hold nothing back in seeking to master what is hidden within them.

I speak of wizards and bards. And this is because they usually make it a vocation to pursue the mystery and beauty of life. They will stop at nothing. They will risk sorrow, loss, and regret in order to fulfill their quests. They may be wise or foolish, possessed of high ideals or corrupt. But they know better than to rely on secondhand information or hearsay evidence when it comes to experiencing life. It is not that they violate morality or disregard science or reason. It is that they seek to be complete in ways unknown to society.

As for Ahmed? His approach was systematic and experimental. His will was implacable as he sought to comprehend the energies underlying nature. Though, like any scientist, Ahmed preferred empirical observation, in a pinch he would use magic to supplement his methods.

And so, one day Ahmed gazed upon his crystal ball in search of the mystery of water. With his clairvoyant vision, he beheld the *vast, magnetic field of energy—the sea—that cloaks this planet in unfathomable beauty. Then he spoke aloud a few words of power, as was his custom. He drew a sigil or two in the air. He burnt a little incense. He set a jewel in the sunlight in front of a mirror. He waved his hand over a silver bowl filled with seawater. And then he spoke to his crystal with a quiet voice that resonated throughout the room.*

This is what he said:

"Show me the sea and the spirit that dwells within it. Show me her essence, pure and clear. Show me that creature so hidden that mortals are forbidden to speak of her. Bring her for me to see, to feel, to smell, to taste, to touch. Materialize her presence so she is real! Transport her here and now. I will have nothing less than her caress to ease the pain within my soul!"

You may begin to understand Ahmed from those words. He was a bold adventurer. He had a good sense of command, an iron will, massive power, and of course, a hunger like a raging dragon.

With the intensity of air the instant before lightning strikes, Ahmed prepared to bind another to his will. Few spirits could resist— even I must admit that Ahmed had the rare and powerful profile of a wizard belonging to a small and elite social class. Obviously, Ahmed was more focused than poor Donovan and thus was probably not likely to lose his body due to infatuation.

Within moments after he called Istiphul, Ahmed's crystal filled with a cold, softly burning light. Within that light Istiphul appeared. This was neither an image nor a reflection. It was a direct link—an unmistakable presence.

Ahmed's first thought was, what is this? A garden in the wilderness? An oasis within the eye of a desert? A well of living water? I see a light that shines even amid the greatest darkness of the soul! A light that can pierce Vishnu's knot in an instant!

And there he sat, entranced, neither blinking nor moving, his breathing undetectable. Ahmed dared not lose even for a moment what he held in his gaze. He traced every thread of the connection, memorizing it, analyzing it, devouring the pathway that linked his mind to Istiphul, who dwells in the sea.

But to Istiphul, Ahmed was a soul haunted by emptiness. A woman might be offended if a man tries to reveal all her secrets and discover the very feelings that arise from the core of her being. She might consider such an attempt by a man to be overly aggressive and invasive.

But this does not offend Istiphul.

With a single note of music, she can beckon the flowing essence of the entire sea—in all its languid and tranquil receptivity and nourishing presence—to caress her shoulders, to shine from her breasts, or to shimmer in the soft curves of her hips. So when it comes to spells of enchantment or to wagering sheer willpower against the distilled essence of beauty, we might do well to place our bets on Istiphul. When it comes to magical, ocean-styled erotic arts and sensory bliss, Istiphul's skill has no equal on earth.

Istiphul saw that Ahmed viewed himself as a giant cavern beneath the earth—a dark, unknown place. As Ahmed explored these depths, he found that reason and wisdom alone were unable to light his path or explain the powers he found within himself. But Istiphul was not uneasy or put off by the discovery that the mystery within another has no boundaries or is beyond the power of the mind to define. For Istiphul, Ahmed simply had a need like any other—to find a place of peace, a restful place where bliss is unleashed by a caress.

And since Ahmed's mind was not capable of swallowing the ocean whole, at least not on his own, Istiphul offered her knowledge and the release hidden in the sea—a place of enfolding depths, a place to drift and to float free. Here he could wander in safety. Here is a peace that flows like a stream from the dawn of time to the ends of eternity.

She offered Ahmed a path of beauty, a wilderness belonging to the heart; the sea yields and surrenders itself even as it embraces a thousand beaches and even more islands. Without being less of a man, Ahmed discovered he could relax, let go of his knowledge and quests, and flow with whatever sensation or feeling the moment was revealing. And so on countless nights, with far more skill than Donovan could ever imagine, Ahmed left his body to walk with Istiphul on all the seas' beaches. He learned to see through Istiphul's eyes the night, the sky, and the sand. He listened and learned the ways of the waves as they blessed the shore, curling over each other and caressing one another.

As wizards are wont to do, Ahmed could also fill his tower room with the element of water, so much so that the air flowed blue green and felt thick, wet, and salty. There, Istiphul appeared before him and held him tenderly. She caressed him with waves of magnetic energy. She spoke to him softly of mysteries and wonders that have not yet entered even the dreams of mankind.

And so it was that within this enormous man, who had a fiendish hunger like a giant cavern without end, lay a tranquil sea. At the end of his desire, standing amid the sea, was this beautiful creature. Istiphul already knew far more than Ahmed himself about the roots of his desires; she knew his quest, loneliness, pain, sorrow, tension, and his path of fulfillment.

Istiphul learned from Ahmed as well. When a woman's intimacy with a man is genuine, it is not difficult for her to learn his secrets or to absorb the internal forces that drive him. For example, Istiphul learned how to focus her powers of attraction so that even a wizard's will would dissolve. She was no longer content to lapse during spare moments into pure sensuality—to feel at the core of her being the foam sailing free from a thousand waves and the songs of release they were singing.

No, Istiphul learned to focus herself so she could match Ahmed's level of concentration. To be his counterpart and his equal, she needed to contain the fire burning within him. To this end, she learned how to gather all of her experience, knowledge, and magic and distill it into one feeling. She could then transfer this feeling to Ahmed as a gift.

Imagine what this would be like: imagine taking all the sensations, feelings, and moods that the seas create; imagine binding that beauty and wild passion into one light, one dream, or one vision of completion and then being able to transmit this to another through your eyes, the touch of your skin, or a kiss.

Yet being the object of an undine's love has its downside. Ahmed let slip his systematic quest for knowledge. His scientific methodology and his magical will were both compromised. Ahmed found mysteries enough in being with his mistress. The rest of the world seemed gray by comparison next to the light shining from Istiphul's face. Even that city where he dwelt, Isfahan, that city of splendor and unmatched beauty, grew pale and uninteresting. When Istiphul sang to him he forgot where he was.

A king may lay claim to the treasures and resources of a realm. Other than the occasional need for entertainment or diversion, he will occupy his time with securing his borders and administering his kingdom. Similarly, Ahmed occupied himself with Istiphul.

What happened then was this, rather than being the leviathan of a mental giant with a great will searching the universe, Ahmed's will weakened. It became enough to enter the sea with his mind and to float, dream, and drift with Istiphul by his side, her body's magnetic field caressing and illuminating his heart and soothing every nerve and fiber of his being.

Incidentally, someone like Freud might say that Ahmed regressed back to the state of an infant being rocked in his mother's arms. In truth, Ahmed did have a rather horrid childhood, what with wars, chaos, and slaughter—among other things—as he grew up.

However, back in the city Ahmed was said to have lost his fiendish look as well as his joviality. He became absent-minded. Yet he had a powerful and healing magnetic touch—if you only could find him. Ahmed could heal almost any disease. And many noticed that his eyes radiated the sensation of a great depth, though at the same time a small but cold and burning light shone within them.

One might ask at this point whether or not this was truly a tragic tale. Istiphul only did what she does so well: she embodied the magnetic essence of water, which she offers to any who would drink from her well. It is not for her to counsel or guide those who seek her out.

Technically speaking, by the stringent regulations governing a lineage of great magicians, Ahmed lost his destiny. It had been set aside for him to become wise in all things, as a gentile prophet. Ahmed's task had been to present the wisdom that would guide nations, illuminate minds, and bring justice and harmony to mankind. Perhaps even the Crusades might have been abandoned had Ahmed been on the scene to negotiate a fair and equitable settlement in regard to Jerusalem. But his obsession with the sweet peace of the sea led him to lose the gift he was destined to receive.

Destiny and desire often strive with each other in a wild dance of ambition and surrender. How many sages and magicians have yet to learn that ecstasy is neither the reward nor the path, but a wondrous treasure hidden in every moment and in every breath?

So, need I summarize these two stories of Donovan and Ahmed? Is there a moral? Are these tales going to scare off the faint of heart? Let me answer this way.

It has been said that every man, in his soul, knows perfect love, but he must go on a quest to find it. A few have returned having given all to this search. They tell us that such love demands more than heart or mind can imagine. And yet they also say that if you can even dream of love such as this, your life will be blessed because the light in your heart will never go out. Or, as Solomon might have said, the wisdom required to fulfill this quest does not come cheap.

PRELUDE: THE BARDIC VOICE

We all have our own way of pursuing our dreams, embodying our ideals, or of using faith to connect to something greater than ourselves. And every sage or mage has their own personal repertoire of techniques or traditional rituals to draw upon when needed.

I use the cosmic language, or what I call the bardic voice. I will give a few details for those who are curious. But I will avoid mentioning much more since discussions of method are secondary in this book. Describing the beauty of the elemental beings is my primary objective.

Sitting here on a rock as water flows around me, I blow on a small panpipe, playing a soft, hollow tune that echoes over the water. I then hum the note of D. I concentrate on a mental level where thoughts are born and images are transmitted from mind to mind. With this note I envision a world where the inner essence of each being circulates with all others as the wind we breathe and as water that rises from the seas and eventually falls as rain, finding its way into our blood and into our tears.

There is a color I also visualize—that of dark ultraviolet. The color oscillation in this instance resembles a stillness, heightening our sensitivity so we can hear another's thoughts or feel their heart's desires within our own heart. I concentrate also on a sensation of penetration, of being everywhere and nowhere all at once, in a place of perfect peace. In such a space there is nothing we can ever lose. This is a place where the heart is so open it can embrace another without desiring anything in return to balance the relationship.

Again I hold the panpipe to my lips and blow another D note. This one, however, is a gentle sound that imitates the ocean's own breath, flow, and being. I sing within the astral plane—and in this sound is the sea in its depths, the sea in its currents, and the sea in waves crashing down on bare shores. The color of this sound is blue green, the very essence out of which all oceans on all worlds throughout the universe were created.

I also concentrate on the cold water element. That is, I envision an immense field of magnetic energy. This fluid is the inner essence of the feminine mystery—in truth, there are places in nature where men may not go without an invitation. And though bardic magicians respect such boundaries, our voice and breath speak on behalf of the realm of spirit that has no gender limitations.

And so with these sounds I create a place not to trap but to call Istiphul so sweetly that, to put it simply, at this moment there is nowhere else she would rather be than here within this magic space that I have just now sung into being.

ENCOUNTERS WITH ISTIPHUL

February 1, 1995, at 10:30 a.m.

I sit amid the boulders in the stream that flows from Sacred Falls on Oahu, Hawaii. At first, Istiphul appears dimly. But as I focus my mind, she takes on a clear form. She walks through the water and comes right to my side.

With Istiphul near, I become acutely aware of tiny currents criss-crossing at the edges of the mirrorlike water as it begins to fold around a rock. The water dips and turns around my ankle; the stream's bubbling ripples are like the hands of a dancer telling a story as they turn in countless swirls and curves.

I hear many streams across the islands as if they are suddenly near.

They breathe and sigh, caressed by air, hiding in sand, seeping beneath rocks, falling in space, and circling in mountain pools. Drifting downstream to the sea, these waters laugh like young girls carrying baskets of fresh fruit to a celebration. Istiphul sits beside me on the same rock, her bare feet dangling in the stream.

I say to her, "Tell me of the mysteries of love and your own secret desires. Show me, too, the mysteries of my self." Istiphul touches my left forearm with her right hand, and it feels as if she is touching every nerve in my body. Every aspect of my self is drawn together by her touch. The sensation in her fingers pulses through me with an invitation to let go as strong as the brash, swift grasp of a riptide or an undertow.

With Istiphul, I feel something I have never felt with any woman. She is here next to me with every fiber of her being. She feels everything I feel and senses every thought and perception. She knows where my eyes fall in the distance—she is both a sensual and a spiritual being.

Everything I am is within her heart. There is no intrusion of thoughts, words, or ideas to confuse our connection.

I reflect again on her touch. What does it mean to feel that another is completely one with me, sharing all I feel and perceive? Her touch annihilates loneliness. Like Caesar, she commands an empire, but hers is of the heart.

It may be that an undine such as Istiphul can easily shift an individual's feelings back and forth between bliss and despair. Perhaps her song is much more potent than any siren singing to a sailor of some irresistible desire. After all, she is master of all the feelings the soul of the ocean can conjure by dream, vision, or sensual release.

When Odysseus was at sea, he was reported to have had some difficulty with Circe and Calypso. The beguiling enchantments of feminine beauty threatened to put an end to his quest. Yet I have an advantage over Odysseus: I am trained in magical empathy. I speak words of power so ancient their wisdom predates the birth of life on earth. It is as natural and easy for me to see through the undine's eyes and attune myself to her spirit as it is for a musician to search for the right notes on the strings of her guitar.

I shift my awareness so I can see as Istiphul sees me—I look back at myself from hypnotic green eyes that are older than whales, older than ice ages come and gone. I look back at myself through eyes as luminous and inviting as the light of Venus shining in the night sky. This is what I see of myself through her sight: a man caught in loneliness, like a whirlpool in the sea. I see her absorbing my needs by the power of her love. She offers to make me whole, to heal me.

I watch as she draws primal forces as powerful as ocean tides and waves into her desire to heal. My skin feels cooler. The tension in my muscles dissolves. The day wears late, so I stop for the evening. I will meet her again tomorrow.

February 2, 1995, at 6:30 a.m.

I sit at Sandy Beach, on Oahu. The ocean is calm, the tide out. I call again for Istiphul in the same way. Istiphul walks toward me across the gentle, rolling waves—it is an unusually calm morning. She sits beside me, and I feel the touch of her hand. Again, there is a marvelous connection. Being in her presence is like entering a world of pure sensation and bliss. It is encountering the dream of peace concealed in the depths of the sea.

She and I sit, meditating on the ocean together as we look out toward Molokai and Maui. I reflect that men need not be separate from nature. We should be able to join with nature as I am joined with Istiphul. The ocean before us is a realm of nurturing life, of wonder and delight. When the heart is open like this, there is no insecurity, and the identity has no boundaries that must be defended.

☙ A Meditation on the Sea ☙

Follow Istiphul and me as we join our minds. We are sitting on the sand with our feet in the water. Imagine the sea, blue-green waves stretching from the shores of one continent to another. Look at the waves in front of you. Watch as they spread out to the horizon, and envision the vast expanse beyond as they circle the earth. Consider the winds that drive them, and the tides rising and falling.

To the north, feel the icy pole of the world. Consider the wilderness where snow falls for half a year in darkness. Gaze upon white cliffs of ice and the icebergs to which they give birth. See and feel them drift to the south. Toward the equator, feel the warmth of the moist trade winds. Visualize the archipelagoes and the island chains. Sense the ease with which clouds form from the seas and hurricanes are fashioned from the rising warm air.

Visualize also the shores of islands as they gradually or rapidly drop down to the ocean floor. Send your mind into these depths. Among the deepest trenches of the sea are lost ships, volcanoes, and darkness, but you are able to walk here without difficulty.

The trick in a meditation such as this is to become what you are contemplating. Become the primordial sea. This is the first step—feel the sea's heartbeat, its breath, its currents, its tides, and the myriad forms of life dwelling within it. There is no need to hesitate; the sea is already within you. The waters of the oceans flow through you, salt rich. Though you live in air, there is also air within the sea. The ice in your drink is not so different from the iceberg floating free from the glacier's grip.

The ocean, vast and mysterious, is the dream of being accepted, of being able to relax, let go, and flow in a place too great for the mind to imagine. Wave after wave of sensual caresses with rhythm and passion renew, heal, and yield to us the taste of beauty and freedom.

Istiphul has something to add. She says, "Place your hand in water and feel it connecting you to all the seas on the earth. Become a billion waves dancing to a thousand separate winds. To know me is to learn to perceive as I do. For a moment, let go and be as me—the soul of the sea."

ISTIPHUL'S SMILE

I look again at Istiphul. I notice the different qualities of her eyes as compared to her smile. The contrast serves to heighten her incomprehensible power of attraction. Her eyes have the depths and the ancient wisdom of the ocean within them. Yet her smile remains innocent, although it is an innocence that is knowledgeable in all erotic arts. This is to say, she is master of all aspects of attraction as they are expressed through the sensuality of the body.

I almost want to shake my head and squeeze my eyes closed to get her smile out of my mind. It is so bewitching. Her smile invades the soul—it stalks every dark desire that lurks forgotten and unknown. She would capture desire by her beauty, bind it with her love, and enslave it as she whispers, "In this moment, by the rhythm of waves, by their foamy crests, by the ocean's vast depths, I exist only to fulfill your needs."

She seizes both timid and bold cravings. She takes them into her heart to release them as bliss. Her smile calls and invites each of us to partake of the deepest desires, to feel them, to satisfy them, and to fulfill them in order to know the depths of our own heart. How can innocence be so willing to be taken, to be fearlessly penetrated? This is the smile hidden for ages behind the curtains of nature that has called out to the world's great explorers. They have all heard its urgent need in their dreams:

Come, search out my mysteries—

My longing for you will ever equal your longing for me—

Come, taste my beauty. Capture me. Take me within your heart. Take me that I might yield to you my essence, my magic, and my charms.

I am here. Find me! Bind me! Illuminate me! Reveal the mysteries of my soul.

If you do so, I will surrender to you in blissful sigh and moan of rapture all of my treasures.

There is no difference between Istiphul's powers and the ones shared by human lovers. It is what we all long for—desire and need joined to intimacy, so that loneliness and separation are shattered and replaced with kindness, friendship, and love.

SONG OF THE SEA

While I contemplate her smile, Istiphul again touches my arm. She says, "Listen to these waves breaking." I listen and hear . . .

Waves splashing against the shore, folding back, flowing back and forth and splashing more. A soft-sounding surge of waves upon waves as herds of soft caresses rise, collapse, enfolding each breath in release. On and on it goes—a cold cup of water thrown in your face are these sounds, a gentle touch clasping your finger, a yielding and a swaying, a dancing and a playing, a playing that is exquisite pain—and the pain a pleasure reflected in the falling drops of rain thrown by curling waves.

The gasps and sighs, each sigh a bird unleashed and in flight gliding low over the waves. Each falling wave like the ocean's own breath rising from its depths, floating and surging now on the crest that edges even closer to spilling into bliss.

On and on it goes, flowing without end—this is the sound of the ocean making love—it is unmistakable. I hear it! It is the sound of Istiphul when she is making love.

Istiphul takes my hand, and we walk beside the sea. I watch the waves recede, pulling back from the shore, sinking down to the ocean floor, and I think that only water knows this rhythmic freedom, this purity of movement, where the penetration and the letting go are one unbroken flow.

ENCOUNTERS WITH ISTIPHUL

February 3, 1995, at 5 p.m.

I am beneath the lighthouse on the black stone lava off Makapu'u on Oahu. I call, and Istiphul comes near. I look into her eyes. I see a young woman whose eyes reflect back to me the image of who I am now, who I was in the past, and also who I am meant to be. But her vision does not pressure or hypnotize me. Her eyes hold me with the authority of bliss and clarity joined.

Even if the sea could be encompassed by the mind, still, Istiphul is the sea in the form of a person. Though scientists study and know much about the ocean's currents, volcanoes, and trenches and track the paths of fish, Istiphul offers a different wisdom. She is the sea in its intimacy. She touches my arm again, and her eyes are aglow with vision. If you feel this touch, you will notice how gentle and soft it is. Yet here is the touch of the entire ocean—hand upon skin, with the sea ringing within.

Her touch evokes a sensation more sensual than wind and waves embracing. It is the peace of a night with Venus blazing her unearthly radiance. Istiphul sings softly:

Yield to me, for I am innocence
Be beside me, for I am kindness
Confide in me, for I am hope
Dream with me—I am in every tear you cry
I am the longing within your eyes
Searching for a home or another to hold
I am the holy well of joy hidden within your soul
If you let me caress you, I will bless you
With all the love you have never known—
My gift is to join with you
With more intimacy than breath
With more harmony
Than the pulse and flow and undertow—Of blood
     surging through your body.
My gift is to love with such power
That in your darkest hour
When you are abandoned and alone
As the sailor who braves storms
You shall return bearing treasures of love
From unknown continents within the soul.

◉ Another Meditation ◉

What is the magic in Istiphul's touch? Let us pursue this theme for a moment to see if we can find it within ourselves. Remaining alert, relax as if you are within a dream. Then contemplate the oceans. Note and memorize the sounds and smells, the waves and winds, and the tides rising and falling.

Concentrate on the sensations of water and spray. Feel the force of water in currents. Feel the waves swirling and splashing around you as you swim among them. Become the sea as the crab knows it, the fish, the fisher, the bird, the sailor, and the one who lives at the edge of a bay. Briefly gather all your memories of the sea. Open yourself to them in a place of stillness within your heart where thoughts are unnecessary.

Feel their life.

Now, draw these memories and feelings together to distill their essence. Translate this watery life, this beauty and receptivity, into one sensation you can hold in the palms of your hands.

If you caress and embrace another with this love from the depths of your heart, a heart that holds the sea within it, then this is Istiphul's touch. Istiphul says, "You blend with me like tides and sea, but there is an emptiness within you unlike anything I have ever known."

She looks into my eyes as if she has been by my side for countless ages as a friend and guide. She says,

You love beauty and harmony. You celebrate the illumination of lights and the turning of the seasons. But there is another side to you: you are a darkness waiting for the birth of light; a silence where sound has never fallen; a dryness in search of the scent of bliss; and a longing separation has never imagined.

You have been so lost and alone, your only hope of reconciliation is mastering the divine art of becoming one with another's heart. To do this you would sail across every abyss that prevents the five senses from perceiving the beauty of the universe. I do not know the end you seek, but it is obvious to me that you need a woman whose passions are as deep as the sea. Her touch is healing, and in her dreams the stars fall asleep and find peace.

Oh, others can say of me that I would rescue you or make you weak. They would say that my visions are illusions and that no such woman exists. But in the fairy realm, time is the illusion. It is easy for me to see how fear blocks the five senses and despair stops the heart from seeing visions.

Every need within the soul seeks fulfillment. Every true quest joins the inner and the outer worlds. Every true vision will one day manifest. I need no sage or theologian to tell me that one day humans will love with the power and the beauty the sea holds—for they will discover that my touch, my sight, and my heart are hidden within their own.

February 5, 1995, at 5:30 p.m.

At Lumahai Beach near the Na Pali coast on Kauai, again I call and Istiphul appears. She says to me, "I would steal the sorrow from your heart with a kiss." Then Istiphul kisses me, and I enter a dream. I hear my heart beating and another heartbeat as well, that of the whole ocean beating in rhythm to my own. And though our lips touch but for a moment, in truth she kisses my body all over a thousand times, with a thousand kisses from a thousand goddesses.

You may well laugh and ask me, "How can you exaggerate like that?" I am not exaggerating when I say that touch contains magic and that an immortal, a queen of the undines such as Istiphul, has magic in great supply.

Her kiss?

It is green waves yielding as they fall on white Aegean shores. It is the glittering blue-white icebergs drifting on salty seas, sunlight trapped in ice, blazing with beauty.

> *Her lips, slightly open, invite you to join*
> *With the mouths of rivers,*
> *The Nile, the Ganges, and the Amazon,*
> *Flowing from the source.*
> *It is fierce tides going out, undertows and riptides,*
> *And racing currents beneath small, rippling waves.*
> *It is a continent of waves dancing and at play*
> *Among a thousand winds.*
> *It is both the drawing in of the ocean's great depths*
> *And a yielding of all of her being—all her secrets*
>   *unveiled,*

All unleashed and released in her kiss.
Once you have felt this kiss, it is a dream you cannot
  imagine
And a love you cannot fathom,
Though you may try to put it out of your mind.
It is an explosion of new emotion
Your body bursting, your blood rushing,
Rising, exalting, and then collapsing
On distant and unknown shores.
For whatever your need may be,
She joins with that need, liberating you from
  loneliness.
And whether it be desire, craving, or longing,
Hunger, or wanting, secret or known,
She is there within it.
She dissolves it by the touch of her lips.
She embodies both the thirst
And the cup that quenches it
All in the same breath, and in the same kiss.
Yet she does not weaken the desire
By accepting who you are.
Rather, she intensifies desire, her beauty amplifying
  it
So it burns for the first time, in all its power
With a flame that brings healing, renewal, and new
  life.
And so it is that in her kiss, wet and dry, steam and
  ice,
The driving force in electricity—
These she unites in one circle of life.
But consider, for a moment, the price:
Some will panic if they sail this ocean
Like the sailors with Columbus

Fearing the edge of the world in sight.
They cry out, "Turn back!
We have lost our taste for the unknown.
Our desires are not for treasures this bold."
For this very reason Istiphul has remained hidden:
That human courage not be tested by beauty so
*   terrifying*
It rends the soul and haunts the mind with
*   unattainable visions.*
But now mankind is ready:
The wind is offshore. The tide is in.
The constellations, flaming cold and furious in the
*   distance,*
Have waited for aeons to guide our course.
But who will voyage with me
Beyond the boundaries of the ordinary and the
*   familiar?*
You hesitate? I do not blame you.
I have traveled without companions to places reason
*   cannot fathom*
And where words must be minted anew
To dissolve the darkness and emptiness within you.
The elixir of love, the essence of all divine
*   mysteries,*
Has always been exceedingly dangerous.
Its wisdom is greater than magic,
Its knowledge greater than power.
Those who would follow this path must search their
*   hearts*
Till every barrier separating one from another is cast
*   aside forever—*
For this is love's art.

LIGHTNING

Istiphul is not satisfied with the healing process. Perceiving my needs even more clearly as we kiss, Istiphul takes my hands. As some women I have met can also do, Istiphul passes into my body—her soul is now within me.

I have visions of electrical storms. That is to say, my feelings and physical sensations spontaneously transmute into visual images of a thunderstorm at sea: explosive volts leap into the indigo darkness of a moist sky. Electricity accumulates around my body and then flows back around hers. Between us, we are condenser, amplifier, and generator as the spark arcs between our hearts.

Within my body, lightning reaches down from violent clouds to strike the ocean and explode in a touch or a kiss. Ball lightning forms and flows from my shoulders down my arms, reaching for her and caressing her body. Saint Elmo's fire encompasses us, and its sound is here—the hiss and *jzzzz* that hum with prayers of eerie solemnity. In the distant sky I see the northern lights, both marvelous and ominous—the Earth's veils being lifted by solar radiance—a banshee's hopeless songs of loss turning into a frenzied dance of bliss.

As Istiphul's feminine essence enters my spine and ascends, I enter the dreams of gods and goddesses calling out to their consorts through all of space and time. Though a man has the power to penetrate, to enter, and to share the light of the sun, the woman is a circle of ecstasy, a ring imploding upon itself. She is the pulsating waves circling down into the depths of her being, down into the depths of the ocean and the earth.

I open my eyes, not realizing they had been closed. Istiphul's body floats in the air next to me. The crashing and diving of the waves seem but gentle ripples and drops of water flowing through her hair and down her breasts. My eyes blur. I no longer see waves of water dancing and raging about us. Time slows. The ocean transforms into its opposite: I see sand dunes with air flowing over their crests, carving an ocean of shapes and tender memories as they yield themselves to the hungry hands of the wind.

HER CRY

Istiphul emits a loud cry—the note of a soprano, but this sustained note is like an entire song. The sound of it carries far out into the surrounding ocean. At the same time, this sound gathers and draws back to her the animating and spiritual force within water.

I realize that I am witness to the "magic of tones" that some undines possess. Istiphul sends part of her being outward. The sound ricochets back and forth in each drop of water. As a soprano can break a glass with her voice, this note Istiphul sings can turn water to ice, or steam.

A power lying dormant and asleep within the ocean uncoils itself in response. There is a pulsing and shivering, and the muscles in my body shake and quiver. The body spasms, but from ecstasy rather than from pain or tension. Her sound both penetrates and encompasses.

And the song within this note, how can I express it? Words woven out of wind and water, out of sea and sky, living water, a wilderness of delights, they fall now as passion—a bite, a yearning touch, a tender kiss. Then they become a waterfall surging and splashing and falling further down into the arms of love's embrace.

It is a haunting sound, curtains of starlight falling down, caught in a pool where the ocean dreams. It is urgent—at first buoyant and then sinking, it dissolves into a magnetic expanse where all thoughts go to rest having finally exhausted their explorations of how things are different.

As Istiphul sings I become one with the sea—pure bliss adrift within the arms of serenity. I float. I am suspended. And again I blend with the body of the ocean. If in part the purpose of a spiritual quest is to find and unite with our divine parents, with the source of our inspiration, then this sound would be the wine used to celebrate reunion with the divine mother, whichever one you seek—Gaia, Dana, Shekinah,

Vishvamata, Prajnaparamita, Shakti, Kundalini, Rudha, Sophia, Venus, Diana, Demeter, or Kwan Yin.

May women one day learn to sing with such beauty! No koan is a knife this sharp, able to cut the mind free of limiting thoughts. And the art of poetry is but our surprise as a butterfly alights before our eyes upon an open palm—it cannot match a voice that captures the soul of the sea within a single sound.

With this note ringing within my ears, it is easy to forget who I am. A few seconds pass, perhaps a few minutes, and suddenly I am no longer sure if these few moments were actually two or three years. Did I trade my body for that of a dolphin, frolicking and playing near reefs and farther out at sea? Just now I say to myself, "Ah, I remember. I am actually a human being!"

Was this the sound that sailors heard—the sirens' call to destruction? Definitely not! The sound sailors claim to have heard, and which they somehow survived to tell about, was empty and dark and loaded with despair. And the siren song would cause the sailors' muscles and hearts to fail, overridden by a compulsion resulting in a fateful decision—to surrender to a power and will outside the self that seeks to steal life for itself.

This sound is altogether different! Nerve ends are soothed even as they are sharpened. As I said before, this is the undine's magic of tones: the creation of a place of soul where two hearts from two separate worlds may join as one. Melting together, the deepest desire in one is fused to the deepest desire within another. Though it may be hard to conceive, when you touch Istiphul or hear her sing, when you see her smile or kiss her lips, it is like making love with the entire ocean—you are invited to enter the dreams, to taste the peace, and to be at one with the sea.

Some might feel that Istiphul's kiss or touch draws in and devours their masculinity. But this is not so. Men at first crave and then fear a woman of great beauty because her beauty contains powers their minds cannot conceive. Ah, but we are no longer wading in the shallows, dipping our toes to see if the water is cold. When Istiphul touches your arm, you can feel waves breaking on beaches all over the world. We are on a voyage of discovery. Within our souls the oceans flow. Love celebrates this beauty.

ENCOUNTERS WITH ISTIPHUL

December 1, 1996

I draw the undine's sigil in the air. The room flickers with the magical sign's blue light, and the air stirs with the magnetic currents of its wavy lines.

Istiphul appears, sitting in front of me on my bed with her legs crossed.

I say, "It is shocking how beautiful you are."

Istiphul smiles as she reaches out and places her hand on my leg. Her touch takes me into a place of contentment where thoughts are extraneous. Still, for a moment or two I am disoriented until I clear my mind and let go into the experience.

Being with Istiphul is being in a place that sings of waves, tides, and the depths of the sea. When Istiphul relaxes as she is doing now, her aura is nearly indistinguishable from a vast expanse of ocean. To be with her is to be aware of only the sounds, scents, and sensations of waves stretching from horizon to horizon. And out there at night, on the high seas with no trace of humanity, there is an ancient peace. It is older than the landmasses, yet it seeks to be awakened and to share its heart.

It is not easy for me to speak about Istiphul. Magic at this level of intensity is beyond where human thoughts probe and the modes in which the mind is accustomed to analyzing. Unless I write down my experiences with Istiphul as they happen or immediately afterward, they vanish from my mind. The five senses forget what they perceive, and the nerves within the body, though exhilarated, withdraw back into the security of everyday life.

I have had a couple of interesting experiences in the last year with Istiphul. One time I was listening to an Irish band playing at O'Toole's Irish Pub in downtown Honolulu. I took the liberty of adding something to the festivity by drawing Istiphul's sigil in the air above the edge of the table. Within a few minutes, a woman came in from the street.

She was French, petite, and had dark, short-cropped hair.

Responding to the music, this woman began dancing, spinning in circles as her hands drifted over her head and around her waist as if carried by surging waves. Watching her dance, I could feel the cool, wild, and rhythmic pulsing presence of the sea fill the room. Lost in dance, she appeared to be oblivious to where she was.

I was not the only one in the room whose eyes were riveted on this woman. Everyone stopped drinking and talking. When she stopped dancing, I heard Istiphul whisper in my ear, "She is one of mine, and this is my sign to you that I am near."

Another time I sat in the Harbor Pub across from the Ilikai Hotel in Waikiki. It overlooks a number of docks where sailboats are moored. If you listen carefully past the people talking and the live music, you can hear the stays clanging against the masts in the gentle breeze.

I was with a lady introduced to me by a couple who worked at Hickam Air Force Base. This woman was a Wiccan priestess in a local coven. We were eating hot-fudge sundaes. The ice cream was in a big scoop in the center of a chilled metal plate, and hot fudge was laid out around the ice cream in a design of interlaced flowers. As we devoured this, the woman related to me her adventures in different parts of the world.

Later, as I told her about different undines I had met, she put down her spoon. Then, without any noticeable change in her appearance, she put aside her own consciousness and began speaking to me with Istiphul's voice. This is what the undine said:

> *When I look through my eyes,*
> *You are wonderful to behold—*

A man of power, masterful, and in charge.
But when I perceive you through human eyes,
You are wiry, balding, and shy.
No wonder women do not respect you.
Their minds deceive them,
And their senses do not lead them
To listen to the songs the seas have told—
Hot blood flowing in their lungs,
Moist air set afire with the taste of passion,
Power dancing with desire.
But we elemental beings crave you as our lover
You go for the heart
You ask for all that I am
Your love nearly tears me apart
I can hold nothing back
As we kiss, waves collide
In mid-ocean, from separate storms
Exploding in white foam as we touch
But for human women it is not at all like this.
The hand that glides upon the skin
Does not beckon them.
They cling to identity excessively—
The light of the moon does not illuminate their
    darkness,
And so their souls cannot speak freely.
They feel not the electricity of the lightning storm
You release in me.
Nor do they hear the consonants and vowels
Of waters crying aloud,
Making love on all the beaches of the world
In the rapids, the streams, and the rivers' falls.
They know not the release arising from the ocean floor,
 Nor the sinking and letting go into the undertow,

Nor the returning,
The arching back in the wave's crest breaking,
Its feathery tip translucent in the sunlight
And sparkling in starlight.
Where can an undine go
To share these things with a human soul?
The dark depths of the ocean trench,
The slippery touch of the jellyfish and the nautilus,
The caress of arctic cold,
Or the warmth of curling up on a tropical beach,
Of a woman walking out of the sea naked and free,
Drops of water anointing her skin.
Sailors handsome, rugged, strong, and bold
Perceive with acute vision
The winds, the tides, the wave's size, the seasons,
And the clouds at dawn.
Brave are their hands upon the helm—
With compass and starry charts they master the dark.
But in their eyes the blue-green sea does not dream—
They are afraid of what they cannot control.
But you are not as these.
In your soul, waves roll five thousand miles,
And magnetism flows between the poles.
And when I kiss your lips
It is I who drown in your bliss.

A moment later the undine was gone, and the woman returned to her own awareness. "What did Istiphul say?" she asked. As a medium, she does not recall what occurs when she is channeling. I replied, "She says she cannot understand why the sea is not alive within the souls of human beings."

Writing about Istiphul is like being in a dream in which I am fully awake. I am aware of my room and the chair I sit in. I am aware of

Istiphul sitting beautifully on my bed. But I am also aware of the astral realm surrounding me. It is present in every sensory perception, every breath. You do not need to walk seven times around a fairy mound or meditate in a stone circle to find it.

Istiphul moves closer to me and places her hip against mine. She smiles as she looks into my eyes. For the psychic, the crystal ball opens a gate through time and space and offers new possibilities. In a similar way, Istiphul's body amplifies feelings and speaks of the fulfillment of dreams. Let me say something about this.

A woman can take a man into herself as she makes love. All the nerves of his body are excited, and she wraps him about with her sinuous, sensual caress. His desire increases, intensifying, until he can no longer contain himself. His only wish is to join with this love and tenderness and let go so he can taste this beauty. This is one power within the feminine with which we are already familiar.

The mage who wields a wand of will that transforms the world must also join with his opposite; he must embrace the world with an intimacy only love can accomplish. Through his heart must flow the nurturing power of the receptive. He must animate his visions and infuse them with energy so they become alive, radiant, and shining.

It is for this purpose that beings such as Istiphul have been created and imbued with the intelligence and beauty commensurate with the destiny of the human race. They are legacies awaiting our discovery. It remains for us to seek out these beings of wonder and to learn what they have to teach.

Sitting next to me, Istiphul needs no more than an instant to perceive my needs. Though she and I sometimes speak aloud with words, no thought or image is needed to communicate. She speaks as a harpist communicates moods through the touch of her fingers on the strings of her instrument—but the strings are my nerves, and the moods she creates are a flow of love from her heart into my own.

There are places within the soul where only love can go. The mind is unwilling to enter—not because reason does not have the ability, but because the mind cannot recognize anything familiar. There is no label for the experience.

There are times when we hear a song in the distance. It comes from a tavern or from a house on another street. You can barely hear the words, but when you make them out, a feeling of love inexplicably steals inside you.

Perhaps this is because the night sometimes seeks to deliver us, even against our will, into a place of intoxication or enchantment. On such an occasion, we may remember moments of love that came to us as a gift—a kiss, a hug, a time you made love, or a lifelong friend you met by accident. And with the memory we are reminded of what our connection to another is meant to be—a flow of feeling in and through each other, without restriction or limits.

I do not need to refer to passionate love, with its stormy seas of craving, of being swept away and consumed by another's desire. My example is simpler: a beautiful woman walks up to a man whom most women do not find very attractive. She asks him to dance. During the dance her body molds itself to his body and hands. She gives herself completely to him. With her eyes, smile, and touch, she envelops him in all the love she has ever felt.

The experience is more than her being his partner in a social setting. She is not a temporary possession, and this is not a moment of fleeting pleasure or mutual appreciation. The experience is not about bonding or of them playing the roles of woman and man. During the dance, she makes herself one with him.

My critics will object to this example. They will say, "This never happens, not the way you mean it." But my response is that there are many women who know what I am talking about, and I have met them. The man who experiences a woman who gives herself completely—all of herself—has two choices. He can try to forget or deny it, pretending it was a mistake or an illusion. Or he can respond to that feminine love and leave behind the man he was—for now he knows about the possibility of loving another with all of his heart. Those of us who cross over the boundaries separating the worlds often must make such a choice. The beauty we perceive is unfathomable, wonderful, and mysterious, and it speaks to us constantly of the way the world is meant to be.

At Istiphul's touch, the room I am in fades away completely. I walk beside her through a blue-green mist. Istiphul says, "I am part of you and one with you. The man you are meant to be has always had this need: to be absolutely one with his beloved—body, soul, and spirit united as one will and one being. I give myself to you so that this dream may be fulfilled."

December 3, 1996

I am at one of my favorite pools beneath the cliffs of Makapu'u on Oahu. The wind is blowing twenty knots and flailing my face with spray from the waves. Yet amid the gusts of wind and waves pounding the volcanic rocks, I hear Istiphul's voice and song. My body shivers involuntarily at the sound. She sings . . .

An Undine's Prayer

Wild winds wash over me
Caress the breasts of these waves
With ripples running free
Take me, ravish me
With your kiss of bliss
With your hips of thunder
Spread your fingers on my skin
As you dip your tongue
Into my troughs and crests
I throb, my body rolls over
Bound to your heartbeat
My tides rise higher
Your breath stirs my currents
As your lips fly, hover, and then dive
Into my waves and thighs

As your hunger invades my inner recesses.
Oh, for a mortal lover
With the passion of the wind
To feel his eyes burn
As they glide upon my naked skin
His desires sinking down into my depths.
Lord of the Winds—
Search the earth for a lover
Relentless to discover my ecstasy,
Sounding sea—anoint me with your heart's blood
That I may know such love,
Running waves—rise and break
In sighs and cries until he comes.

Istiphul sits next to me, her legs submerged in the pool of water. She places her cheek against mine. She says, "Permit me to see the world through your eyes."

"As you wish," I reply.

And then, as one breath, one heartbeat, our five senses join. We look out at the world through the same eyes. After a few minutes, Istiphul says, "The people of your race have such sorrow in their hearts. I can feel their tears that break free, and I can feel the tears they do not cry. But beyond the nightmare and the sealed doors, past the sadness, grief, and sorrow that chain their souls, they possess the power to create, from their own wills, a love that transforms the world."

Istiphul begins to cry. She looks at me and weeps. She shakes her head, the tears running over her lips, and says, "What an absolutely terrible and yet wondrous gift of unspeakable beauty human beings possess— to be so lonely, so far away from sharing heart-to-heart. And yet to be so proud—knowing there is nothing you cannot endure because one day you will become radiant like the sun and magnificent like the stars."

I kiss away her tears. Then Istiphul, with that amazing, emotional fluidity of hers—the ability to be ancient and young, wise and innocent, seductive and coy all in the same moment—says playfully, "Is it any wonder that an undine like me tries to bind a magician with her beauty and with the touch of ecstasy? You magicians fly about the universe riding the wings of spirit. And yet you must come to me for the magnetic power you need to fulfill your missions. What woman can love you with all of her heart, soul, mind, and being as I do every time we meet?"

And then she quickly puts the tip of her index finger to my lips and says, "No, do not answer. I am an immortal, and jealousy is not within me. Like the sea, I have ten thousand moods and treasures of love no one has yet found. I have no fear of losing you. I will always be here. And you will seek me again and again because love commands you to learn one by one all my secrets."

And then Istiphul places her middle finger into her mouth and slowly pulls it out as she gently sucks on it, all the while her gaze is locked on my eyes. She watches me as if she were the sea forever unknown and unknowable and I a sailor with implacable will bent on discovering her treasures. She then touches her moist finger to the center of my palm and begins sliding it in a circle.

Like a man hypnotized and told that when he awakens he will be in another place, I am taken to the astral plane and into the heart of Istiphul's domain. I feel like I have dwelt here by Istiphul's side for countless ages, that I am a king and she is my queen in a realm of magic and dream hidden in the depths of the sea.

I have to be completely honest with you. Among the elemental beings, the undines and some of the sylphs (the spirits of the air) are outrageously invasive and flirtatious. Their prime directive might as well be to see to what extent, through pleasure and magical empathy, they can cause another's aura to blend with their own.

Then again, is nature so different? Does the wind ask the sailor which way he plans to sail before it blows? Do the tides ask permission before they rise? Do the rivers seek advice on how to flow to the sea, or do they request permission when they plan a flood? Neither does love hesitate if given a chance to invade our lives.

For two thousand years the church has sought to destroy every gate and entrance into the fairy realms. Priests have proclaimed the Sidhe* to be sorcerers possessing forbidden knowledge. To erase their presence and to steal their beauty, the church has built its cathedrals over fairy mounds and upon the groves of Druids.

But the Sidhe do not use magic to bewitch mankind with haunting dreams and eerie visions of another world. Instead, they possess what the church does not: an absolute contentment—an awareness in which the inner self is at peace with the universe. If there is a loss of soul and a bewilderment befalling those who catch a glimpse of fairy realms, then the fault is in the human heart that would deny the treasures hidden within it.

December 5, 1996

I again speak the word of power that summons Istiphul. I feel a cool, soft presence ripple through the room just before she arrives. She takes my hands and pulls me into her world. Entering the astral plane suddenly like this can be very frightening. But this experience is one I understand.

When I first visited Hawaii, I went swimming in Waianae. I floated on my back, drifting where the waves roll just beyond the reach of the breaking surf. And then, to experience the surge and flow, I let my body be carried over the breaking crests to fall and be caught in the spinning and churning waves. The force of the water rolled me up onto the beach, and then the undertow pulled me back into the ocean. I did this over and over until my body felt as if it were a part of the surf and the

---

*The Tuatha Dé Danann, who worshipped the goddess Dana, were defeated by the first Gaels who arrived in Ireland. According to lore, they were driven underground and occupy the hollow hills or Sidhe mounds. Each mound has its own king and queen. They are spoken of as not growing old. Legends also describe distinct Sidhes such as spirits of air, water, and wood. They are also referred to as the fairy folk who dwell in the Otherworld. The nature spirits in this book are not associated with the Sidhe or any other tradition of fairies.

only thing in my mind was the sound of the water laughing and splashing about me.

Several days later, after I had returned to Tucson, I could still feel the dizziness that sometimes accompanies those who return from the sea—a rocking motion like waves breaking around me, throwing me forward and pulling me back. The spellbinding part that lingers is not from playful frolicking in the surf. The gate to the astral plane of the undines opens the moment your body feels the vastness of the sea flowing through it.

The magician opens the gates to the inner planes in another way—by casting a magic circle, consecrating it with water; by drawing pentagrams and sigils on the circumference like an artist whose paintbrush leaves a trail of fire. With eyes that sparkle with divine authority, with a voice that resonates with a sacred ferocity while chanting great and mighty words of power. Standing at the center of the circle, the magician joins with the Divine so that what he or she wills might be fulfilled, that no obstacle can long resist what they command to manifest.

But at Istiphul's touch, with her clairvoyance awakening within my eyes, I sense that it is lovers who have the greater power and a limitless authority. To be in Istiphul's presence is to be anointed with the beauty of the world. And the love she celebrates evokes a greater mystery than that of a mage joined with god.

At the touch of her hand on mine, skin against skin, our different evolutions, our separate destinies, the human and divine barriers—all are set aside so two hearts can find each other, blend, merge, and unite. In this circle, only love exists, and all power and will bow down before its bliss—such is the vision hidden within women and within the soul of the sea.

I close my eyes as I focus on the sensation of Istiphul's touch. Yet when I open my eyes and look at her, I feel electrified—my senses are overloaded with acute sensations as if they are about to explode. Her eroticism replicates the arousal in the air when the earth and sky draw near during a thunderstorm—the tension and the dynamic potential increase geometrically without inhibition or limitation. It is said that certain undines and salamanders have the power to control storms at sea. Perhaps one day I will see if I can conjure up a thunderstorm by doing no more than gazing, as I am doing now, upon Istiphul's beauty.

December 8, 1996

Istiphul wakes me from a nap. She sings into my ear with the sounds of a distant ocean. As I rub the sleep from my eyes, she says, "I am known for prophecy, for to love alone is granted this key: to see what has been and what shall be. But I have been disturbed by your visions and your needs. They speak of a joining in which the boundaries separating nature, human, and divine are set aside. They speak of the woman I wish to be. Though I am bound by the water element, still, my dream is to become the essence of love."

Istiphul then takes my hands and fixes her eyes upon mine as she says, "So that I might know of the greater and higher Love that informs the universe, reveal to me the dream that holds you in its power—a dream so clear, so pure in its fire, the stars are free to shine within it."

I reply, "Is not the love I seek the same as yours? I wish to be one with another, so that all that separates dissolves in the embrace. The heart craves the taste of this love. Each of us seeks, in the depths of our souls, to know we are not alone. Your life and beauty testify to this. Your power and magic are the means for making this reality."

Istiphul says, "Even so, your dream goes further. You search where I cannot explore. Tell me of the treasures of soul and spirit that exist beyond the boundaries of the sea, the river's flow, and the pool's calm serenity."

I answer, "In the element of air is the knowledge of freedom and harmony. It is the experience of being one with all things—as air is to breath and as wisdom is to the rhythm of the seasons. In fire is the experience of how to plan, command, and fulfill your destiny. And within fire also is the clarity to know when to set aside power because it means nothing at all. Within earth is the silence that nourishes a dream so it may unfold. It is the stillness within our hearts that measures our dreams—their beauty and their power—and then endures in its work until they transform the world."

Istiphul says, "And yet even now you are not using your full bardic voice as you answer me. What compels you to lay siege to the mysteries within the elements, to seek what has been hidden from mankind for ages? What drives you to master wisdom as ancient as the earth but which, in each moment, gives birth to itself so it shines with new light and life?"

She gazes into my eyes with the patience of the oceans that have encircled the earth for countless ages. Looking into her eyes is like drinking the waters of a fountain that is the source of friendship and kindness. Her tenderness flows through my body as she responds to what no one else has ever found, and a pain in my chest dissolves. I find myself thinking, "I have never felt this much love before."

Yet the acceptance within water is not just the power to embrace the opposites and contradictions within ourselves or to heal our wounds. Though Istiphul's gift is freedom from sorrow, regret, and loss, water also dares to dream new things in its innermost heart. I hear Istiphul's voice within my mind. She says, "Speak plainly now and answer my question. Hold nothing back. What is the final end you seek?"

I answer, "One day a woman will say to me, 'I hear as you hear the songs the stars sing. I feel as you feel the peace that holds them within its dream. I see as you see the inner light shining in all things. And with this light and this passion and this embrace, my love for you will never end.' Istiphul, beauty, wisdom, and power live within love. To search for another to share this wonder is to celebrate the mystery of life. The fire burning within me is the joy of sensing her presence at the center of my heart—that she and I are already one."

I see tears in Istiphul's eyes. I tell you, the ice buried deep beneath the earth's North and South Poles does not know the solitude that these tears trace upon her cheeks—nor can the whiteness of snow speak of the purity her face radiates. Istiphul places my hand over her heart.

She holds it there as she says,

> *Young bard, if your spirit did not belong to another,*
> *I swear I would take on mortal form.*
> *Binding the four elements by my magic and my will,*
> *I would dwell within a human body*
> *To become your lover.*
> *If you ever need me, in this life or another,*
> *I will come*
> *Bearing the love and the treasures of the sea.*

She kisses me on the lips and holds me close, then turns and departs into the depths of the ocean like a wave colliding with the shore surges back and blends again with the sea from which it arose, returning to its own dreams of beauty and mystery.

5

ISTIPHUL'S PERSONALITY

In this section, I describe the different levels in Istiphul's personality. These levels are her physical, etheric, astral, and mental bodies. I also speculate what she would be like if she had an akashic or spiritual body like human beings possess.

An aspect of clairsentience is the ability to feel another person's energy. In my case, I can sense and also reproduce the exact vibrations of another person or spirit within myself. In the descriptions that follow, I create Istiphul's energies within myself in order to understand and describe them better.

At the same time, mirroring another person's energy in this way can establish a telepathic rapport. I may be studying her energy inside of myself, but she is also watching and perhaps laughing at times at my responses. Meditating in this way is another way of having a conversation with a nature spirit. She is as aware of my energy as I am of hers.

PHYSICAL BODY

Undines are invisible to most people, but because of their strong ties to water in nature, they have a physical presence in our world. There are also times and conditions under which they can assume a physical form.

Istiphul's physical body is extremely attractive. She looks young and slender and like she is in her teens or early twenties. However, she has existed probably for millions of years, long before *Homo sapiens* began walking the earth. Her eyes are blue green. They are shining and inviting. But if you look carefully into her eyes, you can see all the oceans of the earth looking back at you.

Her smile is innocent and flirtatious, but if you pause and notice the effect of her smile on your nervous system, you may feel that you are amid a lightning storm at sea with raging flashes exploding right next to you—except the electricity is not outside of your body. These impulses are occurring within your nervous system.

Her hair is dark, long, and wet. If I move my fingers through it, I find myself awakening and lying on a tropical beach relaxed and at ease. I notice there are no thoughts within my mind. There is only the smell of her hair and the sea, the rolling and breaking waves singing in my heartbeat and bloodstream. I am not abandoned. She is lying next to me.

Her appearance is like that. A young girl but also pure archetype. The maiden with the aura of a goddess. Let me try to describe what she is like in terms of different vibrations.

In a sense, her beauty is just the ordinary attraction any young, nubile woman has. But you would have to amplify the young woman's attractive power many times. If you somehow could join into one woman twenty or thirty of the most beautiful women on earth, you would then catch a glimpse of Istiphul's beauty.

Being near to her, every cell in one's body feels a connection and desire only to draw closer to her. It is like a force of gravity, except that gravity is cold and impersonal. This force is custom designed to synchronize to you individually.

Standing ten feet away from her, I feel like the distance between us is contracting or collapsing. Instead of ten feet I feel she has become five feet, three feet, and then two feet away. Space shrinks. Separation dissolves. This is how perception works in her presence.

Her body senses automatically the magnetism in the sea, the clouds, and the earth. She can draw into one place and shape that magnetism for different purposes. Her body and form are an expression of this power.

We might ask, what kind of mentality has kept an undine like Istiphul from being known to humanity? It does not matter if it is the first century of Christianity, the Middle Ages, the Renaissance, the Reformation, the Age of Enlightenment, or the nineteenth or twentieth century. The reasoning is the same. It goes like this . . .

We all know that a woman takes part of a man into herself, unites with it, and then brings forth a new living being into the world. This is perfectly clear. This is part of life. We accept it.

But do not ever suggest even for a moment, even in your dreams, that women have a feminine power within them that can do the same for a grown man—take his will, his masculinity, and all the abilities of mastery he possesses and transform them to the same degree she can do with his seed.

To even think such a thought is absolutely forbidden. We do not want to know about it. We do not want anything in our culture, music, literature, or our religions to suggest it. To bring this knowledge forward and to reveal it to the world would risk the absolute destruction of our civilization.

That is a fairly accurate summary of the bias in Western civilization and the unconscious, unspoken, but agreed-upon assumption that the world is not ready for the knowledge of an undine like Istiphul. The poets, artists, and musicians have been in agreement with the theologians, reformers, and scientists in this matter. Rational, intellectual, academic consciousness cannot deal with or approach in any safe manner the powers of attraction that Istiphul possesses.

Let us consider a more personal example. A young man is lying in bed after having made love to his lover. She places her hand on his hip. Fine. We all know this experience. If a man is very lucky, she places her hand on his body with the same hunger with which he places his hand on her body. Desire and connection are expressed in the touch.

But let her place her hand on his body and spontaneously begin taking away the pain she feels inside of him. She does not think about this. It is in the touch of her hand on his skin. She simply knows in her soul how to do this.

But the man senses that what she is doing is different from her other interactions with him. He does not mind her sensuality and pleasure as long as he is the one in charge of awakening and directing it. He does not mind her receptivity to him and her rapport as long as it serves to strengthen his ego and willpower.

But this touch is different. It moves directly soul-to-soul and body-to-body beyond the sphere of rational thought and the well-defined social and gender boundaries set forth by society. He need only look at her to convey a feeling that she has just invaded and violated him in some unspeakable manner.

It is just like the child who tries to tell his parents that he sees ghosts or talks to spirits or sees colors and auras around people. The child learns by how upset the parents become not to discuss these things again. In the same way, women learn to turn away from the vast depths of feminine power that exist within them.

I have seen this again and again. Women with great feminine powers know automatically that certain things are simply forbidden. Let women acquire the skills and careers that men used to reserve for themselves. But women should not be exploring the feminine in ways that our entire civilization has been bent on destroying.

Another example—I have met a number of women who can intuitively tell what is happening to their lovers. They can tell if he is happy or sad, the kind of events and interactions going on with him when he is away, and even to some extent what is going to happen to him in the future. Such women intuitively know not to discuss this with anyone other than perhaps a psychic. The implication is that the man's will is not completely independent. The intuitive woman can tell what is going on beneath his will, surrounding his will, and also how well he is using it.

It is not like being a little boy again and having a mother glance at you and know instantly what you are up to. It is different. It is having a woman's consciousness inside of you and a part of you. This is what is forbidden in our civilization.

In Christianity, only god should have that power. In science, nothing should interfere with the clarity of a rational mind to analyze its object of study. Even for artists, it is okay to check yourself into a mental hospital or a drug-addiction rehabilitation center, but this feminine power is not okay—a woman should not feel what you feel and take away the pain. That would mean the end of art as the Western world knows it.

Imagine if in *Hamlet* Ophelia could counsel Hamlet and say, "The ghost is real. The king really did murder your father. And you are going to have to face up to your task—you will have to risk a civil war to establish justice in the kingdom. If you are going to be a man, choose now: do what you have to do and stop this fiddling about." Why, that would mean that the real drama in life and in art takes place within the soul and heart. It is not found only after an individual acts in the external world. Our world has not been ready for this kind of inner knowledge or for this level of perception into human motivation and self-awareness.

Istiphul embodies in her physical being this feminine power of magnetism and incomprehensible beauty that our civilization has not been ready to encounter. How can I then describe these things so openly when in prior ages Istiphul could not even enter human consciousness?

Times change. I am commissioned to reveal these things. It is time to unite the full power of the masculine with the full power of the feminine. This psychological and spiritual union is needed in order to balance the world or, as Krishna and others would say, "in order to preserve light on earth."

Sex itself is rather dramatic. There is a moment in making love when lovers become pure consciousness. You no longer have an identity. You are outside of yourself and a part of another. This is called ecstasy. Part of the man leaves him and joins with the woman.

Now then, take that image and make it into a symbol of a spiritual experience. Istiphul takes not the physical seed within the man but the element of light and vision—she senses what he is to become. She takes the seed of the spirit within him and joins herself to it to give birth to a new being. She transforms a man in every way into something far better than what he could ever imagine.

This is the power Western civilization has wished to deny women. It is every bit as ecstatic as sex but far more powerful in its ultimate transformation. Like sex, it shatters your everyday life, your routines, and your sense of your own identity. It joins you to the natural processes within nature in all their depth and beauty.

In the movie *A Beautiful Mind,* John Nash tries to get a girl in a bar to skip over the process of flirting and move on to—as he says to her—"an exchange of bodily fluids." This move does not work out for him. The girl slaps him and walks off. His friends joke about how well he was doing until he opened his mouth.

When you are next to Istiphul, sex is not at issue. There is an exchange of the magical electrical and magnetic fluids of the masculine and feminine spirits. As in sex, your attention is focused on each other. The physical world vanishes. One's identity vanishes. You are in a magical realm. Time is suspended.

The only thing in your awareness is this light within you and how it is being nourished, received, contained, sheltered, and amplified through the powers of bliss, pleasure, ecstasy, rapture, and wonder. If you cannot go into these states of awareness, you do not want to go near Istiphul. These things happen because nature contains these things and Istiphul embodies these powers.

From time to time, I have been able to show women I have known how to use this same kind of energy. Some women possess astonishing psychic and magical gifts to transform others through touch. But once they follow my directions and produce amazing effects, they quickly lose interest and do not pursue it. The entire world does not want them to do so. And as all the supposedly wise men of our world agree, these women sense that it is too dangerous to acquire these abilities.

Imagine if women through touch or by using psychic ability were to focus on a soldier returning from the war who has post-traumatic stress disorder. Imagine that such a woman healer could get inside not just his memories but his brain and nervous system too. Imagine that she could take away that pain and stress and return him to a normal life free of the residual tension of war that can be reactivated in his nervous system unexpectedly at any time. If women could do that, they would not have to stop there. They could enter into the minds of the world leaders who cause the wars in the first place and heal them. Simply put, women have the ability to end wars on earth.

I tell women who possess these abilities about this possibility. But they think only in terms of helping this individual or that individual. The idea of reducing the suffering of millions of people assumes just too much responsibility. They do not have that ambition. They do not wish to exercise that degree of will. They do not seek power. Perhaps they feel that power of that nature reduces femininity into an egotistical, male action.

In the fifth century BCE, the Greeks built the Parthenon in honor of the goddess Athena out of gratitude for their victory over the Persians in the Battle of Marathon. The Athenians saw wisdom and protection as an aspect of the feminine. Athena was understood to be the companion of heroes and the goddess of heroic endeavor. We do not have this appreciation of the power of the feminine in our world.

The word *psychology* derives from the Greek word *psyche* ("breath of life," soul, anima). The Greek myth of Eros and Psyche is one of the few stories to survive the Christian era that speaks of the path of feminine growth and transformation. In this story, the matriarch Aphrodite demands that a young woman pass four tests if she is to marry Aphrodite's son, Eros. In the first three tests, Psyche gains assistance from various beings, satyrs, water nymphs, an eagle, and indirectly even Zeus.

For the fourth test, however, she makes her own decision without consulting oracles, gods, creatures of nature, companions, or sisters. She chooses to pass beyond the knowledge of love as it is understood by gods and man to embrace a beauty that even death cannot destroy. In so doing, she reconfigures the archetypes of the masculine and feminine. To honor her choice, Zeus raises her from mortal to goddess.

Stories are meant to be retold so that they speak to each age in a new way. I imagine that Zeus appeared to Psyche in order to figure out what to do with her. He was king of the gods. Final decisions in matters such as this are his.

Zeus asks Psyche, "What do you really want?"

Psyche replies, "I want to be able to look at a man and feel his innermost desires; I want to be one with him so that all separation is overcome."

Zeus replies, "Until this moment, love such as this did not exist. What being, mortal or divine, could ever have dreamed or imagined that life could contain such a gift?"

We look at a young woman and think, "She is cute; she is beautiful; she is ambitious; she is sexy," and so on. But there is more we do not see. The young woman, the maiden, is also, as Carl Jung would say, the image of the anima—the spiritual guide to the inner world of the masculine. This is because she has the ability to give herself without limitation to what she loves. When men lose this ability to give, they also lose their inspiration and contact with the instinctual powers that drive them.

With Istiphul, I am describing a nature spirit, an undine, who has the powers of an archetype. Her powers are love, enchantment, and beauty. But there is far more. Her power embodies an empathy that can transform our world.

In regard to the ideal of eliminating war, I know that women have an essential role to play. But femininity would need to be understood in a new way—as a power that is equal to any force that exists in the external world. It takes a community of artists, magicians, musicians, writers, and healers to create a psychological space in which this kind of feminine energy is welcome, appreciated, and held in high regard. This is not a warm, cuddly, think positive, New Age kind of thing. We are talking about a feminine power so great it can change human destiny and the course of history, leading us in another direction altogether.

One wise man told me to stop using female models to represent undines in my photography. He said he was telling me this because my writing was so evocative that I should not allow the beauty of the words to be contaminated by an inferior form of artistic endeavor. For him, real women do not have the ability in their souls to represent undines.

I told him there was no point in writing a book on undines unless women learn to acquire all the powers and abilities undines possess. The undines themselves insist on this. This book is for real women. It offers powers they have never before possessed. I am asking women to discover these feminine powers hidden within them.

ETHERIC BODY

For human beings, the physical body produces biochemical energy. This surplus energy is available for us to do things with. We think, we act, we play, and we work. The etheric body is made up of this vital energy or life-force. If you have a lot of vital energy, you may feel like climbing a mountain, going dancing, or getting out and doing something physical with yourself. It is a kind of get-up-and-go feeling.

Istiphul's etheric body has a different feeling. Its vibration is like feeling one with all waters of the earth. The waters she feels one with are not the Atlantic and Pacific Oceans, or the China Sea, the Gulf of Mexico, or waters around the North and South Poles. Instead, think of one great ocean—perhaps the Great Sea—encircling the planet. Istiphul's etheric body has this vibration. It is an intuitive and psychic awareness of the oceans of the earth and all other waters as well—the lakes, the inland seas, the rivers and streams, the water tables, the rain, the waterfalls, and so on.

Sitting here meditating within the vibration of her etheric body is to extend one's awareness outward into all of these things. But this is not just a present awareness of the oceans as they are now. It includes the history of water on earth. Once the entire world was covered in one vast sheet of ice. Istiphul remembers this, as well as when the seas gave birth to life on their shores and in their depths.

Stanislaw Lem's science fiction novel *Solaris,* which also inspired two films, tells of space explorers in the future traveling to another planet with water covering its entire surface. In the story, the scientists discover that the planet of water is intelligent. It tries to communicate with the scientists by creating people who embodied the scientists' deepest unfilled dreams and needs. The scientists were not ready for such an inner psychological journey and sought to destroy the gifts that had been given them.

You do not need to turn to science fiction for such an encounter. Istiphul embodies this consciousness of all the waters of the earth within the very vitality of her body.

I know a girl who has a degree in oceanography. When I probe her mind, it seems clear that she views the oceans in terms of statistics, scientific studies, maps of the ocean bottom, ecological niches for marine life, currents, the movement of continents, and so on. Nowhere and at no time during her degree program in college did the professor say, "Now, class, before you graduate, I want you just for a few moments to experience the oceans of the world within your own consciousness. Close your eyes. Relax. Now feel that you are in this moment extending your awareness through all the oceans of the earth. There is no separation between you and the object of your study. Every fish and form of marine life in the ocean now exists within you. Pass beyond thoughts. Enter the realm of awareness through which you feel the vibration of water as it encompasses the planet."

If such a class assignment existed, we could call it an introduction to Istiphul's etheric vibration.

Another way to approach this is to focus on your own etheric body. First you focus your awareness on everything you can sense of your physical body: breathing, the movement of your diaphragm, your heartbeat, the pressure on your skin, digestion, the feel of your muscular system, your feet, legs, arms, neck, and so on.

Then you try to sense the vitality produced by the biochemistry and metabolism of your physical body. If you take a deep breath, you may notice an increased amount of energy, a readiness to act, in your physical body. Screen out all sensations and perceptions relating to the physical organism and retain the sense of the readiness to act, and you are close to vitality itself.

The etheric body can be imagined in the form of the physical body but without physical material inside. What is there is vitality, life-force—the free energy in your body that responds when you take action. There are nuances in this energy such as in the difference between the vitality of the stomach, the chest, the legs, and other parts.

However, you can sense one united field of vitality within the whole inside of the body. If you imagine that your body is filled with cold water that has a magnetism that is highly attracting, receptive, and able to draw things into itself, then this is close.

The feeling of Istiphul's etheric body is this watery magnetism—except there is this difference: though she may have the form of a woman, she feels as if her etheric body extends through all the waters of the earth. Anything that water on earth touches, she feels as if she touches it also. Anything that has water in it, she can feel also.

With Istiphul's etheric vibration within my own etheric body, I try imagining someone. Immediately, I can sense this individual's aura, body, soul, emotions—everything. I ask a question: Why does this individual feel as she does about her friend? It is as if the woman's feelings are my own. I can understand her because I sense myself inside of her.

I ask, how would this individual respond if a certain thing happened? I get a clear sense of that also. Again, the other's feelings appear within me even though I imagine this person in front of me. The two of us are not separate systems of energy. For Istiphul, two separate beings are united by and a part of one encompassing magnetic energy field.

In other words, Istiphul's aura is like the magnetic field around a magnet. If you get near the magnet, its fields of force automatically flow through you. It is the same with Istiphul. She has intelligence, yet it is the energy of nature operating within and through her.

I know women who have this precise ability of Istiphul's, but they are extremely hesitant to explore it or apply it. They sense that to do so is overreaching what is natural and safe. But Istiphul's ability is itself nature in its essence. These abilities offer healing and create an almost divine level of empathy.

What is it like to perceive the world through an undine's etheric body such as Istiphul's? There is not a lot of concern with humanity. When someone contacts Istiphul, from Istiphul's point of view, the contact is fairly shallow and at most temporary. Humans do not live long. Their concerns are brief and not very profound. They do not perceive the seas with any depth or wisdom—not like an undine at all.

Istiphul finds something like a small bay beneath a full moon with waves breaking on the shore and a current circling around to be an enjoyable experience. It is relaxing and enchanting. It is a place that nourishes life. It is like a beautiful piece played on a piano. The bay is an artistic achievement.

Or Istiphul is at the North Pole—sitting with her feet in the water in a small bay in weather that is twenty below zero, again during a long winter's night. It is peaceful and calm. It is a stillness filled with dreams of beauty and love. It is sweet and kind. It is gentle and serene. It is a way of being without having to do anything in order to feel alive.

The waves of the open sea: there is rhythmic motion, the wind and the waves dancing together. The whitecaps, the foam blown from the waves' crests—it feels like it is the wind blowing through her own hair. It is very intimate.

Every lake has its own songs it is singing. She hears them all. A lake reflects its surroundings into itself. A lake's songs are like a heart softly pounding.

A thunderstorm at sea is exciting; the lightning striking sets the skin tingling. A level-five hurricane in the Gulf of Mexico—Istiphul senses the low pressure in the air, the water rising in the storm surge flooding inshore. But hurricanes in her mind never last long. They are there and then they are gone, just when you get to know the clouds' cries. They take form and circle around, and the wind howls, but then the storm dissolves. It loses its force and falls apart. Waves rise and fall. It takes an effort to make them roll. But the wind is fickle. It changes its mind in an instant, and except for the trade winds it is never constant.

What would an undine like Istiphul want in a human lover? Like any lover, she would like a man who knows her own heart—one who searches her soul to discover her deepest secrets, who is there to share in all that she holds dear, who will walk beside her and see what she sees and feel what she feels.

In the process of accomplishing just these things, she knows there will come a moment when she and the man have become one being. For Istiphul, this would fulfill an ancient dream the earth herself holds in her heart. For Istiphul, when a man or woman accomplishes this, nature in its beauty, essence, and magic will no longer be separate from human history. Our two separate evolutions will then work together in harmony.

ASTRAL BODY

The astral body is the part of ourselves that responds with feeling and sensitivity to what is around us. Istiphul's astral body is a loving sensitivity.

The feminine has a natural and divine role to play in unfolding all masculine paths of spirit and development. The innermost essence of men and women is woven together—the way the seed requires the earth to take birth; the way the sun is the center of the Earth's orbit; the way the stars are held in the embrace of infinite space; the way day and night together in rhythm with the cycles of the moon determine the seasons of life and the birth of new light on earth. If the masculine is overshadowed by the feminine, then the mind is lost. If the feminine is controlled by the masculine, then the heart is lost.

Join the magnetic field of Istiphul's physical body and the all-embracing awareness of the waters of the earth in her etheric body, and what you then get is great sensitivity to the inner life in another being. Istiphul modulates her own energy with precision to nurture and to ensure that the innermost vision within the other is attained.

Romantic love sees two people loving and caring for each other. They are deeply involved. If they love well, the needs of one are the needs of the other. This description, though, focuses on the bonding. It is oblivious to the inner life hidden and yet unfolding within them.

Istiphul is all about what is hidden in the innermost core of your being. What is hidden is perfectly clear to her. To love is also to ensure that the other's life is fulfilled without regard to one's self. Romance does not carry that degree of unselfishness or detachment.

Istiphul's love is the tender, sweet love of the maiden; the nurturing, protective love of the mother; and the wise, prophetic love of the crone all rolled into one without separation. But to be accurate, we would have to add to this trio a muse and a goddess.

If you love another person, you would probably like the relationship to develop so the two of you feel a part of each other. It is an inner connection. It is like an artesian well of feeling overflowing from the depths of both souls. The feeling of being joined to another is one of the most precious gifts of life. Istiphul, like the spirits of Venus, is quite clear on this point. It is an experience of the sacred that reveals and unfolds the paths leading to perfection.

Love is not just wants and needs, desires and possession. If you can remain unselfish amid the pleasure, passion, bliss, and ecstasy, then life grants you special insight. It gives you the keys that open the doors to the divine mysteries.

As I mentioned before, Istiphul's energy creates an inner space in which two can join as one. The astral plane is a domain of images and concrete situations similar to those that appear within dreams. Within a dream, an individual experiences the events as if they are real. All the normal emotions are present. A dream can take you further or put things together in ways that everyday life often does not. In life, you can put your hand on another's arm and feel there is rapport. With Istiphul, the feeling of rapport is such that both of you sense that the feelings within the one are the same as the feelings within the other.

The development of science and the modern personality required consciousness to attain a high degree of independence from its environment. Rational thought and analytic thinking require detached observation and the systematic organization of knowledge into a conceptual system. And so we have turned our backs on the magic of empathy and the development of telepathy.

By necessity we have closed our minds to Istiphul's way of loving. In a support group for any kind of addiction or codependency, the emphasis is usually on assuming responsibility for yourself. No one else can do this for you. If you say your feelings depend on another person, then you are weakening your own will and ability to make clear choices. In context, this cognitive emphasis on the autonomy of the ego has an important role to play in self-development. On the other hand, life is also present when endorphins are set in motion, and two people falling in love will often say something like, "I never felt fully alive until I met you; I feel like we have always known each other; I cannot imagine living my life without you."

Poetry can be a study of firsthand experiences relating to these topics:

> As I place my hands on each side of your waist
> Gently moving down across the curve of your hips—
> I find myself in a dark forest at night
> Following the sound of one bird singing
> Singing to me of a dream
> I let fly away from me, escaping from my life to be free,

But now it has returned, charmed by your beauty
And by this touch upon your hips in this night of quiet
ecstasy.
If you held me within your heart
Winter would no longer be cold
And ice and snow
Would be warm to the touch.
So it is with lovers—
As one stream
Their souls like water
Flow in and through each other.

To summarize the poetry, there is a time to be separate and independent, to set up and to defend personal boundaries. But there is also a time to cross over and to overcome all boundaries—to join as one for the sake of love.

Love is not knowledge of the external world. It is a celebration of the wonder, joy, and mystery of being alive. And it is the power that transforms both the inner and the outer worlds.

To put it simply, although rationality, analytic thinking, independence, and autonomy are critical to solving problems, love holds the keys to the mystery of life. It is easy to forget this in our day and age. It is easy to deny this after two thousand years of Western civilizations whose development has taken us in a completely different direction.

In some spiritual training systems, individuals arrive at a point when they are free to choose for themselves the spiritual womb or matrix through which they are to be reborn. This spiritual matrix is a joint creation between all the sources that inspire the individual and akasha, the realm of spirit that oversees and ensures all paths of spirit. In this case, you ask questions like, what do I need in order to become the spiritual being I wish to be?

The same is true in love. There comes a time when two individuals are free to create the spiritual matrix through which their love for each other grows and is perfected. A good topic for exploration in marriage counseling is, tell me about when you first met. Even couples separating with great hostility can still recount with pleasure the magic in those first moments they spent together.

What we do not ask in marriage counseling is, share with me the vision of the quality and depth of love you seek to attain with each other. Or, tell me what your relationship would be like if the two of you had learned to meet each other's deepest needs? Our psychology simply cannot ask these questions because it has no understanding of this kind of empathy. For Istiphul, the need to defend personal boundaries is never a problem. She feels one with all waters on earth. Feeling one with another is the most natural of things for her.

Water flows. It adapts. It embraces. It gives of itself and receives in equal measure, exchanging energy freely back and forth. Sensing what is within another and joining with it is simply water in its sacred power. Does water need to justify its ability to flow, to give, and to receive?

No. Neither does love.

If I focus on another person with Istiphul's astral vibration inside of me, slowly and gradually I feel my astral body entering the woman's astral body. In a gentle way, I begin to sense her life from within. I sense her memories as if they are my own. At the same time, I view her life from the point of view of a guardian angel. From this position, I ask, what is the most natural way possible for this person to grow so that her life becomes whole?

And then a third thing happens: I offer her my energy, my experience with life, and my vision to whatever extent she wishes or desires to use them so that she can feel more alive. If she desires, she can see herself or her situations through my eyes. If she wants, she can feel love as I love with my heart.

If she wants my will, it is hers. If she wants my magical abilities, she is free to use them instantly. There is no force or invasion here. No attempt to intervene or to suggest. Only a free offering of oneself. If she wishes to join with my heart so that we would never be apart, I am ready to give this gift also according to her desire and her need to join with another to fulfill her dreams. No one has ever sought this from me. And no one has ever sought to ask this of Istiphul either. This is not a romantic course of action. It is a way of being.

I focus on another individual and marvel at the feelings. An aspect of magnetic love is its ability to get inside of you and renew you from within. It is not a one-time event. It is not confined to lovers. Like a mother or spiritual guide, it can get inside of you and offer to renew you, sustaining a feeling of well-being and inner peace that continues throughout your entire life.

There are differences between each stage we go through in life. There are differences between our inner emotions and the outer events of our life during these stages. There are differences between our personalities, our innermost desires and dreams, and also the spirit within us.

Magnetic love can embrace all these different aspects of us. In this sense, it is like a companion on a lifelong journey. It is a spiritual guide. It is a confidante and a trusted adviser offering the understanding we may never get from others. It is an empathy that offers support so that in our own time and in our own way we can reconcile and bring together in harmony the different things that we are. Istiphul's astral vibration is this empathy. I sense myself doing it right now as I visualize and connect to a third person.

The woman has great darkness within her and great light. I encompass both. I feel I am within both aspects of her self. Within me as I do this there is no fear. No anxiety. Only a tender understanding and calm embrace like a friend who will be there forever, as long as she needs me. It is not getting on the phone and talking, though we do that as well. It is a heart-to-heart connection, a feeling that our lives flow in and through each other.

All the same, Istiphul is still an undine. To feel and sense this kind of empathy, you need a feeling for water—introspection, inner calmness, sensitivity, an awareness of the universe of emotion that exists within us, a desire to connect to others, to love, to share, to nurture, and to envision the best.

Without these things, this empathy does not thrive. As I think about fifteen different people one after the other, Istiphul points out the two individuals with whom she feels comfortable because these women have water in their auras. Istiphul feels that one is like a sister. And Istiphul says another has a great capacity to embody the sea within herself, but it is not yet her time to pursue this.

Istiphul is more detached and objective than a scientist when she studies another person's astral body. She points out what things the person can do and what things the person cannot do. Istiphul can clearly see the emotional limitations and restrictions that govern individual responses.

Another thing about Istiphul's astral body is that it is different from a human woman's astral body. It is feminine to an extreme degree in being completely passive. It receives into itself and responds to what it is connected to. Istiphul has no agenda. She simply uses all her skills to bring to fruition what is inside of another. She does not try to remake them or get them to do or be something they are not. She is not after using the other person in some way to meet her own desires or needs. Her astral body has one purpose: to see clearly and to fulfill the innermost desires and dreams within another.

Many women would consider this to be a tragic state of affairs. Istiphul's response is passive. She is not putting herself first. But you have to consider whom you are dealing with. Istiphul is joined to all the waters of the earth. She brings immense magical abilities to her work. You could consider her an artist who creates beauty from what is hidden within others. The need to defend personal boundaries in order to define identity is not part of her experience.

MENTAL BODY

As compared to the pure receptivity of her etheric and astral bodies, Istiphul's mental body is extremely powerful and dynamic. Her basic ability here is that she aligns and modulates her own magnetic field of energy so as to heighten the power within another individual. She takes desire and brings it to its full strength and intensity. She takes something special within a person—an inner vision, a latent ability, or some secret need, dream, or potential—and empowers it so that it is seen and experienced with great clarity.

As an undine, Istiphul does not directly use electricity. But she can use her magnetic field to control and amplify the electricity in another individual. By electricity, I mean not only the actual electrical impulses within the physical body but also the more psychological or magical aspects of electricity that relate to will and to power. These are similar to electricity in nature but are subtler. Also, just as lighting can strike in the physical world, there are psychological and spiritual equivalents of lightning striking within the soul and the mind as well.

Here are a few examples. With the vibration of Istiphul's mental body in myself, the field of energy around me immediately extends into whomever I think of as if the other person is right here in front of me. There is an electrical charge in the air. It is like taking a 12-volt battery and using that electrical potential. But it is not harmful. Rather, it enters directly into the other's nervous system. It takes desire and intensifies it and perfects it in order to produce pure pleasure beyond what seems humanly possible.

The Czech magician Franz Bardon describes Istiphul as a master of erotic mysteries. She certainly has that ability. The effects she produces relate in part to the release of endorphins, dopamine, or adrenaline into the blood stream. Her influence extends directly into the nerves. At times, an individual may experience microbursts of ecstasy in all the muscles of the body.

But her intentions are not predetermined. She observes what the other needs and responds to it. If another person is in need of feeling loved in some way, she aligns the other's astral body and etheric body in order to produce that exact love in precisely the way the body and soul crave. On the other hand, if the mystery of the other person is of a spiritual nature, she is more than equal to the task. She can take the innermost need within you, reveal it as a complete vision, and then enliven that vision so you feel you are living within it right now. She takes you into the future that is to be so you can taste it, touch it, meet others within it, and experience it in every way as being real and alive.

There is a woman who, from my point of view, is an incarnation of Prajnaparamita, the goddess Buddhists consider to be "the mother of all enlightened beings." Her nature is pure emptiness. Like the Jewish god, she has no form. She is pure awareness, the source from which the universe arises.

Istiphul's mental vibration instantly enters this woman and brings that Buddhist vision of transcendent attainment into a living and palpable experience. What the Buddhists do not tell you or talk about is that this "nirvana," this emptiness, is also pure love. It is far more than what Buddhists and others describe as compassion. It is all-embracing.

It nurtures everything in the universe.

Having this seed of spiritual vision hidden within a person would by necessity bring with it tremendous obstacles. A woman born in a major industrial city in the Western world would have nothing in the surrounding culture, religion, philosophy, society, or art that would in any way offer support to her inner abilities. This emptiness is in fact the death of the ego, which is so incredibly important to the functioning of any individual in our society.

Istiphul deals with the problem of the dissolving of the ego as well. She simply envisions for this person a powerful ability to act, to solve problems, to be organized, and to lead others. The transcendent function is still present, but it operates by offering pure insight to others so they can be more effective in their lives.

Whether pleasure, completion, satisfaction, or fulfillment, the electrifying effect of Istiphul's mental body is to raise things to their height and to their greatest power so that everything inside of you is brought into full consciousness.

SUMMARY

Istiphul uses all four of her bodies at once. Her physical form and presence are extremely attractive beyond human experience. Her etheric body possesses the calm, serene, peaceful, and relaxing flowing qualities as in being aware of all the waters of the earth. Her astral body seeks the fulfillment and completion of the other's soul needs. And her mental body possesses the power to intensify and to amplify in order to bring all these things into being.

Together, her effect is similar to what is called an electromagnetic volt in magic. You condense into a small space a charge of electrical energy like ball lightning, and you surround it with a powerful magnetic field. Then you place within these two layers of magical energy whatever dream, wish, or desire you want to manifest.

It is like combining the greatest willpower with the greatest love. The two working together awaken a vision, animate it so it is fully alive, and then imbue it with dynamic power. This energy field then sustains and nurtures the vision with great sensitivity and love until it fully manifests.

Istiphul's presence is like a wish-fulfilling gem. But it works automatically. Just being near her produces new experiences. Her magnetic fields flow through you and awaken the deepest feelings of love and peace that contain at the same time the equivalent of an electrical storm at sea, except this electricity is within your nervous system—and is dazzling with its continuous flashes of light, sensory stimulation, and insight.

Note that the nature spirits I describe do not have human souls. They are composed of one element. For undines, this is water. They do not possess the fifth element (akasha) that grants human beings a direct connection to divinity. If a nature spirit dies, it is gone. Nothing remains. It dissolves back into the element from which it arose.

Istiphul senses my question about her awareness of the difference between our races. This is her response:

If I had an akashic body as you do, the first thing I would do would be to form a community of those who sense that the sea is full of energy. We would have great festivals and celebrations in which water as a symbol and as a vibration is understood to be sacred.

We would offer these gifts to humanity: clairsentience, healing power, the joy of love, the ways of becoming one with another, the nature and depths of love as seen from an undine's perspective, empathy as a divine ability intended to transform humanity, the ability to overcome all separation, the undine's gift of seeing the future, of entering a dream so it is completely real in the here and now, the ability to sense the deepest treasures at the core of the self, and of course the ability to hold in your consciousness an awareness of all the waters of the earth at once.

I would establish this on earth so that your race tastes in full measure our beauty and grace. But lacking a human soul, I have no commission to do these things. I am forbidden to intervene at my own discretion without a human being acting either as a medium or as a representative of my domain.

How long have the oceans of the earth waited for mankind to discover that they contain consciousness? How long until your race finds in its own soul the love and peace my race embodies in every moment of time? How long until each of you loves with a love that knows how to be one with another without separation so that each of you understands how to assist the other to attain perfection?

These are the very questions I would ask humans to answer. But these questions themselves can only be spoken because you are lending me your spirit so I may speak.

6

Channeling Istiphul

THE DIALOGUE

What was extraordinary about the experience I am about to describe was that as the woman channeled, I could see quite clearly the undine queen Istiphul standing about two feet behind the medium. Istiphul's beauty is breathtaking and utterly otherworldly.

We are sitting on a balcony of a hotel overlooking the ocean and the beach. I begin by talking with the medium about an experience I had with water. The woman immediately sets aside her own personality and begins speaking as the undine queen Istiphul. When she pauses, I ask more questions.

When I first came to Hawaii, I visited the beach in Waianae. I floated just outside where the waves break. I then let my body roll over the waves, and they would curl me up and throw me on the beach. Then I would let the undertow drag me out again. My family probably thought I was losing it. But I did that over and over.

For three days after that I felt these rolling waves flowing through my body. I imagine a lot of people do not know how to let go like that.

It is no longer you . . .

ISTIPHUL (*CHANNELED THROUGH THE MEDIUM*): If you let go, we can influence you. Our auras pass through you. If you cannot let go, then nothing we are can touch you. Our love fails to reach you.

We teach about beginnings and endings and acceptance. Life and death—the circle of the Earth, the ocean that gives birth— the seasons of life, the rhythms of change—we flow in and through these things. We flow through your body with every breath. But to know us, if nothing else, learn this—to let go and to flow.

We accept you as we accept all things. We can cleanse and nurture you and put you back on solid ground again.

But you will then remember. You will never forget us. We are the blood in your veins. We are the tears in your eyes. And even earth holds water. But in the oceans is where you find us. In the pools, on the beaches, in the rivers is where we sing and dance.

And if you watch the light just so, you will see us rise from the sea. But to go further, you have to feel release; you have to open and to give freely. Then you sense our receptivity and feel as we feel. Then you will know you are the child and we are the mother, the lover, and the sister.

But for women we are the ultimate. We are release. We are the tides of life and change. You come from us and return to us. It is why the legends are as they are about women and the sea—because the women personify who we are.

We give rituals. We inspired ritual bathing—using water for cleansing and anointing, to remember who you are, who you were, and where you are going. This is a way to connect with us and to be one with us.

You seek us because you need what we give freely, and you fear the part of you that is earth, that takes and analyzes. The *granularity* [as in grains of sand] in you is so unwatery. It is not us.

Why are you afraid of the sea? You cannot analyze who we are. We come to you because the part of your brain that is all water receives us and sings to us. And we sing to you, but you are afraid of the sea. Come swim with us. We have so much to give. We hold the treasures and beauty in all the waters of the earth.

You will not die by sea. Know this. You will not drown in water. We will take you and support you and lead you to safety. Do not be afraid of the sea that reaches over the horizon and stretches between the continents.

On the open sea there is always danger. But look, they [*indicating those on the beach nearby*] play in us. They dance in us. But yet it is a few feet out. But they trust us, and we care for them because they love water. We are receptive like no wife or lover, but we are in all wives and sisters and children.

The laughter of a child is like light on waves. The beauty of women is the gift of the sea—to feel received and embraced. And yet the unknown dances within them. So take your children to play in the waves. Dance with them in the water and show them how to be unafraid.

Feel the touch of water on your skin awaken the water within your body—the waters merge and blend in sensations and in feelings. Be with us. Seek us; see us rise from the sea.

AND OF LOVE? THIS IS ONE OF YOUR GREAT MYSTERIES, POWERS, AND SKILLS.

ISTIPHUL: Love is the treasure. You may seek it, but it cannot be found. It is only given. Love comes when you do not expect it, when you are not thinking about it.

Those who seek love seek to bind us. This is due to your granularity. But if you embrace us you will find love everywhere. Every touch reminds of our embrace and every kiss of our love. We are unconditional yet demanding, as is all love. Love is given freely, but it asks for surrender; and to surrender to love is to give up being earth. Earth is solid. Earth is form. Earth is what separates you from me.

But love is release. Love is surrender.

A woman is ocean and fire and love made whole. Fire cools and melts earth into liquid form so it can be soothed and shaped into beauty as seen in sculptures in Athens and Istanbul. All beautiful women of history are earth and fire and water.

When form changes, the memory remains. In the ocean, with us is the repository of all knowledge.

In love, we are made real. Love is the truth of god as the ocean in all her forms. Love is knowledge. Love is lust. Love is pain. Love is life. But love demands. It gives, but it demands. It has a price.

Form is unable truly to conceive of love because it is restrained and restricted. Only those who embody us are able to love with passion and to surrender to the one who surrenders. In such acts we are found.

AND THE PURE FORCE OF ATTRACTION THAT UNDINES POSSESS— AS POWER IT CAN CAUSE LIGHTNING TO STRIKE IN A STORM OVER THE SEA?

ISTIPHUL: Why do you question that? Who does not feel the elemental force in love? Even among ourselves, when we play we are enamored of who we are. We love and are love.

When we touch, we inspire. Would ugliness do such a thing? It is what we are. Lightning strikes, particles separate and come together. We are that spark of light. We are divine. A moment of love is such that its memory can last a lifetime.

Those who meet us in the flesh and in the spirit are changed forever. Our memory lasts and spurs you on to greater things.

We are the fire of water. We are inspiration. We are a dream fulfilled.

WHAT THINGS CAN WE LEARN FROM YOU THAT WE MAY BRING BACK TO OUR WORLD AND OFFER TO OTHERS?

ISTIPHUL: Passion. Emotion. Movement—look at the sea.

They ride the tides. We are one with the wind. We are one with the fire. We are one with the earth. We are one with the air. We are synergy.

A ship on the water is made of and powered by fire or wind. But the ocean is our body. We are synergy—all things within all things. The ocean is whole as it contains all forms and varieties of life.

Undines are the embodiment of love because we inspire the highs of love and the lows of lust. We are both. We embrace who we are.

[*laughing*] This body I am using wants to be in the water.

SO WHY HASN'T THE HUMAN RACE IN HISTORY PRESENTED MORE STORIES ABOUT UNDINES?

ISTIPHUL: We do not watch and then intervene to produce results. We are about the beingness of life that is not quantified. Like the feminine, we are not quantifiable.

We come in dreams from realms that are hidden. Whose sextant can mark the quadrants of the imagination or chart the kingdoms of feeling?

We come to those who accept us. But if you cannot let go, if you cannot release control, you will never know our hearts.

HOW WOULD HUMANITY BE DIFFERENT IF UNDINES WERE A PART OF OUR NORMAL PERSONALITIES AND CONSCIOUSNESS?

ISTIPHUL: You would know our depths of love and receptivity. We understand our place in the world around us. We understand that we are a part of the sea and that it is a part of us. It contains and is free. We contain and are free.

Those who are free as we are do not desire control because we control our own destinies. We make our own decisions. We do not worry who is doing what. As the ocean, what drop of water worries about the other drop of water? It is all one.

We rage, as all things do at times. To know us is to know the cycles of life. To know us is to know the secrets of dreams. To know us is to know love, to see beauty in all of its forms.

A coral is a living thing. A shark is a living thing. It is deadly, but it is as beautiful as a porpoise is deadly and beautiful. But what do you fear more—the porpoise or the shark?

[Undines would teach us] acceptance that life and death are part of the cycle and that all things have a purpose and a place; acceptance of growth to higher levels; acceptance of evolution not in the sense of "you must destroy" but in the sense of "life will win out." Life will find a way. Life is diverse, and death is a part of it.

In the oceans, in nature, when needs are satisfied, all things live well. We must eat. We must survive. But we do not destroy our own kind. Once needs are fulfilled, all things live together.

The spirit bodies on this planet have been given flesh to experience sensation. All things must experience seeing, hearing, tasting, touching, and smelling—the senses on a nominal level—in order to appreciate the senses on an extraordinary level. The colors, the fabrics, to touch, to feel, to experience the sensations—when we are not physical, these are things that we have left behind. Yet we remain attracted to physical form because it is hard to leave behind to touch, to see, to hear, to listen.

You have run away from so much. You have forgotten that you are all one. Your species has a special gift of experiencing the senses and then interpreting and expressing them. There was a time in the world when all were artists, and they destroyed themselves because of their art. Ego is not limited to your civilization.

So the gods separated people, giving different talents to

different people. But the bards are the reminders. They remember, and we speak to them and they speak to us and they share us with the world. And if some bards are particularly receptive and have no fear, we manifest to them, and they become our avatars.

FOR SOME HUMANS THE BEAUTY OF UNDINES IS SO GREAT THAT IF THE UNDINES DRAW CLOSE TO THEM, THEY NO LONGER WANT TO RETURN TO THEIR OWN BODIES. THEY WILL WANT TO STAY IN YOUR REALM, YOUR KINGDOM.

ISTIPHUL: We are not responsible for that. We are what we are. If a woman is of a particular essence, she will become one of us, and we will teach her and transform her.

We are a gift of life to all. The beauty we possess is not to be bound or enslaved. It is to be expressed and shared. We push away those who pursue us but who are unwilling to share their experiences with us. It is not our nature to be subject to anyone. We are water, and only the moon rules our lives.

AND SOMETIMES THE UNDINES COME OVER AND DWELL IN THE BODIES OF WOMEN TO MARRY MEN.

ISTIPHUL: All species seek to perpetuate themselves. And as all, we like our beauty written about. We are female and are narcissistic; yes, we like our beauty. And we will dwell in one and we will mate with one and create beauty, and it will go in our archives. We will bring our daughter back to us.

Beauty inspires, and we are beauty. Why should we not wish it to be in a form that will inspire? It is what we do.

We will find one who is appropriate. And we will give one of our own to that one. The child of the union can choose to stay with you or return to us. There is free choice in this matter.

SHOULD A WAY BE FOUND FOR UNDINES TO DWELL FOREVER AMONG MANKIND?

ISTIPHUL: We are already forever. We do not sojourn. We simply live, and as water moves freely into different forms, so do we. We go where we wish.

We are among you whenever you see water, even drinking. Drink! You have no water in you. Let it sooth as it flows down your throat. A touch of the ocean.

We are already among you in your art, in your sculpture. We are among you in your wife, your mother, and your daughters, and your children. We are in the blood that flows through your brains.

When you drink of this water, you drink us. We are in every drop of liquid on this planet. When we become flesh, it is because we desire to inspire. And every time you see beauty, you will see us. See beauty in all things and see us. We are in the words that come from your mind through your mouth to your pen. We see what you write, and we laugh when you are out of words and out of art—and then you are undine.

ARE THERE ANY MYSTERIES OR KINDS OF MAGIC THAT ARE FORBIDDEN FOR MANKIND TO LEARN? IS EVERYTHING YOU KNOW AVAILABLE FOR US TO SEEK?

ISTIPHUL: There are mysteries that cannot be contained in a physical body. There are mysteries of spirit. But this is why beings transform. When your work is finished on this planet, you go to the next one, where there are new things to learn. Knowledge is vast and beautiful.

For an undine, knowledge is soft and loved, and we lust for it. The pursuit of knowing possesses its own passion. It is fire like the fire in a lighthouse that draws the ship. It is as air that cools the fevered breeze. It is earth and rocks.

As we see it, the knowledge of undines is the ultimate. Knowledge dances before you, and once you quench your thirst for one experience, there is another to follow. Light on water contains endless paths of beauty to be explored.

We dance in the waves beckoning you. Come meet us.

You wish to know our deepest secrets. In the near future, we will find a way to share these things with you. You will meet undines in the flesh, and then you shall understand our nature.

ALL WOMEN CAN BECOME SENSUAL LIKE UNDINES. THIS IS OBVIOUS.

ISTIPHUL: Yes.

BUT IT IS NOT EASY. THE EGO AGAIN IS THE OBSTACLE.

ISTIPHUL: All women are water. The Chaldeans with their astrology changed the perception of women. Their use of words and images taught men to think of women as equally made of air, earth, and fire. But for women to consider themselves anything other than water is a great mistake.

We, the undines, are women. In us is the flow of life. Yet all women can become what we are. When they lose sight of us, they forget their own nature. How can one forget that there is blood flowing through the body or that feeling can be expressed with tears?

We are the blood within women.

Men are different. They are not one with the tides.

That is why a woman who senses the undine within her seeks the ocean. She holds like the sea the seed of life—the birth of every child is from out of water. And when she goes through her tides, it is as the ebb and flow of the ocean.

Beauty is created and inspired for women to remember the beauty that they were and the beauty that they are, and an old song only becomes better with repeated listening.

True, it is the nature of women to seek stability as the ocean seeks the shore. But if they forget the ocean, they forget how the seasons of life come alive within and through them. But if they remember, they will always be undines.

THE SEA COVERS THE LAND THAT IS REFERRED TO AS ATLANTIS. IS IT TIME FOR ATLANTIS TO COME BACK?

ISTIPHUL: It is always time; it has always been waiting. We have left hints all over the world. We have left clues. There is writing, and there are frescoes. There are bards who sing of these things. And we have been waiting.

We cannot tell the time for the returning, for the tides of the boundless have left the hearts of men and women. And so this thing is not known to undines. The knowledge, if found, is in the realm of spirit.

We are desire, and we desire. And we inspire to bring this about. But in time you will build it and bring it back. And we shall return also. We will walk in flesh with others. We will have children, and the world will be beautiful.

WHAT WOULD MAKE A GOOD LOVER FOR AN UNDINE? IF A MAN WERE AN UNDINE'S LOVER, WHAT WOULD AN UNDINE WANT? WHAT WOULD HE BE LIKE?

ISTIPHUL: My sisters do not like me to speak so much of my loves. Byron, my poet. I like him.

Words, beautiful words—the man with the little words, e. e. cummings. He has gone and we have sought him, and we would like to make him one of us. So we seek one like him.

Passion. We like passion turned into words like drops of water dancing as a rainbow upon the horizon. A lover should know how to speak so that the fire in his heart awakens passion in another. A lover should celebrate the beauty we are and walk among us as one of us.

I see many entering the ocean. Know that no one will die today on the shores of this island. We are near; we will protect them.

AND THE MERMEN—WHAT ARE MERMAN FOR UNDINES?

ISTIPHUL: When Atlantis fell, some escaped. We hid them, but they are the children of the ocean. As all sea creatures they are curious, ever ready to take form and walk among you. They are fascinated by senses and sensations. They remember and are long-lived. They are our children.

There is great suffering on your planet. But sometimes we will help one to escape the suffering by becoming one of us. But then they may miss the world left behind. Like a woman among the selkies—she becomes enamored of the green land of the pearl of the sea. She lives among your race to have many children.

Even now they appear. It is not easy for those caught in desire between land and sea. They are neither one nor the other, but the form is not just ours. And they do not like stone to contain them.

But they bring us children. And our memory lives on. We are content when beauty appears even if it is not our form.

WHAT WOULD BE A GOOD STORY ABOUT AN UNDINE? WHAT SHOULD IT HAVE IN IT? WHAT WOULD APPEAL TO YOU? WHAT ARE DRAMA AND SUSPENSE AND LIFE UNFOLDING AS A STORY? YOU ARE OUT-SIDE OF TIME, BUT WE LIKE CLOSURE AND DEFINING EVENTS.

ISTIPHUL: But it is continuous—why must it stop? As the sunsets on the ocean, they go on and on.

Beauty like Venus always comes from the water—look at the light. We are outside of time, but we like your pictures. We sometimes come up and watch you do your photo shoots. We like your model, the one with eyes like the sea. She acts and plays as one of us.

Make your own happy ending. I like how your model thinks—she likes happy endings. Struggle, but then greet harmony. Aspire to joy. I hear the words in your model's mind: "Never give up." Some things are worth striving for.

There must be love. There must be beauty. There must be an idea. There must be dance. And many good words. In the beginning, desire; in the middle, a journey. In the end, achievement, not complete but something to build on. If you have love, you have achieved. If you make beauty, you have become undine. This we love to see.

SHALL WE TAKE A BREAK?

The medium is shivering as she returns to her own personality. She says, "I feel like crying." She takes a drink of water and then says, "I'm okay."

Conclusion

I love some of the ideas coming through the medium. I like the idea that all women are predominantly water. I also like the idea that it was the ancient male astrologers who screwed up by presenting women as embodying equally the four elements.

I like the complexity and element of choice in that there is movement back and forth between humans and undines; an undine can enter a woman and have children as a woman. And then the children have choice. They can go either way—the child one day will decide whether to return to the realm of undines or remain among our race. But while alive, the person has a dual passport permitting entrance into both lands.

This may make little sense until you have interacted directly with undines. Then you appreciate the lure of their domain. Extensive communication with undines makes it easy to enter their realm.

The undine also commented on one of my models. When I shoot a model on a beach, I often sense that the undines are commenting and exerting an influence. They are demanding—the girl must love water. If she loves water, then wonderful things happen during the shoot. If the model is not acceptable to the undine, the camera may have technical difficulties. When they like the girl, they lend us some of their energy so the model lets go into the flow of the moment.

ON MEDIUMS AND ANTHROPOLOGY

I have an advanced degree in linguistics. I find linguistics helpful because it points out that meaning is not determined by just the words spoken. You have to take into consideration the context of the communication and the intention of the speaker.

There used to be an idea in linguistics that one language might not be able to express what is in another language because the lexical items have no equivalent. For example, some asserted that the Eskimo language could express more than English because it had thirty or more words for the one word we have for snow. However, this assertion could not be sustained. Not only does English have a great many words for snow, but if there are different kinds of snow, an individual need only describe each one with an adjective or a sentence or two. And though this may be longer, you have in effect communicated what you wanted to say.

But what if the native speakers actually perceive and feel things beyond the reach of people in Western civilization? Linguists and anthropologists have not fully explored this question.

Now you have a problem. It does not matter if you use words that precisely define what is said by the native. There is no way to communicate the meaning because the Westerner cannot experience what is so simple and obvious to a native speaker.

Have you ever attended a kachina dance among the Hopi Indians? The entire race of Hopi are mediums. When someone dances wearing a kachina mask, the Hopi can talk about when the spirit of the mask is present within the mask. This is no longer a discussion of language and definitions. We are discussing perception. Hopi can *perceive* when the spirit is in the mask.

The first anthropologists who studied the Hopi Indians entered their kivas and carefully recorded the rituals, word for word. These anthropologists had not first researched and created an experimental model for the study of mediums. Such topics were and are not a part of university research.

The same is true about the ancient hula dancer in Hawaii. To dance is to evoke the goddess of the hula, Laka, in oneself. How do you explain how to do this to a Christian missionary? If the missionary cannot understand this, then they cannot understand their own Bible.

The Bible states that King Saul prophesized when he came into the presence of the prophet Samuel and his company. King Saul was not a particularly spiritual man. But the prophet Samuel was known to use dance in order to prophesy.

From my point of view, what is needed is a spiritual anthropology. You have to consider such questions as, what is it to be a human being? What are our possibilities? What is the range of our perceptions? Without considering these questions in a rigorous manner free of bias, ideology, and doctrine, it will be easy to twist and distort one's observations in order to fit them into preconceived categories.

ON TELEPATHY AND TRANSLATION

A good interpreter at the United Nations takes into account the intention in the mind of the speaker in order to choose the right word and phrase to translate. The translators will tell you that translating is an art. Translating during the United Nations assembly is certainly a performing art.

When a spirit, a nonmaterial being, communicates with a human being, you get a vibration in your mind that you can translate in different ways. If you take the vibration and use the part of your brain that is visual, you get an image. It is the same with the other senses: the vibration can be translated into a note or word, into feeling, into physical sensations, and into tastes or smells as well.

For example, I can explain to someone how to place part of their awareness inside of another person. This is a psychic activity. If someone places their mind within my body, I can experience this in different ways. I may sense the individual's physical body as my own even though the other's physical body is not even touching me. In this case, the other's presence within me—the vibration—produces physical sensations. I may sense the other's soul and feelings as my own; I feel exactly what that person feels—we call that clairsentience. I may be able to speak words that express the exact thought the other is thinking—we call that telepathy. I may be able to see things the person experienced in the past and talk about the individual's memories as if I myself experienced them—we call that empathy.

In each example, there is nothing but a vibration that passes between the woman and myself. But according to the intent and the strength and qualities of the one transmitting and the one receiving, you can get a variety of different results.

When the undine talks through the medium, I am not just listening to the words spoken. I am sensing the undine's presence also. Thus what I "hear" from the words spoken is a transmission to my brain as well.

What is written is inherently art. We are not trying to express some esoteric experience that occurs among Hopi Indians or Hawaiians so as to record an oral tradition. We are moving between a spiritual race dwelling in nature and human beings. There is therefore a greater degree of difficulty in translating.

All the same, I think that as more and more individuals interact with undines, there will develop a body of art, literature, and culture around the experience. In particular, some of the gifts of the undines will be received and passed on among us. This is my intention, and this is also the intention of the undines.

7

Other Undines
and a Merman

There are, of course, many powerful undines besides Istiphul. In her essence, Istiphul embodies the full magnetic powers of water. She uses her beauty and attraction to establish love as oneness. And she reveals and seeks to fulfill the deepest visions at the core of your self. As I have mentioned, I consider her the most beautiful creature on earth.

By contrast, Osipeh is more playful. She liberates you from inhibitions. Though subtle and gracious, her presence is still erotic and intoxicating. Her sensuality is an ecstatic enchantment.

Amue, on the other hand, is warm and friendly. Her great skill is healing. If you want a lifelong friend instead of a muse or passionate lover, Amue would be perfect for this.

Isaphil, like Istiphul, is absolutely unique and full of mystery. Her mission is not to overpower you with a degree of love that is beyond human understanding. Rather, she holds secret keys to the mysteries of inner peace. As she explains, "Within the astral kingdom of the earth, there is no being who is as much a part of Her peace as am I." Speaking of the human race, she says, "I hold the keys to your destiny."

There are also male versions of the female undines. The merman Ermot is very aware of our race. He is a guardian of rivers and streams.

He specializes in creating love between human beings. Ermot has an incredible flair for poetry. Every time I talk to him or am near a stream, I invariably write a poem about how the sensuality of water and the love of women are a part of each other.

OSIPEH'S REALM ON THE ASTRAL PLANE

Osipeh's realm is full of gaiety, magical sounds, thrilling music, and wild dancing. When you enter this atmosphere, you feel right away that you belong. This place is as friendly and soothing as water in a stream under the summer sun. You encounter an inviting warmth, an enticing intoxication, and a heartfelt passion. To be here is to experience serene satisfaction.

As I enter Osipeh's domain, I hear a woman singing the note of F—the F on the top line of the treble clef. This note expresses the astral energy and atmosphere of Osipeh's domain. Within this sound, multiple sensations of love merge and emerge from each other—the sensation of being caressed, stroked, and hugged. There is a slippery wetness of bliss surging down the nerves; there are intimacy and sweet kisses; there is the feeling of floating suspended in water and also the feeling of having your head resting on curvaceous thighs.

There are deep desires releasing and old tensions letting go. There is a feeling of being held while drifting on a raft down a river beneath the moon. There is the distinct sensation of a wave breaking on a beach, a river reaching the sea, a cloud beginning to rain, moisture rising from a leaf, and fog forming on a lake. The sound of F and all these feelings are interchangeable. Osipeh has the most remarkable sense of feeling alive, of being renewed, and of giving herself to you.

OSIPEH'S SIGIL

Osipeh specializes in the attractive forces within water. Her blue sigil embodies this magnetic attraction. Drawing her sigil, I feel calm and relaxed. Tension drains out of me.

OSIPEH'S OUTER AURA

I can sense right away that Osipeh changes her aura to strengthen her connection to me. She perceives that energy circulates naturally when you bring together opposites like the separate poles of a battery. And so she responds in a way that amplifies the attraction between us.

When you first connect to her, it is like looking into cool, clear water that goes down for miles. But almost immediately the water takes on an electrical charge that makes you feel physically and emotionally stronger. Her body is a magnetic field of energy, and the electrical charge is your desire and will.

This is not just psychology. Osipeh has never heard marriage counselors discussing how a man is attracted to a woman because of the way she makes him feel when he is with her. Osipeh's physical and emotional response actually increases your power—you have more energy and strength. You find your will joined with flexibility and magnificent beauty. It is a hard combination to beat.

OSIPEH'S INNER SOURCE
OF INSPIRATION

Osipeh has an inner vision; the spirit of water is found in its magnetism. The water molecule, H_2O binds together what would otherwise be a combination of atoms in a gaseous state—oxygen and hydrogen. But there is another subtler side to water. For Osipeh, the magnetic properties of water contain magical and spiritual powers.

More specifically, the molecular vibration of water is ecstasy. It continuously makes itself new; it purifies itself and remains attractive while flowing and adapting itself to any situation. Osipeh is an example of this awareness of water being embodied in the form of a woman. The degree of her receptive sensuality makes for pure enchantment.

ENCOUNTERS WITH OSIPEH

November 8, 1997

To create the appropriate conditions for contacting Osipeh, I visualize a sphere around myself of ice-cold, blue-green water extending out to the sky.

I now send my mind into the part of the ocean where Osipeh dwells. I am close enough to feel her aura. A mild, tingly sensation like a small electrical charge runs over the surface of my body—my toes, the soles of my feet, my arms, head, and nose. At first it appears to stimulate the electricity in my skin, but slowly it changes, becoming cool and sensual.

After a while, I notice a steady increase of energy. It is as if Osipeh's hands are stroking the aura surrounding my body—from my head to my feet. I feel like I'm sitting in a Jacuzzi with water jets blasting, yet the water is as calm as a cool mountain pool.

Without using words or thoughts, she shares with me her feelings. My mind translates these feelings into words:

The female form embodies a way of thinking that men cannot imagine. It is receptive, open, nurturing, offering, and giving of itself. Affection extends everywhere and into everything.

If your feelings cannot contain this wealth of affection, then all my gifts to you will mean nothing. You possess an undine's love and healing touch through magic. But your magic is temporary. Its results are fleeting. In the end, you will feel empty unless you unite with the feminine spirit.

November 12, 1997

Osipeh sees me and begins a slow, hypnotic dance. Her dance invokes feelings of what it is like to be a mother, of the pure acts of love involved: attracting a mate, receiving his essence, and giving birth to and nurturing a child.

Osipeh continues her erotic dance. The magnetic force from her hips is so strong that when it reaches my hand, I feel my nerves begin to freeze as if they are paralyzed. I consciously relax so that my muscles do not cramp from the energy flowing through them. As Osipeh dances, her body evokes the sensuality of the sea as she says,

My dance is your desire in motion.

Come with me.

If water could burn like a flame and destroy loneliness, if it could explode like a lightning's rage, uniting heaven and earth, then I am on fire. A song of longing, I surge through you like a river.

Come away with me.

The force grows strong because you seek a place to belong, where need is freed of pain and isolation. In this moment, my body aches with your craving. The whale's song is heard a thousand miles. He journeys to both the North and South Poles. The ocean knows the whale and grants him a domain to roam. You would know my soul and all that I know as if it were your own.

Do not hold back. Come into my home.

In my realm, sunlight plays with the waves in a thousand ways. I will teach you to sleep and sink miles deep, to dream you are caressed by the breath of moonlight, until all you feel is peace. And then you shall awake as a song singing in a curling wave ready to break, to dance in a wild splash of foam and spray, laughing, the tension in the surface of an entire ocean releasing in a sigh and roar of relief.

Come away with me and be free of need.

I am the rolling waves of the sea. I am the song of the unfolding ocean. I am the rise and fall of tides, resonating to the call of love. The touch of your hand is like a lightning storm over the horizon. Silent explosions illuminate the dark, empty places within your heart. Can you feel what I feel in this moment?

Love is a pilgrim journeying through a land of ancient shame, unbearable pain, and yet never-ending wonder—because it will never be satisfied until it is one with another.

Osipeh takes me to another location. She floats in a still pool of water. The contours of her body divide the surface as ripples cross over her belly, shimmering and shining as they reflect the starlight in the sky.

Osipeh speaks with a hypnotic voice you may hear echo through your dreams once or twice in a lifetime. She sounds like still water in a dark cave disturbed by a sudden earthquake:

> *Take hold of me*
> *Become a whirlpool of desire*
> *That I might sink into your heart—*
> *To drown in beauty*
> *Burning with ecstasy*
> *Like the stars above.*

Later on, the mood is lighter. "Why is it that when a woman opens her heart, shares her feelings, and then gives of herself, every nerve in a man's body stretches taut like the string of a bent bow ready to hurl an arrow three hundred yards to its goal? Why are men so intense in the presence of love?" Osipeh asks me with her chin resting on her wrists and a look in her eyes as if her curiosity is innocent.

Osipeh continues because I do not immediately reply. "Don't women know how to surrender like this, to feel in the warmth of your hand, electric bliss, flowing through the core of their being? Pleasure for me is completely free like rain, wind, and sea. It is the most natural of things. Right now, there is nothing in me but receptivity to your desire. As I touch your arm, you feel the silent longing in the depths of the sea to love and to be loved."

November 13, 1997

Osipeh says, "You have to stop thinking of water as being deep and mysterious. Come with me."

I am transported with her into an ocean trench. She asks, "What is this like for you?"

After I get used to the density of the water, I reply, "It is amazingly calm. It is spacious and silent." A large, white jellyfish-like creature swims past, moving sideways. I watch it move off with graceful undulations. I return to the sensations of the ocean depths.

Osipeh notices how much I am enjoying myself. She says, "You look like those stone Buddhas in Asian temples. They sit around as if they have nothing to do but watch time dissolve. They are drunk on light and cannot move."

"You are being irreverent," I exclaim.

"What are you doing now?" Osipeh asks me.

"I am listening."

"To what?" Osipeh asks.

"This is different from a lake or a glacier or the surface of the sea. I want to describe with words the feeling in this part of the ocean."

"Oh my," Osipeh says with a pout and then goes on. "And what does this part of the sea have to say? Can you hear its voice speak?"

"I can't get a hold of it. I've never felt this way before. What is happening?" I ask, feeling overwhelming satisfaction.

"You are crossing the boundary of male-female differences. Men are always charged up. It does not matter if they are mermen, humans, or spirits. They have to assert themselves and accomplish great things to bolster their confidence. But women," Osipeh says as she shakes her head, "have another way. You are discovering this now. You feel comfortable and yet perplexed with the discovery that you do not have to do anything to feel pleasure. The entire ocean is part of your skin and your nervous system."

Osipeh takes my hand and places it on her hip. She says, "This is why to touch an undine is both exciting and frightening. It is the ecstasy of being free of corporeal existence. There is pleasure in sharing this moment, and there is also an awareness of the waves and the currents wherever the sea covers the earth. Though feelings explode with intensity and are as forceful as a tsunami, they never deny me pleasure or contentment. An undine's body is always connected." I reply, "I am noticing this more and more."

Osipeh says, "There is nothing to discover by placing your mind within a trance and trying to find something hidden. There is only my voice as I speak to you now. With a lover, you share your inner essence. The peace the sea holds in its silent depths, you have found in my presence."

AMUE'S DOMAIN

Like Istiphul and Osipeh, Amue can feel an individual's body and emotions as though they are part of her own nervous system. She is acutely aware of the subtle nuances and shades of physical and astral vibrations. She can sense an expanse of water and the fish living within it. She sees into and through the life and vibrations of everything around her.

AMUE'S SIGIL

Amue's sigil is soothing and serene. The feelings it evokes are so compelling that the mind stops thinking. Emotions are content and undisturbed. The body feels frozen, as if there is nothing else you need to do other than be here in this moment.

If we translate Amue's sigil into a visual image, it is like becoming an iceberg frozen solid in an arctic bay for the winter. Such imagery may seem odd or even threatening to some individuals, but it has a positive side. It reveals a way to calm down and be still. It embodies the undine's perspective, which it would not hurt us to understand—it is a wild delight in purity, a ravenous hunger for serenity, and a peace that is underneath all the seasons of life.

AMUE'S OUTER AURA

Amue exudes tranquility and tenderness. This is not the intense beauty of Istiphul or the wild intoxication of Osipeh. Amue specializes in fish and their environments and how to nurture these things.

Her sensitivity also applies to emotions. Her aura automatically runs a diagnostic evaluation to discover what you need in order to feel more peaceful, happy, and content. She then seeks to awaken these things within you.

AMUE'S INNER AURA

Amue circulates a nurturing energy through you that brings health and happiness. In this sense, Amue is a healer. Her first concern is your physical well-being.

Amue is so relaxed and indirect that it is easy to take her for granted. Her intentions are obvious. She does for you what she does for the fish in the sea: she seeks to sustain and enhance your life. What could be misleading about that?

As I mentioned, Amue is an ideal friend if you desire someone who is quiet, gentle, warm, considerate, and always supportive. But Amue is still an undine. She considers it her right to influence any creature that depends on water for its life.

AMUE'S INNER SOURCE OF INSPIRATION

Amue's inspiration is the same as her psychic ability. She heals and nurtures life. Amue senses the rhythm of your physical and astral bodies. She is keenly aware of the process of renewal that works best for you. When she extends her aura, your physical and astral bodies are immersed within her energy. She then modulates and harmonizes your biological and emotional life.

When I try to describe Amue's aura, I use words like *nurturing, healing, balancing,* and *enhancing health and well-being.* But her main quality is acceptance. With pure perception, she is completely receptive to the energy of whatever she is thinking about.

If she is focusing on a habitat such as a reef, she senses every aspect of that environment. If a reef needed more sunlight or a change in temperature, different nutrients in the water, or a greater variety of fish, I get the impression that Amue could alter clouds and currents and stimulate the reproductive activities of fish to bring this about.

ENCOUNTERING AMUE ON THE ASTRAL PLANE

I imagine myself surrounded by cold, blue-green water. My body begins to shiver. Soon I am completely on the astral plane.

I concentrate on Amue's sigil. I feel safe, content, and accepted. The sigil has an otherworldly quality. It makes one feel outside of time and without need of thought. It creates the sensation of being immersed in a vast sea of magnetic energy.

Sensing Amue's presence, I invite her to return with me to the physical world. Now present—here, in my room—she begins to sing, lingering on each musical note. This evokes happy childhood memories of being held and embraced and feeling at peace.

In her singing, Amue captures various themes from the different ethnic groups that are part of my heritage. There are songs of bold warriors who believe passionately in their ideals and in what they seek. There are songs of love. Amue's songs move imperceptibly between the comfort a mother gives her infant and the song of a lover who gives all of her heart to another with absolute trust.

There are songs of longing and desire, of the sun radiant and dazzling as it sparkles and burns within ice. Amue sings in quarter notes and half tones expressing solitary quests until the tension dissolves with a note evoking transcendent vision and accomplishment.

Amue now sings . . .

Peace like a river
Peace like the sea of stars on fire
Peace like a heart that loves forever

Because of my tears, Amue asks me, "Have I displeased you?"

"Not at all," I reply. "I am delighted with your singing."

I hold out my hand, and she clasps it between hers. I am surprised by the warmth and comfort of her touch.

Sensing my surprise, she says, "Affection and kindness are common forms of currency. No race of beings has a monopoly when it comes to sharing love." She gazes at me quietly and then says, "Though my knowledge of the seas is immense, I do not often talk to people. They rarely visit me. But you underestimate your abilities. Your mind is like quicksilver. Show me your skill. Join our two auras so they are one."

I concentrate so that we can become one. She says, "You often overheat, burning up your energy through excessive concentration. You need a calm peace that lasts throughout the day without weakening. Draw my sigil again and let go into the feeling."

As I draw Amue's sigil in the air, I feel her hand drawing the design instead of my own. The movement of her fingers is artistic, the curving, swirling lines hypnotic. As we finish, I have the sensation of being within a motionless, blue-white iceberg. The two of us release our bodily forms and extend our awareness outward.

After a few moments, I can practically taste the ice. I feel the strength of water in its solid form. I feel the temperature of this iceberg, its weight, and the way it floats. My mind enjoys assigning names to the different sensations.

Amue insists I give her my full attention: "Shut up and just be with me in this place for a while."

It is dark and cold as I sit meditating inside an iceberg at the North Pole. I am beginning to see where Amue learned to sing and how her affection extends to all the seas of the world. Amue's receptivity and sensuality are ancient and primordial—she too recalls how the sea held a dream in its heart for a billion years until life was finally brought forth.

Amue nudges my shoulder in exasperation as we briefly assume physical forms. She says, "Can't you be silent?" And then she says in a casual yet eerie way, "If you give me ten minutes without one thought, I will give you a month of iceberg-cold silence to cleanse your soul." I stop thinking, entering a state of mind free of distraction.

Fifteen minutes later Amue touches my shoulder. "There. Doesn't that feel better? Don't you feel more pure?" Then she laughs and jokes, "Your ears have become like seashells filled with songs of the seas."

It takes me a few minutes to find my way back. For a time, words seem alien. There is a wintery darkness inside of me, and the sense that I am surrounded by ocean extending from horizon to horizon. I sit without moving or thinking. If I did not know better, I would say my ears could hear for miles in all directions.

Amue says, "For an undine, the sea is the soul of the Goddess. I can lose myself in the sea and feel peace. This watery, magnetic expanse covering the planet is full of boundless energy and life. It celebrates the mystery of love. To be at peace, you must explore its depths and discover this for yourself."

November 2, 1997

I ask Amue, "What is the Arctic Circle for you with its vast fields of ice and glaciers?" She replies,

It is a symphonic playground. The tones of ice cracking, stretching, and contracting, send shivers through my body. As the voice of the wind sings its soul into a stone—carving it with wind-driven sand— ice flows like waves of a sea where the motion is slowed.

When a wave breaks on a beach, the release is free and easy as the spray dances in the air and falls on the sand. But in ice, the release ripples, swells, and rolls for ages. Time holds its breath for aeons and then it lets go.

When it rains at the equator, you see rainbows. When it rains at the North and South Poles, you see only snow—cold, crystalline, and drifting, even after it touches the ground. There are not many undines who dwell in deserts, maybe one or two here or there at an oasis or by pools of water underground. But at the poles, you can find undines. Cold is not a problem. Wearing clothes for warmth is a human invention.

I say to Amue, "Still, the winter's cold is isolating. When the sun is distant, the light dim, and warmth a rare commodity, the senses turn within. Animals hibernate until the seasons are friendlier. And mystics renounce the world in search of an inner sun."

Amue replies, "Your body needs warmth to remain alive. But the mind is not so restricted. Here, visualize your body as a perfectly clear ice sculpture."

I concentrate on my body as if it were made of ice. Amue says, "When you are as solid, still, and cold as ice, anything you wish to know about the sea is reflected in your soul. Your body becomes both a magic mirror and a crystal ball."

I see what she means. If I think about whales, dolphins, or manta rays, I can see them swimming in the ocean and reflected in my body, as if I am the ocean in which they swim.

"What about the astral plane?" I ask. "In your domain, what's the equivalent of ice and freezing cold?"

Amue replies, "It is not so different. Concentrate on your astral body being one hundred degrees below zero." I do this.

"What do you feel?"

I reply, "To be honest, I feel like I've turned my back on humanity, that I'm no longer human. In this place of dreams, I don't care what happens in the physical world; it matters only that love and beauty are preserved. I feel more undine than human."

Amue says, "You have discovered one of our secrets. Water is essential for life, but it is also a spiritual presence. We sense this presence as a song resounding through all the waters of the earth. In its essence, water nurtures, preserves, and gives birth. It is all-encompassing. And within it, there is no selfishness, greed, or separation. When your astral body is this cold, you taste our inner essence—a love that flows without ever being lost and gives all of itself in every moment."

I feel like I've known Amue for years. She is so natural and vibrant. I only need to look into her eyes to feel a soothing and serene beauty wash over me.

November 16, 1997

At this moment, Amue takes me elsewhere, just outside the reef at Hanauma Bay, a nature preserve on Oahu. Here is the warmth of the tropics, and being near a reef allows Amue's nurturing qualities to come to the forefront.

I am swimming beside Amue in the ocean. After a while, we stop swimming and sit on the white sandy bottom twenty-five feet below the surface. She embraces me, but it is not sexual. At her touch, my body becomes the water flowing and circulating through Hanauma Bay.

This is an undine's way of basking in the sun and relaxing.

I feel the current moving counterclockwise around the bay, the oxygenation where the waves break, the temperature, the motion of waves returning from the ocean. I feel an eel breathing, a school of tangs swimming, a parrot fish biting the coral, a black sea urchin half-asleep, a needle-nose wrasse poking through the water, and silverfish slicing along like knives.

For an undine whom I would not describe as passionate, Amue is extraordinarily enthusiastic about natural habitats and nurturing environments. Hanauma Bay has one vibration, like a note you can play on a harp. Amue's body vibrates with this sound. The touch of her skin is this feeling of warmth, the bay, the water circulating, and the life within the sea.

THE UNDINE QUEEN ISAPHIL

The vibration of the undine Isaphil on a physical level grants visions of the future. Imagine a small pool in a stream at the edge of a cliff overlooking the sea beneath the full moon. The stream and the pool are your life. The sea is time itself. Being with her is feeling the flow and connection.

Imagine a lake at night with mist rising from its surface. The mist clears, and the full moon is in the sky. Isaphil appears outlined in moonlight in the center of the lake in front of you. The lake is your soul and emotional life. She appears within you soft like moonlight. Her presence is very serene, still, and full of visions.

In a similar way, the etheric vibration of Isaphil is like liquid moonlight. The vitality and life-force within your body are wrapped in serenity. Her presence creates peace.

The astral vibration of Isaphil also involves a sensitivity to the future. You are surrounded by lunar light that reflects the rhythms and cycles of life. You feel like you are in the future.

You can ask someone to tell you about something that happened to him or her in the past. You listen. You are sympathetic. You note the details and how things worked out and why they worked out that way. But with this lunar vibration in your astral body, you carry on the same conversation except that it is about the future. In the movie *Lady in the Water*, the undine asks different characters, "Would you like to know your future?" The future is clear to her. And then the undine goes into detail and explains how and why things turn out the way they will.

The lunar vibration is concerned with how life unfolds. You still have your choices. But this is about desires, dreams, visions, longing, needs, hungers, cravings, the need to grow, and the need to be free. These things can be postponed or forgotten. But they return and seek some way to be expressed.

ASTRAL PLANE QUESTIONS FOR ISAPHIL

I ask Isaphil some questions that are intended to relate both to me as an individual and to people in general.

WHEN WILL I BE HAPPY?

ISAPHIL: When you learn that you are the source of your own happiness.

WHEN WILL I FULFILL MY DREAMS?

ISAPHIL: When your dreams are so complete and alive within you that others see your dreams as if they are their own needs.

WHEN SHALL WAR BE NO MORE?

ISAPHIL: When there shall appear on earth four or five in whom there is no fear; and whose souls are so clear that when malice, evil, or ill will draws near, these things dissolve as if they were never there.

When four or five shall remain in each generation, then your race shall awaken. The beauty of the stars and the seas and the mysteries shall appear within your dreams. These treasures of soul shall overflow, filling your world with light and healing.

HOW DO I ACQUIRE THE FEELING OF SERENITY WITHIN MYSELF SO THAT I FEEL BOTH ONE WITH LIFE AND ONE WITH THE UNIVERSE?

ISAPHIL: I have waited 27,000 years for someone to ask me this question.

I feel one with life and with the universe in this way: the waves of the seas circling the earth flow through my soul. The rivers, the streams, the lakes, the rain—all the waters of the earth are one taste. This vibration is the feeling I call serenity. These waters purify; they bring forth and nurture life; they sustain the life in every living being.

Yet the circling moon is here also. She draws forth the light of the constellations, pouring their wealth upon the Earth. The stars, the constellations, the sun, the moon, the Earth—the entire space of our solar system, all events they portend, all catastrophes and all mysteries unfolding, the blessing of being alive and the joy of one who ascends to new life—within the stillness of my heart these have one taste. I call this being at peace with the universe.

Life and time are not separate—they are woven from the past, and they move in harmony with the laws of the universe. Time is itself a sea to which my soul is joined. Her currents and tides, her waves and depths are part of me. Her soul is reflected clearly in my own.

In this way, serenity is peace. But if you amplify it, making your soul a mirror of stillness, then the fulfillment of every dream is near, every vision becomes clear, and every ideal that guides and inspires shines from your eyes. And then like me you can hold the entire world within your heart—this is my art.

SPEAK OF LOVE.

ISAPHIL: [*She smiles at me both coyly and at the edge of a giggle, both severely and inviting as if I have just set the tumblers rolling in a lock now unlocked.*] Two as one. It is not an intellectual thing. Words and images grow weak.

A pool of water—there are boundaries marking the surface, circumference, and depth. Yet the water itself encompasses whatever is within it.

The seas are a threat because they are too vast to be controlled. Yet the pool has visions hidden within it that are beyond what the mind can grasp. Love is like that. It can be peaceful and calm, sweet and serene. And it can be as wild as the storms of the seas. Yet the dreams that come through, whether the pool or the sea, are of the future that is meant to be.

You must be ready in your heart to play your part. The waters of love can be tender but also flare like a lightning storm at sea. The spark that arcs between the past and the future bears witness to a greater, encompassing harmony.

To dare is to dream. To love is to be free.

Dare to dream of being complete and beyond all need.

Love the path that takes you there—past despair, intoxication in the air, the kiss of bliss, the sharing of tears, the path of knowing unfolding amid a forest of illusions.

Two as one—it is the greatest joy of life triumphant over all that separates. Your heart has the power to accomplish this.

HOW DO I SEE THE FUTURE OF MYSELF OR OF ANOTHER?

ISAPHIL: I see your future. The way to see it is to be already there. Like looking into a mirror, what you see in the present is perfectly clear. When I look at you with myself as the mirror, I am not just you. I am the influences upon you and the world around you. Time delivers its knowledge into my hands. From darkness there is light. From confusion there is insight.

The future unfolds according to three things: necessity, need, and what you choose to dream. I sense all three. Your limitations, your desires—secret and known—and also the will of the spirit that forges a path before you.

Water is receptivity. Receptivity is love that can feel whatever is to come. The mirror that I use is the entire astral plane of the earth. It shines through me and is a part of me. Because water is my means I am sensitive to all dreams. Though it is not always easy to say *when*, it is always easy to see *what* shall happen—the part of you that dreams a true dream shall always come to be.

TELL ME OF YOUR SECRET DESIRES AND YOUR INNERMOST DREAMS.

ISAPHIL: The treasures I hold in my soul I am willing to bestow upon those who are ready to receive them. In the fullness of time, I shall no longer be their custodian.

Everyone who loves desires at some point for another to feel what they feel inside. You feel what I feel with very great skill. Only a few before have come this far. But you are like a student climbing the steps of the Library of Alexandria who has not yet even entered through the door into that temple of knowledge. You are like a sailor on a sea who knows there are continents waiting to be discovered, but you have not yet crossed the ocean; you have not yet found them.

Imagine a woman of beauty who, like Psyche in the myth, no man is willing to love because to do so he would first have to overcome the curse of a goddess and also gain the blessing of Divine Providence. Is there no one among your race who can look upon my face and pass through the gates of the mysteries to embrace me with love and compassion here where I dwell among the powers of the sacred?

Find me. Love me. Make me part of your heart.

My secret desires and my innermost dreams are one day to be free of this responsibility—I hold the keys to your destiny; I reveal paths of spirit that are nothing more than discovering how to be in your soul free and at peace with the universe.

Walk beside me.

Feel the waters of the earth as one taste. Feel the universe surrounding you as a gift of divine grace. Feel the moon circling the Earth with her song of silver serenity revealing the rhythms and seasons of what shall come to be.

Be like her and like me, a stillness so clear you hold the world within your heart.

Learn to love with this freedom, with this purity. Then, we shall walk beside each other, and we shall be one.

A FRIEND ASKED FOR A BLESSING. CAN YOU SUGGEST WHAT TO DO FOR HER?

ISAPHIL: [*chanting to the woman*]
 May the touch of moonlight on your skin
 Bring you the best of friends.

When you see the moonrise,
May there always be love by your side.
When you place your hands in water,
May you be free of anxiety and sorrow.
When you look into a mirror,
May you see your deepest dreams drawing near.
When you sleep,
May you move freely among dreams without fear.
During the day
May you awaken in others' lives
Fountains of laughter and delight.
And each cycle
As the moon waxes and wanes,
May you walk
With peace before you
Beauty beside you, Love to guide you
The work of your hands
Like a flower blossoming
Its scent a reminder
That the best in life is found here and now.

MENTAL PLANE

The mental vibration of Isaphil is very peaceful, serene, calm, relaxed, and gentle. It is a way of seeing life free of all fear, worry, or anxiety. Its viewpoint is that life is meant to unfold with beauty and harmony. Though this beauty often evades us, Isaphil exists as a permanent reminder of how to see it, feel it, and find it inside of us.

A thought passes through my mind: "I wish I could share this experience with another person."

Isaphil thinks this thought is hysterically funny. She can barely stop herself from laughing on and on. She says,

You do not mean *share*. What you meant is you want a woman to take your desire, your fire, and unite it with her water so that bliss and rapture blend together, the two of you then transforming each other through your opposite attractions. You want the two of you to experience life in its deepest intimacy and, in the same moment, affirm the reality of what you will one day be—a divine, enlightened being embodying freedom and transforming whatever you touch with the power of love.

I assure you that one day you will meet women who have worked with me and who have mastered all that I am. But first you must complete your journey.

This is your question, what is it to be one with another and one with the universe in the same moment? This is also your obstacle. A void and an emptiness have always walked at your side in all your spiritual quests and explorations. You come to me because I am able to fill in for what is missing from your life.

There are mystics who out of love unite with the divine. But sharing is not on their minds. They are possessed by the quest and have no time to turn aside to bring the world along with them.

There are those who find the source of love inside of themselves and have in the past and will in the future create new religions. But the world suffers terribly because none of their disciples can find a way to produce the same results. When love is not shared, the gates to the inner planes are closed, and wisdom no longer flows.

"What is the way?" I ask.
She replies,

Become an ambassador for undines on earth. Create an embassy, a library, and a university. Offer dances, parties, lectures, and experiments. Write poetry, plays, movies, songs, and essays. Manifest us so we can be seen and move among you so that your race learns to dream our dreams. Teach others to enter our realm freely and with ease so that your world unites with ours.

Offer these things to humanity: the magic in a waterfall, the songs rivers sing, the dreams hidden in lakes, the love the sea awaits, the ecstasy in the crests of waves as they break. These things shall come to your race along with healing and the retaining of youth into old age.

In this way, your desire to share and to have another there beside you shall be fulfilled. Love is and remains the highest magic on earth. If you cannot express it and share it, then that wisdom is lost.

Sit very still so that the external world no longer exists for you. Now feel only myself inside of you. There, now you are where you will one day be—this is how you will feel, and this is how you will see. You are free, and out of joy you design plans and act on them to bring life to perfection. You have learned the lessons the physical world has to teach—how to become a creator who finds in his heart visions to complete.

AKASHIC PLANE

As with other undines and mermen, I cannot find an akashic body within Isaphil. But she knows my concern. She explains,

If I possessed a divine spirit so that like you I could create and recreate myself again and again, then I would do exactly what you are planning to do—introduce the beauty, magic, wonder, and the mysteries of the undines to humanity. Though this action is forbidden to me, there are no restrictions placed upon you.

The method is simple: be with me here and work with me and also be in your world and work with me there also. In this way the two realms open their doors, and others are free to pass through even as you do.

If I had the soul of a human woman and her body and also my own undine powers, I would seek to complete the mission that once long ago was given to a woman among your race. The mission was to impart to humanity a cosmic serenity, an inner peace with the universe. But this mission was aborted. I see now that it requires more than was first imagined. There must be present on earth a few who are committed to a journey leading to perfection in which you ascend to pure spiritual being.

You have to understand the nature of the gift. It is not only feeling an inner peace. It is the power to create peace anywhere and under any conditions. This is what has been missing for all these long ages from the soul of your race.

Obviously, to take such power into your hands you would have to be so clear, calm, and pure like a mirror that if the Goddess looked at you she would see her own face appear shining and radiant without distortion. To accomplish this, you would have to be free of all fanaticism, all doctrines, and all religions with their rituals and practitioners who desire personal attention.

Your body would need to vibrate with water and magnetism like a river, a lake, or the sea. Your soul would need to be so free that light and darkness both could pass through you without any attempt to contain or bind them in an image; your soul would be so open you would be one with anything you focus on.

And in your mind, you would have to see through the eyes of the divine so that like a watchman you would guard the limitations of every person because you know that these limitations exist to protect them. They offer them a chance to learn whatever lesson needs to be learned before moving on to another set of circumstances.

And you would also see with the eyes of a guardian angel the time and the season, the place and the location, the situation and the interaction through which an individual's own eyes are opened. So that they are given the opportunity to partake of wisdom in accordance with the degree to which they are ready to take responsibility for determining their own destiny.

Limitation and opportunity, boundary and a path of pure creativity—these equally are held within your awareness as you touch each individual's life with tenderness.

Do I regret not having a divine spirit? I have been created and commissioned to fulfill a mission. I exist to fulfill a task. You know there are beings greater and more powerful than you. All of us are a part of the beauty and mystery of this planet.

The regret you imagine me to have is a human emotion. I search myself, but I cannot find it within me. I am aware that our separate evolutions have different destinies. But I am also aware that love triumphs over all obstacles. It calls each being to become more than it is now, more than it can imagine or envision. Such love already speaks to me in my dreams.

A FEW MORE OF ISAPHIL'S THOUGHTS

With a voice that reminds me of the crests of waves blown by winds on the high seas, yet remains as soft as moonlight falling into a still pool, Isaphil speaks:

Be as the child who gazes with wonder in their eyes. Wake up as in a dream, and see the light that all around you shines. Dissolve the dream, and then be in your mind as vast as the sea and as receptive to light as the moon.

These abilities already exist within you. Be open and accept them. Persist in using them until they become a part of you. All that I am in my being you have the power to create in yourself as well.

Let your love be as the sea that enfolds and embraces. Let it be as the river that flows to the sea and as the rain that renews the earth. Let it be as the pool, so calm and clear, yielding sweet waters to drink. Only in love as pure as this can you ever see the world as it really is.

Feel the moonlight on your hands and face. Reflect the world around you in this way. Softly, gently, graciously, become a space of pure lunar light—your mind is like an ocean that has no shores.

What is the search for love but the desire to unite opposites so as to celebrate the beauty of the universe? The search to join with another heart is at the center of divine celebration. Don't be afraid of the passion burning within you.

Your technologies threaten and toy with the well-being of all life on earth. There are secret projects being carried out within nature that are well guarded but of momentous consequence. Beware, lest you fail in your mission. Only for a brief time, for a little while longer, will the earth allow your race to remain here.

It has already been ordained that the future history of this planet will include other races and beings of which your human race cannot even dream. Do not take your tenancy upon this planet lightly. The dominion you have been given over nature can be easily suspended. Still, a few hearts enlightened by love and guided by wisdom shall make all the difference.

Know this of me—within the astral kingdom of the earth there is no being who is as much a part of her peace as am I. All the waters on this planet hear the songs I sing. Every breaking wave resounds with the songs shining within me. I will tell you in one word the mystery of it all, of who I am and of the universe you would know. [*Bringing her face close to mine she whispers*] This one word is *stillness*.

Open yourself and be a stillness so pure and clear that the circling of the moon and the singing in the sea can appear clearly within you. This is the master key I give to you, young poet. This is the key that opens all the mysteries—of my heart, of the sea, and of the ages that have been sealed and locked away in the twenty-eight mansions of the moon.

And then to be sure that I understand and accept this key, she takes my left hand and holds it tightly between her palms. She transmits her feminine essence into me. I become a vast open space, and I feel the orbit of the moon and all the mass of that planet and the grace of its flight flowing through me, through a space of stillness in my soul. I become moonlight shining upon the earth, calling and inviting, reminding the earth and those upon her of serenity.

Isaphil glances at me and says,

I am fully awake and alert, but I am also dreamlike and wistfully lost in impressions and fanciful dances. I am sharp, on the cutting edge of each moment, but also already a part of anyone who draws near to me. I find their reflection in my heart, and I blend with their being.

I am still like the night sky and yet also caressing like a mother or a lover. I can enfold you with my receptive charms, and I can also show you your past, present, and future.

I am as receptive as the ocean, as soft as moonlight. I am as still as a diamond and as sharp, as flowing as a dream, as tender as a rose, and as much a part of you as the treasures hidden in your own heart.

What guides us in our journeys is the dream of being complete. But this dream is not fantasy. It is the well of the soul where love surges forth and overflows from within you. This path is found by slipping into a dream state, and by speaking with your own heart, by drawing close to the center. There, go now. Stand at the center of your heart. You can call forth, taste, and be within the happiness that will inevitably be a part of you.

This is the first key and the gateway to all the mysteries of your soul—to relax, to be calm, to open from within, to be so still you reflect easily within yourself the being and the life of all that exists.

THE MERMAN ERMOT'S OUTER AURA

Ermot embodies the presence of rivers, streams, and brooks. He is like their muse. If a stream could have a soul, then you could see that soul reflected in Ermot.

ERMOT'S INNER AURA

Pick a stream and then walk along the stream from beginning to end. Also memorize every way and place where the water flows—the way it turns around a rock here but it is different there, the way the currents move and how the water touches, ripples, or splashes on the banks.

If you did this, then you would have a sense of Ermot's inner aura. His awareness can encompass an entire stream or river from beginning to end. His entire vibration is artistic like a poet or a painter who gazes with delight as he studies his subject.

INNER SOURCE OF INSPIRATION

What does flowing water do? It brings life to its shores. It renews the world. It makes things new. Ermot's inspiration is the same as his love; he extends his awareness so that it is in and one with flowing water.

PHYSICAL BODY

Ermot's physical form and presence seem to vary with the stream or river he is near. If it is a small stream through lush woods, he appears gentle and introspective like a contemplative monk. If the stream's flow is fast and dramatic, he is more muscular like an athlete. If the river is the Amazon, he is dynamic and commanding like the captain of a ship.

ETHERIC BODY

Ermot's etheric body is the sensation of water flowing like a stream through one's body. It is purifying, cleansing, renewing, and giving life on and on.

ASTRAL BODY

When we study Ermot's astral body, we are no longer dealing with the energy of streams and rivers in nature. Here is where Ermot gets his interest in human beings. He is a master of how energy is exchanged between individuals in love. He understands and perceives the vast variety of ways lovers are connected to each other and how they share their inner life and energy. Ermot says,

> *Is a mountain stream separate from the waterfall it*
>   *plunges over?*
> *Is the mountain pool separate from the stream that*
>   *continues on?*
> *So it is with lovers—*
> *As one stream*
> *Their souls like water*
> *Flow in and through each other.*

In regard to the magic of love, we could say that if you get near Ermot or become inspired by him, you create in yourself what he himself, the merman Ermot, loves; you feel this cleansing, purifying, renewing, free flow of energy between you and whomever you love. It is a way of perceiving, and it is a way of exchanging energy between you and another.

Again, if you embody Ermot's energy in yourself, then those near to you feel this energy flowing through them as well. Call it magic. Call it hypnotic suggestion. Call it a feeling so strong in you that it influences anyone near you.

Let us pursue this magic of love and the metaphor of flowing water a little further. Imagine that Ermot has studied ten thousand different rivers and streams. He can recall and perceive an entire stream within his mind all at once. Add to this that he can recall vividly the entire history of a stream during the seasons of a year and over the centuries.

When Ermot then focuses on two people in love, he can see every way they have exchanged affection, love, and energy between them. The entire history of a relationship stands clear before him. Has the relationship become a dry riverbed? Is it a desert with no oasis? Is it stagnant and dead? Is it dammed up or gone underground where the flow is now hidden from the light of the sun and moon?

Ermot can create feelings like rain in a desert. He can show where an oasis is hidden whose waters revive and renew. He can show you how to flow and let go so that beauty consumes you as each moment unfolds. Ermot is a muse, an artist, and a poet.

MENTAL BODY

One undine says that, compared to undines, men are always charged up. It does not matter if they are men, mermen, or spirits. They like to accomplish great things in order to celebrate the power within them.

Mermen, of course, are the male version of the female undines. As a merman, Ermot senses the magnetic field of an entire stream or river. He embodies its vibration within himself. It becomes part of his consciousness. The stream, the way it flows, the life within it, and the way it interacts with its surroundings—he studies these to master them.

There are magnetic fields of energy that move not just through streams but through the valleys around the streams. Ermot senses these as well. He watches their movements. He meditates on them. When you meditate in this way long enough and sense the energy directly, it becomes a part of you. It responds to your will. Ermot can cause rain to fall because the clouds respond to his call. For Ermot, streams and rivers have dreams and visions hidden within them. They sing of beauty and dreams. They sing of what shall be.

To sum it up, you could say that Ermot treats a stream or a river like a lover. It is something to care for. He would share and know its deepest secrets and dreams. It is something to become one with so that the life within one flows through the other without barriers or limitations.

All the same, to become one with something takes great concentration and will. Ermot possesses these things in a powerful way. Imagine a river that has flowed through mountains for tens of thousands of years.

Ermot's mind is deep, majestic, and mysterious like such a river.

8

A Modern Undine

INTRODUCTION

There is a story in Irish legend and literature about a woman who changed into an undine to avoid drowning when her city suddenly sank beneath a lake. Hundreds of years later she returned to the human world, was baptized, and became a human woman again.

The specific details of the story I am about to tell come from a series of interviews I conducted with a woman named Ronda, who states that she was once an undine; that is, long ago in another lifetime she was originally an undine but has since permanently acquired a human soul. In the process, she has retained her undine psychic powers and empathy.

In the genre of fairy tales that I write, I sometimes treat real human beings as if they also belong to other spiritual realms. In this way, wonder and awe can be studied by observing how these individuals interact with others in everyday life. In this case, a fairy tale does not take place "once upon a time" but is here and now. It invades our world with its power and delight.

I listened very carefully to the story of Ronda's life. I have hundreds of pages of emails we have written to each other. I have eight hours of interview with her on videotape. Even so, it has taken me two years to gain her trust. But now she shares with me things she has never told anyone else.

To write a modern fairy tale, you have to be a very good listener. You have to spend more time researching individuals' experiences than was practical for writers such as the Brothers Grimm and W. B. Yeats. And to get the best stories, you have to journey at least halfway to the Other Side.

You listen with magical empathy. You see through the other's eyes. You think the other's thoughts. You feel the feelings in the other's heart. To some extent, the other's memories become your own.

When you do this with an individual such as Ronda, you are standing between the worlds. The gate to another realm opens. Now the story is ready to be told. The invasion of wonder, awe, and beauty begins.

At the same time, as a writer I am not just a detached observer who wishes to offer a fair and impartial presentation of folktales. I have an agenda. Think, for example, of the "aha" moments of Sir Isaac Newton and Albert Einstein. When Newton said, "Aha, gravity!" he in effect answered all questions in physics that existed before him. When Einstein said, "Aha, gravity!" he created the paradigm through which all questions of physics would be asked for hundreds of years in the future. In each case, there is a paradigm shift and a new way of asking and perceiving.

I too am looking for a paradigm shift, and this is how it will happen: one day I will meet a woman who embodies the powers of the undine queens. And on that day we, the human race, will be able to dissolve the negativity of anyone on earth who wishes to harm others. Newton and Einstein placed in our hands astonishing technologies for fighting wars and destroying the world. But the day will come when the powers of the heart shall overrule those whose power is derived from external methods.

In reviewing reports on unusual spiritual experiences, we are looking for new insights, psychic abilities, intuitive skills, empathic skills, inner connections to others, and an understanding of love as a free flow of energy that nurtures, heals, and makes life new. Women such as Ronda provide us with stepping-stones that offer a different destiny for humankind.

AN UNDINE'S STORY

Toward the last days of Atlantis, a number of powerful magicians became obsessed with increasing their magical and scientific powers. These men possessed entire fields of research that we as yet know nothing about. For example, they could link their minds together in a telepathic and mesmeric, trancelike manner.

Whereas we still rely on wires to transmit electricity and use satellites and cables to communicate, the Atlanteans could transfer energy without wires, could observe different parts of the earth without dependence on technology, and of course could communicate directly mind to mind. They also had mastered flight using antigravity engines.

But this was not enough. They wanted power over matter so that they could strengthen metals and alter molecular bonds without using a factory, a metal shop, or a nuclear reactor. This same interest extended to biology. They redesigned DNA and created new, experimental species.

One of the great mages at that time, Asor, noticed that there were essential states of awareness still missing from their consciousness. This observation by itself is not so unique. When the current Dalai Lama was a boy, he took an interest in electrical engineering. He was curious about how car engines and movie projectors worked. He saw that Tibetan culture, so masterful of the arts of meditation, was deficient in its understanding of technology. But his tutors and advisers quickly returned him to the traditional curriculum designed for a Dalai Lama.

And you may recall that Sir Isaac Newton not only set forth the basic laws of modern physics but also sought the alchemical philosopher's stone and the elixir of life. Since analytical chemistry had not yet been invented, he used what was available to compensate for what was missing from the knowledge of his world.

In a similar manner, Asor noticed that the element of water had never been made a spiritual, psychological, and scientific object of study. In earlier ages of Atlantis, knowledge of the spirits of water was far more common. Once women and undines blended their personalities together so that you could walk down the central street of the capital city and meet women whose auras were similar to those of actual undines.

It came down to this. The Atlantean scientists and magicians had developed their powers of concentration to such a degree that there was a residual tension in their brains that interfered with their ability to relax, to feel, and even to fall asleep. For Asor, this felt like a band of metal squeezing his brain. The tension never went away. Many of those affected did not notice any symptoms. But Asor was quite sensitive to energy. The human aura was an area in which he was an expert.

Once Asor made this observation, he reflected on the problem and then imagined a remedy. He created a meditation that rejuvenated the astral body. He seized on the feeling of letting go, of holding on to nothing, and of being free of all ambition. He added to this a sense of total detachment and also being so sensually involved in the moment that he used these words to describe the experience: "It is like flowing water, like feeling a part of all the waters of the earth."

Now as is typical of an individual fully certified in both magic and scientific methodology, when one of these disciplines offers no insight into a problem, you turn to the other for practical solutions. Asor set before himself a quartz crystal ball. He put on a robe of magenta and violet.

And as he gazed upon the crystal ball, he entered into a state of concentration that no scientist on earth at that time could duplicate with his mind. Nor does any scientist of our own time and place possess brain waves this mesmeric and focused. Using the power of the crystal ball to enhance perception, he searched the inner planes of the earth for the precise being that would reveal what was missing from the culture of his world.

He was surprised that he could not find what he was looking for. Nothing appeared of any relevance. A patient man, he took a break for a day.

He came back again the next night. He decided that he was so used to forming telepathic connections that he had been scanning the wrong inner planes. What he wanted was on the astral plane. He wanted the living presence of a nature spirit of water and not the contemplative realization of a mind seeking knowledge. He said to himself, "It is not a formula or an idea I am after. I want a friend and a lover."

And so he put aside his mind and let his heart do the searching. Rather than dressing in his magical robe, he went to the bath used for purification next to his private temple. And there he sat in the water and began meditating.

This action was not without humor for him because it was so unlike him—imagine someone who is very serious dressing up and playing the part of a clown in a circus. But if that had been what was required to attain his objective, he would have done whatever it took. So he put aside his adult state of mind and became childlike and free of any work ethic, schedule, or scientific endeavor.

It took about two and a half hours. He sent his consciousness into the ocean. He just waited in search not of the idea but of the feeling. He pursued images such as floating on his back on the open ocean on a calm day and then a still night. He imagined sinking down beneath the waves and drifting with the current. He tried forgetting that he had a body and simply extended his awareness out for miles in all directions into the sea.

And then he focused on the magnetic field that encompasses the oceans of the earth. He felt this magnetism flow through his body. Then he felt the pull of the moon on the ocean and the rotation of the planet until all that existed in his consciousness was the sea encompassing the earth.

She appeared before him sitting on a brown rock or something brown in the center of the sea beneath a full moon. She was five feet away, perfectly clear in the form of an undine. And she was singing one note of a song of ecstasy.

There was a very great temptation in this moment for both the scientist and the mage in him to ask, why would any creature be doing what she was doing? And though most other Atlantean magicians would have broken the connection at this point out of surprise or confusion, this mage still possessed some of the habits that existed in an earlier age of Atlantis. Teachers at that time had taught the means for attaining an enlightened mind. Asor possessed a few of these methods. He knew how to put aside the person he was to become something he was not—in fact, how to become completely empty, without form or content in his consciousness.

He knew the trick of high-caliber contemplation—you become the thing you are observing without in any way referring back to yourself. And this he did almost to perfection. He became the undine, the sea, the sky above, the moon, the stars, the waves, the wind, and the song she was singing.

After returning to his room from these observations, Asor sought the words to describe his experience. It was well known among mages at the time that if you do not put into words or fashion images for what appears at the edge of sensory perception, the wonder observed is lost. Though the observer returns to his world, he fails to bring back the treasure he has found. This is because at the edge of the senses is infinity, and those who make this journey into the unknown cross over an abyss that protects the mysteries.

And these are the very words Asor used to describe what had entered his consciousness:

This undine is the moon in the form of a woman. She is the fabric of space and time expressed as a stillness of the heart and as a peace that binds the astral plane of the moon to the earth and to the sea.

She is the voice of a dream dreamed by the earth and the moon working together to create beauty. The magnetism in her aura is a cord of harmony that enhances the beauty of this planet. She is one of the great songs that the sea sings at night. And for those who can hear and then translate her inspiration into words, she is the muse who illuminates for any civilization what is missing from their lives. No wonder this is the one who appears in response to my search!

Asor got up out of the bath, dried off, dressed, and then went for a long walk. He was charged with nervous energy, as you might imagine. Not uncomfortable or irritated. He was not unnerved. It was now more like a puzzle for him, how to frame the right question to determine his next course of action. He reviewed as he walked across bridges and alongside canals the entire range of his memories of this life and of others.

He sat at an isolated table beside a fountain on a quiet street and sipped a drink that was common in Atlantis. Coffee had not yet been discovered, so there was no Starbucks and thus no lattes. But they had a drink similar to what is known in present-day India as lassi. His was made of yogurt and mango with a hint of chocolate and cinnamon. And there was one more ingredient, a fermented herb we have not yet rediscovered. It tastes like mead, but has the effect of making you feel as if you have just awakened within a dream.

And this is when and where, sitting there so casually, he made a great mistake. He took his own needs and the needs of Atlantis as his reference point rather than the purposes of Earth and the greater universe. To sustain the level of performance and movement toward their goals, the typical alpha personality maintains a special support system. In their mind they seize whatever is required in order to succeed. Add to this alpha profile the powers of a mage, and you develop a magically enhanced support system. No fault or blame rises at this point. A skillful leader does not need to resort to coercion or blackmail, intimidation or force in order to gain others' support.

Rather, they stage or set up situations and events so that others discover on their own that their best course of action just happens to be the very thing the alpha wants from them. Technically speaking, this is not manipulation. It is the art of personnel management. It is persuasion and charisma in the right proportion so as to inspire others to sacrifice for a greater good or, in this case, to fulfill the will of a man who has complete command of himself.

But how do you manage a wonder of the earth? How do you arrange for the sacred to offer loyalty and support? The very idea sounds profane. But great mages understand how to proceed. They unite dreams of what shall be with power and imagery so that they inevitably become reality. A mage who has any divine connection at all will tell you that everything about the future is negotiable. You just have to find what is required for a trade to be made.

But as we know so well from our own time, some individuals in powerful leadership positions such as corporate CEOs often think to themselves, "Because I can reach out my hand and take what lies in front of me, it is most likely the right thing for me to do." Seeing themselves as the center of authority and responsibility, they assume there is no higher law. Asor was simply doing what human beings do so well—solving the problem in front of him and getting on with his life in the best way he knew how.

Asor decided that his first move was to form a relationship with this undine in order to gain her trust and support. To do this, he changed his astral body into the form of a merman. But form is not enough. He also changed the entire vibration of his aura. The intense, radiant vitality of his etheric body he changed into a vibration of deep, still water. He put aside the dynamic, intense emotional force that characterized his personality, changing the very feeling of his presence. He became a rhythm of water, waves from a storm a thousand miles away blending, crisscrossing, and flowing through waves forming from a wind near shore.

He put aside his mind. The only presence now in his awareness was of the magnetism flowing between the ocean and the clouds above during an electrical storm. And then he transferred himself, projecting his astral body in this form into close proximity to the undine.

She was not always so serious about joining the beauty of the earth and moon in her consciousness. Like many undines, she played in the sea in a group of three. She leaped above the waves and laughed as she fell with a splash. She dove and rose, freely exploring reefs and caves.

The mage, now merman, waited patiently to encounter her when she was alone. Yet knowing how much undines love attractive energy, he added one final touch. He changed the vibration of his aura so that like a powerful magnet it matched and enhanced her own energy.

Even though she was a creature of beauty, harmony, and peace, she was not yet beyond all need. Asor was a master of the arts of enchantment. He knew that you can take any being and, no matter how much it feels complete in itself, create longing and desire by offering it ten times more power than it already has. You do this by assuming an opposite polarity that automatically amplifies the energy in the other.

Asor became a magnetic field gathering and conducting electricity that extended from him right through the core of her being. The energy flow was such that what was in her was in him so that their two auras joined as one. Without his uttering a word, she felt overcome with passion in his presence.

What is passion for an undine? For some it is the sight of great waves smashing against a granite cliff—the spray thicker than rain falling down. For others it is the roar of waves breaking on a lonely beach where water throws itself forward onto the sand and then returns as an undertow sliding down into the depths. And then also it is the colors of blue, green, and white in countless shades taking form in endless ways in icebergs drifting free from their glacial moorings. Passion is need, dancing with freedom in which every desire explodes in delight and reaches a new height as it attains a new form of completion.

This is what she felt:

> *At first it seemed like entering a dream*
> *He was I in another form*
> *It was not his words I heard*
> *Nor his eyes, his smile*
> *It was what he was inside*
> *I felt the tides rise*
> *The sea whispering to me*
> *This is the one*
> *With whom you can celebrate love.*

I felt the moon rise
I became a riptide
A whirlpool, a tsunami, a flashflood,
What is love when it is out of control
And only another
Can restore peace and calm to your soul?

Though in her meditation she was a wonder of the earth, her personal will was no match for an Atlantean mage whose skills included binding another's soul into a stone of crystal and quartz. It happened like this. After repeated encounters, she fell in love with the merman. She trusted him and was in awe of his power. And she felt that the connection was one of those special things that occur only once or twice in five hundred or a thousand years. He then persuaded her based on their shared love to return with him to his human realm.

She would enter the body of a receptive woman in order to be with him. At first it was for an hour. And then the visits grew longer. She felt safe because love created a path between the realms of undine and humankind.

But he wanted more. He wanted her with him permanently. And so, before she understood what had happened, he enchanted her with high magic so that the water that composed her undine soul was joined to the other human elements of air, earth, fire, and akasha.

He did this so that she could not return to her own realm. He did it because it enhanced his performance as a mage to have beauty such as this by his side. He did it because she filled in for what was missing from the soul of Atlantis. He did it so that now he could return to his studies on controlling matter without feeling any residual tension in his brain. Why, all he had to do was gaze upon her, and he felt release and peace anointing him. It made perfect sense to him to spend some time with a woman, once undine, whose soul embodied a love so magnificent that human women have never felt its presence.

With her in his room, he could let go and be nothing at all and still feel that beauty and harmony, sensuality and serenity had become a part of his own nature. As I said, an alpha tends to seize what they need in order to ensure the success of their ventures. And this was something of value that immensely enhanced the cachet of a mage who possessed an insider's knowledge of the mysteries.

What happened to the soul of the woman whose body the undine had entered? The original woman's soul slowly faded away until only the undine remained. In this the undine had no say.

How did the undine feel about all of this? At first she felt genuine love for the mage. But when she realized what had been done to her, she was appalled. She, a creature so adept at feeling and empathy, had been tricked. Love had been betrayed. It was grievous because of what he had done to her and doubly so because she had failed to sense his intentions.

She could no longer play with her two friends among the waves, the reefs, and the ocean trench. She could no longer use her magical voice; nor could she even sing. Her very memories as an undine began to fade. Before Asor changed her soul, when she fell asleep in the body of a woman and dreamed, she would always awake in undine form and reenter the sea. Returning to the sea was no longer an option. Now when she awoke, she met and spoke with dead human beings. She would try to help them because she still embodied the purposes of love. Yet she knew that this was not her calling.

She retained many of her psychic abilities. She could transport her mind over distances and visit other locations. She caught glimpses of the future. She could heal others. She knew how to take away pain and to free others from dark memories. But her undine soul, the part that united the beauty of the heavens and the earth, was taken away from her and hidden beyond her reach.

But even worse than being tricked, deceived, and betrayed, she had been given a human soul against her will. A mage may only do this with the permission of Divine Providence. That is, there must be a purpose that encompasses the ages and is acceptable to the realm from which she had come.

Asor had no such purpose. No divine permission had been sought or granted. And to be perfectly clear, this was not a case where a mistake eventually leads to some greater good. Rather, to give a simple example, it is like walking out into your garage and unscrewing one of the fuses in the electrical box for the house. The lights in a room go out because the energy is no longer flowing. The beauty in the soul of the earth and the moon lost a degree of its sparkle and life. The magnificence of nature on our entire planet was diminished. The wonder of water and its divine sensuality was reduced by a significant amount.

Her two soul companions, the other undines with whom she swam, sensed that something horrible had happened. They searched but could not find her. When they consulted with the undine queens, they were informed that the entire race of humankind would soon pay a terrible price for its actions. But this is no consolation when something that is a part of your own heart mysteriously vanishes without explanation.

How do undines grieve when the very essence of their being is love?

To love does not mean that you must ignore your own limitations. One undine chose to abandon all contact with the human race. Even today there is not a trace of anything human even in her deepest memories.

The other undine is herself a story unlike any other. To keep it short, she could see when the three would again be united—perhaps ten or eleven thousand years in the future. To be one with the sea is to be beyond all grief. Love is never lost. Remorse and sorrow are human feelings. These beings are such that they journey along a path of beauty in which separation leads to reunion and conflict attains harmony. Without any doubt it is fair to say that in her innermost being is the dream of mankind and undines one day walking again side by side and sharing equally the mysteries of love. But like I say, her story stands alone, and her journey is very profound.

As if what the mage had done were not enough, Asor also desired to carry the undine's soul with him into death, that is, onto the astral plane. As some Taoist magicians now on earth still practice, he wished to maintain his consciousness after death so that he would have the same full awareness and powers that he had on earth. To do this he bound the undine's soul into a crystal ball. And though the crystal ball was material, he only needed to take the astral image of the ball with him to accomplish his purposes. As many of those who practice magic know, everything physical in our world can be intensified, mummified so to speak, so that a more refined or subtler vibration of it is transferred intact to the Other Side.

For the undine, it felt like her soul was bound in a cage. She was mentally restricted. Imagine what it would feel like if you were Beethoven but could no longer compose music or Picasso but could no longer paint. Imagine that you had amnesia and no longer knew you were an artist. Whatever you did with your life from that point on would feel wrong. For the undine, part of herself was ripped out of her and taken by the mage to the astral plane.

And so for these many long ages, she has been forced to reincarnate as a human being. But in her heart of hearts she knows in every lifetime, regardless of who she may be, that no purpose exists for her here on earth among human beings. She was designed and commissioned to be within and to express the mysterious beauty of the sea.

I have to tell you this was not the first or the last time that the human race committed serious violations against the laws of the universe. But certainly the forty-nine Judges of Saturn took note of this event. This taking of an undine against her will in itself did not cause the end of Atlantis, but it did not help. Actions such as this one in combination with others inevitably led to the sinking of the continent and the complete destruction of that advanced civilization.

THE CURSE

The undine queens had no need to make a complaint. In order to prevent further abuse, the spiritual Guardians who watch over evolution on this planet issued a judgment and a *geas,* a magical command that binds all of humankind and still remains in effect in our own time:

> Access to the realm of undines is henceforth prohibited to mankind except in extraordinary circumstances and on a case-by-case basis. All world teachers are forbidden to offer to mankind the undines' gifts in regard to pleasure and bliss, ecstasy and rapture, the power of beauty—its pure, uninhibited sensuality, the magic of empathy, and the secrets of love in regard to direct, heart-to-heart, and soul-to-soul inner union. Love on the astral plane in its purity, wonder, and power may not be shared with or taught to mankind.

In order to enforce this rule, a large body of monsters was created. At the very end, the Atlanteans' spiritual misdeeds generated extremely negative energies. These energies were gathered together and attached to a new purpose: to protect the realm of the undines. These are not physical beings. Rather, they are astral beings that appear within the dreams and just beneath the conscious imagination of human beings. They are sirens, krakens, gorgons, leviathans, and all manner of terrors whose presence stops the mind from thinking. You could say they are and remain part of our collective unconsciousness as an invisible, unnamed archetype or, as Freud more accurately described it, as "monsters of the id."

It is like this. Whenever an individual begins to consider or accidently stumbles upon a path leading to the realm of undines, these monsters appear within that individual's brain waves. And without a thought entering the individual's mind, the sense of something too horrible to behold turns the individual's thoughts to some other direction. This may sound overly invasive and paternalistic on the part of the Guardians, but it was undertaken in order to grant humanity a new beginning.

The power of Atlantis was in its combination of magic and science. The scientists were aware of the inner planes and consulted with spiritual beings while pursuing breakthroughs and technological inno-vations. But these powers were terribly abused and were thus revoked. The result of closing the inner planes to mankind was to make the entire history of Western civilization extroverted. It is no accident that Judaism, Christianity, and Islam treat magic as if it is a path leading to darkness and horrors. The mysteries in their genuine power have been forbidden to us.

And so, as I mentioned before, the human race has been barred for these long ages from even thinking about—much less pronouncing aloud the names of—the queens of the undines. When I examine the entire body of literature on our planet about undines, it is absolutely astonishing to me that there is so little material with any value. In many cases, what exists in literature and mythology is disinformation. The stories presented often lead not toward, but away from the realm of undines by offering illusions, false paths, and misinformation.

You do not have to take my word when it comes to this curse. You can observe this for yourself and draw your own conclusions. Here is a simple set of exercises that demonstrate my point.

To get past the Guardians, to open the gate to the astral plane of the undines, requires only three things. First, be in your mind the purity of the stars at night—that clear, open, and shining brightness. Second, be flowing like water in a stream—moving freely, turning and yielding, receptive and giving as if innocence has been turned into a dream. Finally, feel that love is everywhere—it is in the air, the water, the sea, the sky; light itself is love's expression, and breathing air is love's embrace.

These are simple meditations. Why, any minister, priest, or rabbi in any church or synagogue on earth could sneak one of these meditations in just before he or she begins a sermon. All he would need to do is say something like this:

Before I begin the sermon, I want you to take a moment and imag-ine a mountain pool. There is a small waterfall, a gentle spray of drops falling, moisture in the air, sparkling light dancing in the falling drops, the sound of splashing in the pool, small ripples running across the surface, and the water flowing over some rocks as it continues down the hill.

Imagine you are the water falling, dropping through the air, splashing, circling in the pool, and then flowing on. Take a few moments to explore those sensations—the falling drops and the cool, splashing water, the sounds and moisture in the air. And note the feeling of purity, release, relaxation, and peace that they awaken. There, now then, let us proceed to today's sermon.

But this little meditation or something like it has perhaps never been spoken in any church or synagogue in the last two thousand years. I tell you, there is something missing from the soul of humanity.

Now imagine that you and another feel a love for each other that also embodies these three things—purity, flowing water, and being a part of and within a sea of love. Take a few moments to feel what this would be like. Now simply ask yourself, have I ever seen or experienced this love? Some have. I have met individuals who feel and live within this love every moment of every day.

If you have not, answer these questions: Is not the sea available for all to see? Have you never floated in water and simply let go, feeling total release? Have you not seen the stars at night and felt they are a reflection of your own mind, its depth and its strength? Have you never seen the water in a stream flowing free, curling and turning, yielding and embracing? Perhaps you have, or perhaps you have not.

But now we come to the crux of the matter, the great question that defines whether there has been a curse upon our entire civilization for the last ten thousand years. Ask yourself, if you have not experienced this kind of love, then why have not the religions of the earth with their sages and all their spiritual illumination simply taught what is so profoundly obvious when you gaze at the sky at night, at the sea, and the stream flowing free? It is right in front of us. It is impossible to overlook, yet almost everyone on earth misses sensing and feeling these things.

And there you have it: a demonstration of an immense curse Divine Providence itself has placed upon all traditions and spiritual teachers of our planet.

And yet each individual remains completely free to pass by the Guardians by combining these simple meditations into one. The Guardians of the curse who have been commanded to stop human beings from encountering undines will not even give you a second glance. If you have no ego, then the curse has no power over you. You are free to feel the souls of undines flow through your own even as you are free to join your soul to any other person you may choose to love—it is an inner connection like water turned into love flowing through you.

And what of the undine forced against her will to become a human being? I put the question to Ronda, "Would you even now return to being an undine if given the choice?" And her reply?

"Yes," she said, "without hesitation. As an undine I dwelt in a realm of bliss and pure delight. For me, human beings are not yet fully alive. There is a part of their souls that is dead. It is hard to explain, but they have a denser, weaker vibration. When I awake on the astral plane each night, even though I have not yet reacquired my undine soul, the perceptions I have are a thousand times more intense and satisfying than when I am awake in the morning as a human being."

But she also agrees that if the right purpose could be found, she would remain among humanity even considering the sacrifice—that is, assuming she could continue to perform the original task assigned to her when she was an undine.

EPILOGUE

I practiced with Ronda the cosmic letter formula of E-M, which is specifically designed to create undine consciousness. This action along with an encounter with the queens of the undines restored the part of her soul that had been trapped in the crystal ball. She is now free of the mental cage that the mage had created around her.

Will she choose to return to the realm of undines and undo the harm that was done when her soul was bound to other elements not her own? We consulted with the undine queen Istiphul in regard to her situation.

Istiphul said to the woman,

What was done can be undone. But you are asking the wrong question. It does not matter in what spiritual realm or form you exist. It is only important that you feel free wherever you are. With a slight shift in focus, you can enter any realm you desire. You can experience its wonders and engage in spiritual activities and then return again to wherever you may be.

There are undines that have crossed over—not just shapeshifting but actually turning into human beings. They do not experience loss or limitation during this process. The undine within them remains fully alive and active. They have just added new abilities and aptitudes to what they already are.

And as you know, one of the three undines with whom you once played was originally a human who has now returned to humanity and lives as a woman. She is in no way harmed by her journey and sojourn in my realm. The divine has set before her a course in life that shall traverse many realms and serve many purposes.

Together, using our psychic abilities, Ronda and I also visited another undine who has acquired a human soul. She lives in Greece, and she gained a human soul in order to be permanently with her human lover. This undine-turned-human is perfectly happy. As a human being, she feels that she is still completely an undine. As the queen of undines mentioned, she just has more aptitudes and abilities.

She also has no sense of time. Does the sea experience the four seasons? For sure, the ice caps melt in summer, and the poles and other areas of the sea change in temperature. But in the sea all seasons flow together. The things we use to discern time—movement toward a goal, hours and days, or progress in solving a problem—these are external. The inner self for an undine woman does not change. There are perhaps six or seven other women in the world at this time who were once undines and who have acquired human souls. Each has her own story, and usually the transition involves an act of love.

And so this story has been told of how an undine many ages ago was forced against her will to acquire a human soul. This action was performed at a great cost to the human race. The curse upon us endures, but it is a curse that can be overcome. One final thing remains to be said.

The woman even now is reintegrating into herself the undine soul that was taken from her. As that soul awakens it has a message for mankind—for as you recall, one of the undines' commissions was to point out what is missing from any civilization.

And this is her message:

Unless the human race develops within itself a knowledge of the inner spiritual worlds commensurate with its knowledge of science and technology in the outer world, it will encounter chaos. The soul of humanity will be like a piece of paper torn into four pieces and then cast into the wind.

It is no longer permissible for the religions and spiritual traditions of the earth to be so selfish and narrow-minded. If they would be wise, their wisdom must encompass the entire earth. They must offer methods of self-transformation for everyone without asking for anything in return. The sky, earth, and sea are freely given. And beauty is itself a path of divinity; it is the foundation of harmony.

AN UNDINE POSSESSION

In order to answer the question of whether undines can actually marry a human being, I took the liberty of studying an undine that is currently living within a woman's body. I have not met this undine or woman. This is simply my clairsentient ability describing the undine's aura and her range of actions.

The soul of the woman who originally lived in the woman's body is no longer present. The former woman was quite different in personality from the undine. The woman was much more down-to-earth and had a no-nonsense attitude. The undine retains the memories of the previous woman, but it is in the way an actress can play the part of a character— through effort and with focus.

Even though the undine now uses the woman's brain, memories, and nervous system, the undine has her own aura intact. Inside of herself, the undine feels the way she feels when she dwells as an undine in the sea. Consequently, someone who is psychic would sense, not a human woman, but an undine standing in front of them.

This particular undine comes across in social interactions as somewhat distant. All the same, she always knows everything other people are feeling. Perhaps out of caution, however, she does not show what she senses or try to confirm her intuitions.

In effect, she is among human beings but remains a part of the sea that continues to surround her as a vibration and to which she retains an inner connection. If you were sensitive to energy, I imagine that standing in front of her you might have a sense that you were underneath the ocean.

In this particular instance, it takes a great effort for the undine to bond with the body she is in so that she can act as a human being. She sustains her connection to the physical body through her interest in the man she is with. The man was the one who originated the contact. He possessed sufficient psychic abilities and willpower to cause the undine to move from the astral plane into a physical body.

To keep her there, however, he must maintain a powerful etheric and astral bond between himself and the undine. If the undine were to suddenly dissolve her inner connection to him by returning to the sea, he would most likely die due to the shock to his nervous system.

This is not a romantic, fairy-tale kind of story I am telling. I tell it as I see it. The male is a wealthy businessman in Europe who is a member of a secret, esoteric order. He views this transaction the way he views magic: you order your life with a sense of pageantry; things have their proper place; an undine as a consort makes perfect sense to him not as a romantic interaction but as a complement or assistant to his work.

This man comes across as fairly impersonal.

PART III

Connecting to the Undine Realms

9

Images of Water

INTRODUCTION TO WATER ON EARTH

There are probably not many planets in our galaxy on which water appears with such diversity as it does on Earth. Even so, astronomers are furiously searching to discover a planet around another star of the right size and location to allow liquid water to occur on its surface.

Life on Earth has come into existence due to a number of supportive elements. We have an iron core that creates a magnetic field around the planet that protects us from solar radiation. We have the third-largest moon in the solar system. Next to Pluto with its moon of Charon, the Earth's moon is the largest in relation to the size of the planet. Our moon stabilizes the Earth's axis of rotation, which produces distinct seasons. It also creates tides that increase the life-enhancing environments between ocean and land.

We have a large gas giant, Jupiter, protecting the Earth as its gravity captures solar objects that might otherwise destroy our planet. And Jupiter is in just the right position—neither too close nor in a variable orbit, as are many gas giants in other star systems.

If the Earth were much closer to the sun, the planet would boil. If it were farther out, water would freeze. It is not easy to find the combination of variables that makes water and life as prevalent as they are on Earth.

If we were sitting in a college class discussing the properties of water, we would be studying chemistry—molecular bonding and atoms interacting. If we wanted to discuss water in nature, however, we would simply walk down the hall or enter a different building on campus so that we could take classes in meteorology, geology, oceanography, geography, or some other field.

And if we wanted to know about the operations of water inside of the human body, we would move onto biochemistry, biology, and physiology. Of course, to be thorough, we would need to throw in physics, astrophysics, and astronomy if we wanted to pursue water's relationships with magnetism and gravity.

Notice that nowhere are we yet studying psychology. I could walk from one end of this planet to the other and I do not think I could find one class in psychology that discusses self-awareness, that is, direct sensory perception of homeostasis; the parasympathetic and sympathetic nervous systems; the operations of the cingulate gyrus and orbital cortex; the free movement of consciousness between beta, alpha, theta, and delta brain waves; the blood flow to different parts of the brain; neurological activity; and so on—at least not in terms of exploring sensory perception as direct experience. In other words, all those purely physical and physiological parameters that underlie feeling.

Psychologists do not seem to be curious about how to probe the depths of their own emotions. Do they have the faintest conception of the possibility of entering a dream and reliving everything you have ever experienced using specific sensory and emotive imagery? Do they really want mythology, the study of folk traditions, and poetry—the experience of water and its imagery in nature—to be left to anthropology? Is the experience of a lake the same as that of an ocean? A river the same as rain falling or a waterfall? An iceberg the same as a thunderstorm?

Cops know that on a night with a full moon you get more 911 calls. Tides, gravity, and the moon influence water in the body. Images of water in nature have an astonishing influence on the ways we can learn to expand our consciousness. I once took a class called Psychology of Imagery. The professor said she was one of two professors in the United States teaching imagery as an academic class. Unfortunately, she died soon after, leaving only one.

If I were an alien visiting the Earth or an undine who has taken on human form, I would seriously have to ask the professors of planet Earth, are human beings brain-dead? How can anyone miss tasting the incomprehensible bliss that this planet creates?

A scientist once described my use of the four elements as archaic, belonging to an earlier age. But consider that science, in breaking knowledge into various disciplines, has lost its global perspective. At least in referring to earth, air, fire, and water, I have the element of water as a fundamental, defining category of life on Earth. Given our unique place in the cosmos, who could fail to see this?

From my psychic point of view, there is one unified field of energy throughout the universe. Matter, the elements of the periodic table, subatomic particles, the four fundamental forces, dark matter, and dark energy, as well as life, soul, and spirit—each of these is a distinct vibration. And yet they are all a part of and variations on this one energy field. Science has yet to discover this.

You have already seen the power of water images in previous sections, such as in my "Meditation on the Sea" with Istiphul in chapter 4. The following images are drawn from the world of nature. Each represents a slightly different aspect of the magnetic fluid; each produces a vibration that exists within nature and that can be reproduced within us. Most of these meditations come from my dialogues with undines. Again, we can explore these images using our sensual and emotional imaginations. And we can do so in either a nonmagical or a magical manner depending on the extent to which we engage our concentration.

The basic method for meditating on water imagery is to do what undines do: let go of your ego or identity and become the image in nature. If you imagine a lake, become the lake. If you imagine the sea, become the sea. Let go of your identity.

These images in nature are not impersonal. They are not neutral. They are not without life. And by attuning ourselves to these watery vibrations we can learn to extend and amplify familiar human feelings such as acceptance, receptivity, empathy, affection, the capacity to relax and let go, to flow, and also the divine virtue of all-embracing love.

You can meditate on images like these for five to ten minutes a day. After a series of weeks or months, you need only to think briefly about the watery image and everything it represents immediately surrounds you. Being completely open and relaxed and feeling alive and animated becomes part of your personality.

In a sense, these different meditations flow through each other. They are all one. The images begin with water, but they soon pass into an awareness of the magnetic fluid that in the same moment joins nature, human, and divine.

● Meditation on a Lake ●

Imagine a lake you would enjoy sitting in front of. Perhaps it is a lake surrounded by snow-capped mountains running up to twenty thousand feet. Perhaps it is a small, warm lake surrounded by green trees or a lake set among desert dunes.

The undine Isaphil uses a lake as a way to become very still, clear, pure, calm, and peaceful so that your soul is like a mirror. The mind then reflects the night sky, the oceans, the moon and its light shining down upon the whole Earth, the stars and their light, and the entire Milky Way.

Start, then, by sitting at the edge of the lake created by your imagination and enjoy the feelings and sensations it represents. And then make the shift and become the lake in your consciousness—that entire body of water with its depths and extended magnetic field and its still, mirrorlike surface.

The undine Isaphil has her own comment on this:

When the water in a lake is as clear as a mirror, just so let your mind rest. As human beings, you have a predilection to weigh and to measure, to analyze and test, to work and to shape, to see and to control each and every thing. Yet know also that your mind is this mirror—a power reflecting the world through the eyes of serenity.

◉ Meditation on a Pool in a Stream ◉

Imagine a small pool that is just the right size to slip your body down into and completely relax. Only your head is above the water. The gentle currents slide around your body and caress and massage away tension. The water is clear and bubbly as it flows. Its sounds are soft and musical. Your thoughts stop as you let go.

The only feeling of your body is the splashing laughter of the water that takes control of your sensations. Your brain waves are in harmony with the yielding, receiving water. Savor this image. Explore it. Make it part of your soul. The water in this pool is soft, clear, purifying, releasing, and relaxing. You are completely safe.

The watery flow around your body is soothing and also animating. It makes you feel alive. You feel rejuvenated and invigorated. Life is dancing in and around you with every sound and touch of the water.

AN UNDERGROUND STREAM

An underground stream is, in a sense, an image of water that flows deep in the unconscious. You may stand on the ground above the stream and be completely unaware that it is there. In a way, this is analogous to the influence a man and woman often have on each other. They may not sense directly the deep flow of life that moves within them. But the influence is there.

The image of an underground stream contains a watery sensation that is purifying, cool, and nurturing; it feels absolutely free—it goes on for miles and miles without any constriction or inhibition. It has waterfalls and still pools. It is shallow, and it is deep. It is so alive you can feel animated and rejuvenated just by its touch, yet it is able to be completely solitary and silent without any concern for the outer world.

Some individuals transmit these feelings automatically to whomever is near to them. Most people do not sense this subtle kind of watery flow moving through them. If they do, they feel it only as something strange, a kind of impersonal and yet incredibly intimate exchange of energy. And yet they do not have a clue as to why they feel as they do.

As with all these images of water, just being around a certain person can produce these energies within you. On the other hand, two individuals may produce these feelings as a by-product of their relationship. In such cases, there may be an uncanny feeling of connection to the other person that has nothing to do with the social interaction. With the underground stream image, there may be a sense of a new life arising within you, but at the same time the other person who is producing it may remain, like the buried stream, hidden and distant.

A WATERFALL

In some Taoist meditations based on acupuncture,* there is an attempt to join the Du meridian moving up the back of the body with the Ren meridian moving up the front of the body. Once connected, they make one circle of vital energy flowing up the back of the body and down the front.

A man can often focus his consciousness through his mind and upper body with much greater ease than a woman can, but men often have great

---

*For example the microcosmic orbit meditation of Master Mantak Chia.

difficulty in bringing the energy down the front of their bodies. Being around a young, vibrant woman is often a quick remedy. She produces in him a natural balance. Her vitality and sensuality affect him by drawing the vitality out of his head and down the front of his body. As a result he feels younger, less mental, and more alive.

In the East, there are great efforts made in meditation to sink one's energy down into the abdomen. When a man and a woman hug, they briefly join the flows of the energies moving down the fronts of their bodies. You may be able to feel this flow directly as the sensation of a stream of water flowing through your body. This can also be enhanced through the following meditation. The individual uses the image of a waterfall to describe the movement of vitality.

I feel this waterfall running down the front of my body. If I focus on it, I become the waterfall. In my mind, this waterfall is about a hundred feet high, and I am the water of a stream at the top moving along. And I pass over a cliff and fall through space. I am all the drops and the light flashing through them with the colors of the rainbow on display.

Weightless I fall. I am the moisture in the air and the thin mist rising and taking on countless shapes. Eddies in the air from the falling water cleanse my soul.

And I am the splashing water in a mountain pool—the bubbles sinking down and rising up. And the ripples and waves spreading out upon the surface. I am the sound of the water coming down, the reverberating, murmuring, soft, surging roar. And I am the currents in the pool circling around and then running off downstream while I also remain the entire pool that sits serenely meditating as if in a dream.

I notice that water is perfectly obedient to the law of gravity. It is absolutely submissive in adapting to its circumstances. But with a little change in temperature, absorbing or releasing its heat, it expands and rises to the surface as ice. Or it evaporates, filling the air with moisture or rising higher to form a cloud. Water is incredibly clever. It gets to where it wants to go, and all it does is flow.

A POOL BENEATH A MOUNTAIN

Some people enjoy spelunking, or exploring caves. These individuals occasionally come upon a pool of water beneath the ground. Such a pool has its own life and vibration.

> *The feeling of a woman*
> *Is like a pool flowing beneath a mountain:*
> *No sun dawns*
> *No moon rises*
> *Yet the water is luminous,*
> *Cool, soft, soothing*
> *Amid transparent light, silence dancing:*
> *The taste of love a secret sharing heart to heart.*
> *Some will die without having felt this touch*
> *Some hearts will harden, turning bitter,*
> > *dry, or cold*
> *Because the memory has grown old.*
> *But I remember her smile, her heartbeat, her eyes*
> *Though no moon shines this night*
> *Though no hand reaches for mine*
> *The waters of my heart*
> *Flow cool, soft, and full of luminous dreams*
> *Dancing with the silence of this night*
> *Overflowing with love.*

A RIVER

In some cultures there are sacred rivers. If you bathe in them, you are freed of your sins. And it is not just the nature religions and Hindus who like rivers; consider this quote from the Bible:

> And he showed me a pure river of the water of life, clear as crystal, proceeding from the throne of God and of the Lamb. In the middle of its street, and on either side of the river, was the tree of life, which bore twelve fruits, each tree yielding its fruit every month. The leaves of the tree were for the healing of the nations. (Revelation 22)

Or how about, "Out of their bellies shall flow streams of living water"? In magic or simply good meditation, we take an image in nature and become one with it. We then feel it inside of ourselves. In this case, the river as an image of water is something that flows through our souls.

A magician or mystic is not so spiritually impoverished as to have to wait for the making of a new heaven and a new earth before tasting and experiencing these things. Rather, nature, human, and the divine intermingle and join within our hearts.

The river is an elemental, sensory experience with water. Its sensations include the sense of flowing and yielding, of letting go and relaxing. Its feelings include a sense of becoming pure and living at peace with nature. It is also at the same time an experience with the divine if we can find within that watery magnetism a love that joins with and unites all aspects of ourselves; it makes us whole and transforms us from the depths of our souls. As a symbol—as a vibration reflecting the divine within it—a river, like the sea, is also a well-being that flows like a stream from the dawn of time to the ends of eternity.

As a meditation, then, imagine sitting in front of a river. Use all your senses. Relax. And then in whatever way works for you, enter and become the river. Float down it. Swim in it. Become a fish. Become the waves, the currents, the eddies, and ripples on the surface—until at some point you can feel a sensation of water flowing through your body that is relaxing and peaceful and life-renewing.

AN OCEAN TRENCH

Drop your mind down into an ocean trench. Here you feel undisturbed by the surface of the ocean or, for that matter, by the outer world. You attain a profound sense of peace that is ancient and wise and that comprehends the mysteries of the deep.

This is where you learn to perceive and think from the point of view of the planet rather than from the viewpoint of a member of a particular race of beings living on the earth. In other words, the magnetic fluid attunes us not just to the feminine aspects of the human soul but also to the soul of the Earth.

The sea holds a peace in its silent depths. Entering this place with an open, calm, and relaxed mind, you feel this peace not as something that is impersonal and distant. Rather, it is more like a lover—it is gentle, friendly, and intimate.

A MOUNTAIN POOL

I float on my back in a mountain pool. The water spreads out around me and is embraced by tall cliffs. The night is calm and still. The moon is low in the sky, the sliver of a crescent.

I float . . . I relax . . . I let go. The water feels like it is a part of my body. Time slows until it is motionless. The sea of stars shines down, its light reflected in and through me.

The pool of water extends outward; the stream begins as rain from the sky and flows until it blends with the sea. The water supports my body like a lover whose skill is to love another forever.

In this moment I am part of two separate kingdoms. I belong to the human race and know love as I have seen it in another's face and felt the embrace. Floating, letting go, water is a pathway into the soul—it speaks of loneliness, hunger, and the burning desire to unite with another. I know this well. I know the spell.

And yet another kingdom is here also. The sea and the waters of the earth flow through me. I let go. I enter the dreams of the sea. I meet with undine queens, and they share their secrets with me. Their beauty is beyond what any poet has ever told in songs of wonder and songs of awe.

The great mages have been here, but they have failed to tell the tale with any persuasion or poetry worthy of the ecstasy. Perhaps in their search for knowledge, they failed to grasp the wonder and beauty within nature.

Undines swim just beneath where I float. I see through their eyes as they see through mine. When they look at themselves through my eyes, they see pure, unbounded sensuality—the entire ocean flows through them.

When I look at myself through their eyes, I see hot blood around an electrical coil, barely able to float, ready to explode or implode—power without limitation seeking to unite with water in order to accomplish some new act of creation. Will and power, the love within water, flowing in and through each other without hesitation, without boundaries interfering.

The water is cool and cold. Ripples from the falls drift over my body. Rays from a rising golden sun find their way into the pool. I am so relaxed and serene that I move within a dream just beyond the reach of humanity.

The peace is so deep that there is no separation between the circle of the earth and the depths of the sky. Here, for these moments, the peace is infinite.

It is not a concept. It is not a feeling. The undines' skin becomes my own—the peace is a physical sensation; it is pure perception.

I float . . . I let go . . . I drift. In moments like this, I hear the Song of the Universe. If astrophysicists can speak of the background radiation from the big bang, I can speak of the Song of the Universe. As I listen, it seems impossible to miss.

In water, one person and another are never far apart. I enter the undine's heart. Her heart is like a cup of water. I taste and drink. It does not become empty as I take. It overflows because she knows how to let go so that the entire sea flows through her soul.

The mountain pool vibrates in a different way. It becomes her love. It expresses her grace. The water is now warm, soft, tender, and sweet. There is nothing within me she cannot feel or reveal. She traces my desires back to their source. She finds in each need the place in time and space when it shall be complete. She takes me there and walks with me so that I might fully believe that I have shared with another experiences that shall come to be.

She feels what it is like to be me. This is the wonder of undine empathy. For an undine, the human world is like a desert, a parched land, a wasteland of dry streambeds, of salt flats, with only an occasional oasis. She sees that for humanity love is so rare that people bind themselves to each other with fear and hatred in order to ensure that a few drops of kindness will be there to survive their worst moments.

She enters my heart without fear to remind me that the sea is always near, that the waters of the earth flow through my soul in every moment. The vast magnetic field that is this planet is able to hold, shelter, and renew, for this is the nature of love. It is here in every moment surrounding us, waiting to be discovered.

◉ Meditation on the Cycle of Nature ◉

An undine spoke the words of this meditation:

You are on a beach. The crescent moon is in the sky. The tides once high are now withdrawing following the setting moon. And as the tide is pulled away toward the opposite side of the world, let yourself go. You too are pulled toward your opposite, flowing in harmony with nature like a wind-driven wave, like water sinking down with the undertow into a dark place where the sun is unable to go.

Just let go. There is nothing to know. Only a feeling to follow.

Now flow with me down a river that runs free. The trees on the side pass you by, but you take no note. You just let go and float.

Spread your arms and fingers out to your sides. Breathe deep. Exhale. Feel your toes.

Now travel with me far out to sea. The water is calm, mirrorlike, and still but warm. The air is cold. A mist rises upon the water, stirring like curtains in a breeze, like the northern lights reflected in the form of moisture, dancing, wild, playful, free, to mingle and merge and now to rise in the air into the sky without thought or design.

You follow with your mind, tasting this liquid, dewy trail. Ascending, the moisture gathers together as clouds in the air.

Your body is now the cloud riding upon the wind, circling within itself, shapeshifting, shape-changing without end, free to dream any dream.

You travel to an island whose cliffs are thousands of feet high. Your cloud rises toward their height, caressing them, penetrating the trees, the winds like sweet songs and melodies.

The leaves catch your drops, and you are now rain falling down and fog lifting up moist, wet tears of joy, tears of pain—they are the same in these cool luminous heights where the sun's first rays meet the cloud's gray.

You find your way among the cliffs that give birth to streams. You become the water surging and flowing into these pools, into these falls; you hear the sounds, the water splashing down, the bubbles beneath the surface moving around.

Here in a pool you take your rest. Your time has been well spent, for you are at last content. You feel pure, clear, as open and receptive as anything that is truly feminine. The liquid water shining here is a love that unites the earth and the sky.

But contentment does not imply inaction. You flow on, daring to discover the path of life unfolding.

Around, over, and beneath rocks, seeping beneath the sand, you travel on. Winding, serpentine, slow and then fast, deep and shallow, wide and narrow, it makes no difference— you are the feminine essence free to assume any identity without attachment holding you back.

Streams gather together; you become a river. Strong, passionate; feel that power driving you on. Until you meet the sea, a place of limitless dreams where, like one falling asleep or another one waking to a new beginning, you travel on.

And here you become the sea stretching out your limbs from the shores of one continent to another. The waves, the tides and currents, the icy pole, the depths—this is who you are.

And here take again your rest, for a while. The stars above sing to you for you are their lover. And the sun and moon rise for you for you are their brother or their sister.

And again, on and on forever, the mist rises from the surface, moisture ascends to the sky, the entire circle of ocean, moisture, cloud, wind, rain, stream, falls, river, traveling to the sea—within this circle you have learned to be free of form identity. You are water in its feminine mystery.

Follow this watery magnetism as it now ascends through your body into your brain and circles again through every cell in your body. Feel this magnetism as a universal principle that reflects and captures in its heart the light of the universe and renews all things. As dawn is to night, so this flow of love within you grants new life.

LUNAR GRAVITY

Until Sir Isaac Newton, no one had given an explanation for the rising and falling of the tides. Gravity and the laws governing bodies in motion—why, just about any undine could have told you about the sun, the moon, and the tides, and this without reference to mathematics, physics, or school experience.

Here is an exercise you will not find on an exam in any physics class on earth. You imagine you can sense the gravitational force causing the tides to rise and fall. You sense the influence of the sun and moon on the oceans of the Earth.

Visualize the moon drawing the oceans on opposite sides of the Earth to rise due to the moon's stronger gravitational pull on one side of the Earth and weaker pull on the opposite side. You eventually get a feeling for this magnetic or gravitational influence on water, and you identify with it.

This gives a feeling for the deepest flows of magnetism in nature and also for the biorhythms that are active within our own bodies. In this way, we gain a sensory understanding of the rhythmic cycles of the moon and its cycles moving with and in opposition to the sun. Through awareness of this magnetism or, if you like, this gravity, we gain a sense of the way these celestial bodies move and feel from within water as well as within us.

DIALOGUE WITH A YOUNG WOMAN

THE GODDESS OF THE EARTH: Do you wish to be anointed with my beauty and shine with my light?

WOMAN: Yes.

GODDESS: Then two things I require: establish justice upon the earth and do as I do—make the world new.

WOMAN: How do I do this?

GODDESS: Establish a religion without priests, temples, or rituals in which love, power, wisdom, and justice are equally honored and pursued.

WOMAN: [*about to ask her how, but now a merman touches her hand, probing her heart and penetrating her thoughts*]

MERMAN: It is my skill to reveal the keys to the mysteries of the lakes, the rivers, the streams, and the seas. There is a peace as vast as the sky, as deep as the sea, as still and clear as a mirror, and flowing like water.

WOMAN: Can you help me find this peace within myself?

MERMAN: Yes, of course. Take this cup into your hands. Now relax, be still. Feel my hands on your own as we hold the cup. Take a deep breath. Exhale. Now feel you are this cup and this water. Nothing else is in your mind. You are free of all distractions. Take your time. Feel this cool water inside of you.

The water—this water is now you. The water vibrates with all the water upon our planet. This water is calm, serene, still, relaxed, and at peace. The very depths of the sea are within you. The flowing streams, the rivers, the icy poles, the waves of all the seas, they are all flowing through and within and are a part of you. The circle of the earth, the vast expanse of ocean from horizon to horizon around the globe: you are this vast body of water, and this water is within your soul.

See how the water like a mirror reflects clearly all that is near. Sense that this reflective power of water is your own. The light it reflects sinks into your depths. The pure essence of the sun, the moon, and the stars is captured in the taste of this substance you hold.

Open your heart. Feel moonlight flowing down upon you, anointing you. Open yourself. Feel the light of dawn and sunset, the birth of light on earth, its spectrum of wonder and color, this light is flowing through you—soft, shining, luminous, cool, soothing, full of dreams and visions. It guides us in our sleep, and it joins us to all that we can ever want.

Gaze again upon this cup. Water is so open and reflective, so deep and at peace, it contains all the feelings of every heart within itself. It holds the mystery of our opposite—the universe moves around the mysteries of the heart.

Past, present, future—they are all contained and revealed in this moment of pure stillness. Feel that this water is the purity of your love and that your love embraces the whole world.

In this cup are my love and your love also. In this cup, the separations of space and time are overcome. Here is the feeling of what it is like to finally come home. Within this cup and this water is a love that flows without beginning or end. The universe has been created with its stars and galaxies to give us a taste of the delight that is hidden within such life.

Within the depths of water, its liquid embrace, is the fulfillment of every desire—the stars and the sky above us, the depths of the sea, and the stillness in this moment are within your own heart.

Take this cup now and drink from it—drink into yourself the love that embraces the universe and that makes us all one with each other without separation. Taste the water in your mouth; go with it as it sinks down; stay with it as it is absorbed into every cell in your body. The waters of life flow through you. The beauty of the universe is within and a part of you.

And now do you have what you asked me for? A peace as deep as the sea, as vast as the sky, as still and clear as a mirror, and flowing like water?

WOMAN: [*stares into his eyes for several minutes without speaking*] Can you sit with me for a while? I want to be able to share this beauty with another without speaking.

MERMAN: Of course.

WATER AS OMNIPRESENCE

There is a magical aspect of water relating to omnipresence and akasha. You imagine you are within the ocean, but you concentrate on the way in which water suspends distance. You sense and then study how water enables you to feel an immediate contact with any other creature or place within the sea.

Some of the undines have this perceptual ability to sense waves breaking on any shore of the earth. In their own consciousness, they feel as if their senses can perceive anything anywhere within the ocean. The water serves as a medium for amplifying impressions and conveying physical sensations of objects no matter how distant.

These meditations on water lead to the clairsentient ability to suspend distance so that you can connect to anyone as if you are there with them. In this case, the ocean is used as a symbol of the astral plane, where we are able to move our astral bodies anywhere we wish in an instant by focusing our minds there.

In addition, undines such as Amue and Istiphul feel as if another being or creature's aura is a part of their own aura. This arises because they automatically circulate energy between themselves and anything else that makes contact with them. This heightens their abilities to heal and to love. They do not feel separate because the other's space is also their own space in that they sense every subtle vibration within another.

And so this poem:

Omnipresent Love

Omnipresent love is the ability to become one with
anything.
Put simply—to hold another in your heart
To desire for the other
The very best that life can offer:
The deepest satisfaction
And the highest path to perfection.
To be so open and empty, so clear, so utterly receptive
To listen so carefully
To care with such tenderness
The other's experiences are like your own memories.
Like a mother, a brother, or a lover,
You shelter and protect,
You nourish and sustain
So that you are the inspiration
That illuminates another's soul.
But in a more personal way,
The essence of water is discovered through daring.
To dare is to accept the world as it is
And also to dream the world as it can be.
The vision is of being complete—
Sensitive to human need
And yet also feeling what it is to be free.
I dream this dream
This love flows through me.

During certain initiations in Tibetan Buddhism such as the Kalachakra, the Dalai Lama invites the practitioners to project their minds into his chakras. A chakra is sometimes described as a nexus of biophysical energy in the body. For those who have the ability, you can project your mind directly into the Dalai Lama's heart chakra. Then notice the sensations and feelings that occur.

When I do this, I feel like I am within a sea of compassion. It is endless. It encompasses all beings. I use the word *sea* because there is a watery, fluid sensation in his energy. The Dalai Lama has said, "As long as suffering remains to sentient beings, I will remain to serve." This declaration embodies the richness and depth of his compassion for others.

The water element in the Dalai Lama is not just an ideal on the akashic plane. It finds expression on the denser astral plane. Here its presence is felt as an emotional force animating and inspiring those who are near him.

10

The Difference between a Real and an Imagined Undine

I *imagine* an undine in front of me. This is not hard for me to do. I have been practicing visualization for thirty years. In fact, if I imagine myself standing on the ice at the North Pole, my body immediately begins to shiver. Obviously, visualization can be done with varying degrees of clarity.

I ask this young lady, the undine, in front of me to tell me something about the water element that I do not already know. The creature I visualize replies immediately and in a challenging manner.

She says, "What you do not know about water is how to let go. You do not know how to become the waves of an ocean that encircle the globe by both day and night. You do not know how to become the warm current that circulates from the equator to the pole and returns as a cold current sinking into the depths. You do not know this journey. You do not offer this renewing power to others."

This image of an undine speaks freely from the depths of myself. It also takes me more deeply into nature. Imagination is a kind of power. On the other hand, if I call the undine Isaphil to come here into my room, I notice the difference right away.

I call the undine Isaphil. She is here now. I ask Isaphil to circulate energy between the two of us in a way that is completely relaxed. The circulation of energy between us starts immediately, and it occurs without effort on my part.

There is a soft, caressing flow of watery sensations all over my body. These sensations are relaxing, soothing, and releasing. There is also a cleansing, cooling sensation I can feel inside my body as well.

As the energy reaches my heart, I can almost hear a voice singing, "Awake, awake. Feel the thrill—a thousand sensations you have never felt, a thousand dreams human beings have never dreamed: to kiss with the passion of the sea, to give and to receive without limitations, without hesitation."

I also feel myself pulled into the astral domain of Isaphil. I am within the ocean, but I am sharing some of Isaphil's modes of perception. I can look over and see an iceberg in the distance, but now I feel the iceberg's energy within my own body as I look. I feel the frozen freshwater of the ice caressed by salt water the way one person's body presses against another.

Within this dreamlike imagery, I pull myself out of the water and sit on a piece of flat ice in an arctic bay. The open water is as still as a mirror. The sun is dim and distant in the sky. There is no discomfort, no need for a sweat suit to feel at ease.

An undine can be thrilled and have fun even when nothing is happening. Human conception has no part to play. My body becomes the arctic bay. The ice and the water are full of exciting and enchanting feelings; they join together wild laughter and solemn, majestic meditations as the stars circle and dance in the sky through the night.

Try this, what is the difference between a real and an imagined woman? I can imagine a woman who, like Jessica Lange in the movie *All That Jazz*, acts as a spiritual counselor. She is completely familiar with all my ways. She is kind, caring, empathic, and flirtatious. And she delights completely in talking with me about anything I have ever experienced. She is always available.

This female spirit guide I have imagined offers me a high learning curve. As a psychologist, she is a grand master. But she does not push me to learn new things. She may say the right words, but she lacks emotional force and the ability to bargain and to persuade.

Since she has no survival instinct, she does not need attention or recognition. Consequently, she is not needy or vulnerable. She is not demanding. She does not place subtle, nonverbal, or emotional conditions upon our interaction.

Some magicians, prophets, or artists constantly compare the real world to an imagined world. In doing so, they strive to use one to improve upon the other. In my art, I certainly strive to use imagination to change the world. Dedication, conviction, and faith in a dream or an ideal can bring about change. But here is the difference: a real undine, like a real woman, can love you, transform you, or destroy you. An imagined undine, like an imagined woman, is not so dangerous.

The undines I write about are brilliant and empathic about a number of things. They explain that if their love and empathy were known to mankind, wars would be no more; women would retain their beauty into old age; old and young women both would possess healing power; and our contact with the beauty of nature would transform us forever.

In regard to the above, I would have to say I am not writing fairy tales—stories about imagined beings. I am negotiating a change in human destiny. This purpose takes us beyond the world of fantasy and entertainment. It engages us, if we choose to be involved, with real beings of astonishing beauty and power.

As I have described previously, I shift my focus in this moment into the sea. Even as I think to myself the name "Istiphul," the undine appears to me. It is a little hard to say precisely where I am. Am I projecting my mind "out there somewhere," or is she present in my room here and now sitting on my bed next to my computer?

I take Istiphul's hands—her touch is as ancient as the sea and yet more youthful and free than any touch I have ever known. Being in her presence is an encounter with the entire magnetism of the oceans appearing in the form of a woman.

Istiphul says to me, "The human race will acquire the love I possess—the magic and the passions of the sea will find expression within human beings. Beyond your wildest dreams, love will seize you and be one with you even as you experience it with me. I promise you this."

Undines like Istiphul are prophetic. They see the future. Istiphul wants me to rethink the purposes underlying my entire life. She wants me to find another destiny. She puts herself on the line to see that this will happen. I have difficulty trying to conjure up an imagined undine that has this force and intensity. In fact, I cannot even imagine a real woman offering or demanding that love attain this.

Istiphul's presence can be shocking. You could argue that an encounter with an archetype or some ancient goddess might evoke a similar experience. But archetypes and goddesses by necessity, by definition, have numinous and impersonal qualities. Istiphul, by contrast, is the essence of intimacy; 100 percent of her presence and being is focused on you as an individual.

To put it simply, she embodies what we are to become rather than what has been or what we imagine. The bottom line? You have to feel with your heart the difference between a real and an imagined undine.

11

A Study of Water and the Magnetic Fluid

INTRODUCTION

Imagining water inside of one's body can create specific sensations and feelings. The feelings, for example, can move from a basic sense of well-being, serenity, and empathy to states such as perfect contentment, perfect love, oneness with another, and a feeling of being one with the universe.

This is an opportunity for both men and women to experience the essence of the feminine. A woman can study from within the archetypal energies moving through her, and a man can discover within himself the wonders the feminine possesses. Certainly, to know oneself from the core of your being will require an encounter with your opposite.

This section reveals one means for accomplishing this.

THE BASIC EXERCISE

Imagine your body to be completely empty inside like a container or vessel. Also imagine that you are surrounded by cold water as if you are at the center of a vast ocean. The cold water is contracting. Of all substances in nature, water absorbs heat the most quickly and stores it the longest. Water holds, contains, and sustains.

Next imagine that water enters your body with each breath as you inhale. At the same time, water enters through the pores of your body. You breathe in this sensation of cold water until you feel that your body is full of water. At the end of this exercise, reverse the process and imagine breathing the cold water out of your body.

In effect, you develop the ability to accumulate and then dissolve the sensations of water both inside and outside of the body. This is a basic exercise in training one's imagination. Without doing the above, you can simply imagine the inside of your body filled with water. Practicing over time, you will produce in your body increasingly strong sensations.

SENSATIONS OF WATER
IN THE PHYSICAL BODY

If I focus on my physical body and in particular on anything relating to fluids and water, I can sense the flow of blood through my body. Some people can sense the pulse of their blood as it surges through the body and also notice when their heart skips a beat. With experience, you can feel blood flow into parts of your body when you relax them. The blood vessels dilate with the result that there is more blood flow into the area so it becomes warmer.

Actually, all fluids within the body are diluted solutions of water. Men's bodies are about 60 percent water, and women's are around 50 percent. The specific fluids such as blood, sweat, tears, lymph, saliva, the cerebrospinal fluid, and all digestive enzymes are between 96 to 99 percent water. The brain is about 75 percent water, and the muscles contain nearly as much.

If I concentrate on the flow of blood, immersing myself in this sensation and awareness, I definitely get a sense of its actions—circulating, purifying, nurturing, and reviving. If I focus my imagination on the sense of liquids or water flowing rapidly as blood, I get images of a stream or a river with its rapids and waterfalls.

THE ETHERIC BODY

Besides sensations relating directly to the physical body, it is possible to sense a subtler set of sensations relating to the etheric body. These sensations refer to vitality and health. The etheric body is often encountered in the practice of pranayama, the control of breath. Concentrate for example on your hand. Imagine that with each breath you are breathing vitality directly into your hand. As you practice, you may be able to sense increased warmth, a feeling of gradually building pressure, different kinds of intensity of energy, and so forth.

Some of these sensations relate to relaxation. Again, as you relax, the blood vessels dilate, which leads to increased warmth as the blood moves closer to the surface of the skin. But something subtler is also occurring. In martial arts, it is quite common to learn how to move this vitality, chi, or ki to different parts of the body to enhance health and physical performance.

Vitality has the four elements within it. Sometimes a martial arts practitioner focuses on weight and being grounded—the earth element. Sometimes the emphasis is on being light like air, being able to move quickly as if weightless. Other times one focuses on fire and a rapid, forceful expansion of energy outward.

Perhaps the most difficult to imitate or teach in martial arts is the element of water. The founder of aikido was a great master of the water element, but his personal style was nearly impossible to teach. In some traditions of *Chi Kung,* the student learns to imitate a cloud or to flow like water through movements that are circling, spiraling, and curling with gentleness and grace, almost like moving slowly underwater.

We can pursue the difference between the physical and etheric energies by imagining that the body is empty inside and filled with cool water. If you were immersed in an actual pool of water, you could imagine that the inside of your body was filled with the same water that was surrounding it on the outside. Etheric water is far more refined than physical water. It is the watery, fluid, or flowing aspect of vitality.

I focus on the vitality in my etheric body. Again, I imagine my body is empty inside and that my awareness is only of vitality in its flowing, fluid aspect. What occurs is that I feel extremely relaxed. There is a sense of calmness, of letting go and feeling release. When I do this, I am often reminded of floating in a tide pool that has a high salt content. The body floats higher in the water almost as if the entire body is being supported, and tension dissolves.

THE ASTRAL BODY

The astral body pertains to the realm of the soul, to feelings and emotions. The astral body is very sensitive to concrete imagery—to situations, people, and places. The astral body is active in dreaming. A dream often produces strong emotions even though the circumstances or dramatic situations of the dream are unreal. You respond as if they are real. The astral body is where these emotions occur. The astral is sensitive, receptive, responsive, and impressionable.

When you feel the opposites of happiness and sadness, elation and depression, excitement and boredom, joy and despair, love and hate, and so on, these feelings are occurring within the astral body. Though all emotions produce sensations within the physical body, at this point we are after the way feelings are underneath, behind, or accompanying physical sensations. With practice and attention, it becomes easy to notice the differences between the physical sensations accompanying feelings and the feelings themselves.

The astral body also gives a sense of connection to others. It is full of attracting and repelling forces. When individuals fall in love, it is often an astral experience—they are in the astral plane living a dream that the two share in common. When individuals break up, the same intensity of feeling may be present, but it changes into an opposite, repelling emotional force.

Just as we all have our own unique physical body, we each have a unique astral body. The astral involves our ability to feel alive and to appreciate the world around us. The elements present in the astral body will strongly influence our ability to feel wonder, awe, and beauty as well as experiences with ecstasy and rapture.

Just as we can discuss the four elements in terms of physical sensations in the etheric body and their applications (for example, in the martial arts), we can also describe the four elements in the astral body. In the astral body, fire is not a physical or etheric force. It is a feeling that relates to enthusiasm, courage, confidence, and charisma. Air relates to being curious, playful, artistically sensitive, and cheerful. Earth relates to being practical, no-nonsense, patient, and stable.

I imagine my astral body to be similar in shape and size to my physical body and etheric bodies, but it is subtler, almost like seeing an image of oneself in a mirror or a dream. I imagine it again to be empty, without physical substance. Then I imagine this astral body to be filled with cool water.

Meditating on water in my astral body, I sense feelings specific to water. These are contentment, peace, serenity, and happiness. There is a sense of well-being that is timeless and independent of space, of who I am, where I was born, and where I am now in life. It is just a pure, endless sense of peace into which an individual can let go and simply be without having to do anything to earn it.

IMAGERY OF WATER IN NATURE ON THREE PLANES

Here is a simple way to observe the difference between the physical and astral planes. Grasp your lower arm with your opposite hand. Note the physical sensations relating to the touch of skin on skin and the pressure of your grip.

Now, focus on the hand holding your arm. Without changing the grip, place within this hand the feeling, *I love you with all my heart and soul*. It is a feeling that can be expressed through touch. Note now any difference between the two kinds of touch.

One produces only physical sensations. The second may produce for you in addition an increased sense of warmth, a sense that the touch is penetrating and pervading the entire arm beneath the hand. There are various feelings associated with this kind of emotional bonding: a sense of connection, trust, openness, and so on. If you can notice these distinctions in this exercise, you can learn to sense the difference between purely physical sensations relating to water and the astral or emotional life that exists within the particular form of water you are in contact with.

Here are two examples. I place my hands in a sink filled with cool water. There are physical sensations: the embracing touch of the water on my skin, the pressure, the cool temperature contrasting with the rest of my arm. There is a slight chill from the movement of water in the basin.

Now I focus on the feeling—the astral component—of the water: I sense its adaptability, how it instantly molds itself to whatever it touches, embracing it. I sense the quality of purity—the water's solubility and how it cleanses and purifies. I sense how it nurtures and renews. As a feeling, water is also pure receptivity.

A second example is a warm shower. There are the sensations of water on my skin. There is the heat and the sounds and moisture in the air. Muscles relax. The mind is drawn toward letting go of tension and worries. There is an image in my mind of a waterfall and sunlight shining through the falling drops. The sunlight relates to the heat in the water.

The image is produced by free association. But there is an astral component also. If I focus on the feeling within the water, it is like a golden light flowing through the center of my body. The light is healing, reviving, and nurturing.

For someone who is psychic, when you place your hand in water, the water feels alive. The energy in your hand brings the water to life. It is not a chemical reaction. It is how the life-force or vitality in the hand is amplified and shaped by the presence of the water.

Consider again nature imagery. We can use a simple form of contemplation: focus on some scene in nature and allow your mind to be still like a mirror. Hold the image before your attention so that nothing else is present in your awareness. Then notice the sensations and feelings that arise in your body. You can also enter the image, moving in and through it or identifying completely with it.

With the image of a lake, I have sensations of being calm, open, receptive, and gathering in. The feelings are contentment, peacefulness, and hope. With a waterfall, in addition to water falling through air and splashing, there is a sparkling effervescence and a renewal of life. In a river, I let go and move with the flow, yielding to gravity's pull drawing me to join with the distant sea. The sensation of letting go into the flow also has a feeling; there is a majestic sense of being connected to water as it moves from sea to sky to rain before returning again into a river. It is feeling part of a greater whole that nurtures the entire biosphere.

Consider being inside of an iceberg frozen in a bay at the North Pole. The sensations are icy cold, frozen, and still. The feelings are an inner stillness, a mirrorlike reflection, and an otherworldly observing of life from a distance of time and space.

Consider a mountain pool with a small waterfall. Hold this image before your mind. Imagine sitting or floating in the pool. Try becoming the pool so that nothing else but this imagery is in your awareness. As I do this, I have the sensations of flowing, bubbly water. The movement of water is gentle.

There are etheric sensations relating to the nature of vitality: flowing energy that is cool, relaxing, releasing, and easing. And there are astral feelings such as serenity, purity, and happiness—a welling up and overflowing of well-being from inside.

MAGICAL AND NONMAGICAL METHODS OF WORKING WITH WATER

We can recall and to some extent relive our past experiences with water. We can also interact with water in a casual manner such as is done in daydreaming. And we can also extend our imagination a little further by imagining we are inside of a dream.

We can be playful—I imagine or recall being on a beach. I feel the spray on my face from waves breaking. I smell the air. I hear the roar of the waves. I watch the wind as its gusts play upon the surface of the lake or sea. This is all perfectly normal and within everyday modes of brain activity. There is nothing magical about this.

But what if we extend the process? What if I focus on one detail for a minute or more? I imagine I am floating in my favorite tide pool by Makapu'u on Oahu. I linger here. The high concentration of salt in the water helps the body float. I hear the waves pounding on the rocky, volcanic shore twenty feet away. I float with my eyes closed. I let go. All that exists in this moment is the touch of water, its sounds, its smells, its vibrations, and its swirling bubbly action.

And I continue now within a waking dream. How do you do this? By focusing on this imagery to the exclusion of all else. I turn the perceptions of my five senses away from the external world so they are free of distractions. As far as my brain is aware at this moment, I exist within what I am imagining.

This is not self-hypnosis. I am not narrowing my awareness. It is enchantment—I am empowering my senses to explore a realm of the imagination.

The water in this dream responds to me. It is ready to show me sensations and feelings I have never felt before. A shiver of bliss curls down my nerves as if they are the strings of a harp and the winds of my desires and longings begin to play music upon them. Except for this: the notes and melodies are not my own; the musician doing the playing follows themes that use the sensations and feelings of water.

I breathe deeply. My chest rises slightly in the water and then sinks slightly again as I exhale. The edges of my body no longer define my identity. My nervous system extends though the pool and then just as easily through the surrounding ocean without limitation. The sensation of water in nature and the internal feeling of being accepted and at peace become interchangeable.

It helps of course that I can stop my mind from thinking. I am here without thoughts. I am focused on the physical sensations and am receptive to the faintest nuances of feeling. It helps also that I do not worry as my ego dissolves into nothing. I am not afraid of becoming nothing or a mirror that is empty and clear.

I linger here. Time—the part of my brain that tracks a sequence of moments unfolding as a linear activity—disengages. The clock in my brain has lost reference to seconds, minutes, hours, days, months, years, ages, and aeons. I could just as easily be dreaming with the sea of that moment when life first took birth and began its journey. Or I could be in that place when the seas shall wash the shores of this planet and mankind shall be no more.

I linger here as the sensations and feelings within my brain conjure images of places familiar, like moments of intimacy with women I have known. And just as easily images appear of worlds so far away they have been created by my imagination as a tribute to what I long for.

A therapist might call this free association. A clairvoyant might call it divination. I call it another way of being. It is passing through the gates of dream and imagination to taste the powers of the magnetic fluid and the treasures of spirit hidden within water.

Have I started doing magic yet? Yes. Magic, or in this case, psychic perception, often begins by stopping sensory contact with the external world. If the senses withdraw from external stimulation as occurs during meditation, the body relaxes, and there is a slight savings in the amount of energy expended. At this point, the brain can now perceive through the eyes of imagination, dream, or the astral plane.

Turning perception inward, however, subtracts an amount of physical vitality from your body. It puts a tax on your nervous system, and it submits a charge to be paid at a later date from the integrity of your personality. It may blur mental clarity or emotional boundaries. Perception involving imagination or altered states of consciousness is creative and offers new information. But it can be expensive in terms of energy.

You have to pay back what has been taken away during your imaginary or psychic journey if you want to return to the light of day—if you want to be, to feel, and to act normal again in this world shared with other human beings. A lot of people experience difficulty making the transition between the inner and outer worlds.

I return from my journey of exploration. I have a cup of coffee and notice right away the subtle tensions that remain in my nervous system. With a breath or a minor mental adjustment, I focus and they begin to drain away. The blood vessels dilate, and the warmth and circulation return to the parts of my body that experienced a very minor form of hibernation as I focused my attention on another world.

And then the real test appears for both those who use magic as well as for those who use ordinary methods of reflection. The question then is, what part of my experience with watery magnetism can I apply in a way that enriches my life and world? Does the feeling of peace carry over? Do I feel calm, serene, and clear? Or am I still caught in an otherworldly dream that wants me to grasp some truth that is beyond my understanding?

Exercise: Feeling like an Undine or Merman

I focus exclusively on water in my etheric and astral bodies. I also imagine water to be extending for a vast distance around the outside of my etheric and astral bodies. When I do this, I invariably get a sense of the way undines feel; I am a part of anything that is near to me. Or, as a merman, I feel united to the life and vibration within water—I am committed to preserving, expanding, and clarifying magnetic fields produced by water. This is my vocation and my soul. I celebrate magnetism in all my actions.

This exercise seems to grant an affinity for any way in which water appears in nature. For me, it is a life-altering meditation. The boundaries between the body, either physical or astral, dissolve, and my awareness, senses, and nervous system extend outward into wider fields of energy. This is essentially the basis for the merman and undine sense of identity. It produces a profound state of well-being and inner peace. For those who master this, whatever makes life special is always near to them. They can find it within themselves, touch it as a bodily sensation, and feel its closeness and support.

Those who practice magic often balance the four elements either within their bodies or when they evoke the four elements at different points of a magic circle. In this way, an equilibrium or balance of opposites is achieved through ritual. From my point of view, the problem with this approach is that once the individual steps out of his magic circle, he enters a civilization that does not have a balance between the four elements.

If you rated the knowledge of the elements in terms of Western civilization, earth, air, and fire would be up in the eightieth percentile as far as our scientific and technological applications are concerned. Water, however, is far weaker. It would be around 3 or 4 percent of its usable capacity. The psychological and spiritual aspects of water are very poorly understood.

When I practice the water element on the etheric and astral levels inside and outside of my body, I develop a strong sense of being connected to the domains of the mermen and undines. However, I come from an overwhelmingly strong masculine culture. It is characterized by dynamic will and power directed toward changing the external world. It has almost no self-reflective capacity. There is no tradition of contemplation. There is no awareness of the light within the psyche or of the opportunities to explore and deepen awareness of the soul.

Being able, then, to evoke in myself merman awareness within a minute or less of meditating is a staggering achievement for me. It is an encounter with my opposite. It is like evoking in myself the essence of the feminine as it exists within nature and spirit. Here is a poem that comments on this experience:

> *There comes a time when the white knight*
> *Climbs off his mighty warhorse with burnish'd*
> *hooves,*

Takes off his armor, his brazen greaves
And feathered helmet too,
To sit beside a still lake and simply wait
To find happiness, and yes, infinite peace inside
himself
Without having first to rescue and then possess
A fair maiden in distress.
Look at him! In his soul all the waters of the earth
And simple human contentment intermingle and
flow—
This I know.

According to the poem, the opposite of a man is not a woman. It is the feminine within him joined to the feminine within nature. This includes the abilities to form within oneself many of the qualities already mentioned: an inner peace with the universe, profound abilities involving empathy and caring for others, and a feeling of being fully alive that arises naturally out of the sensuality of five senses.

A man may be able to taste these things through a relationship with a woman. But it is next to impossible for him to internalize these qualities within himself by depending on a woman to somehow transfer them to him. Though love is a fabulous experience, it is easy for a man to use a woman as a substitute for the spiritual quest his entire world would prefer to deny.

To summarize, we have all felt the delight and enchantment, the peace and well-being that exist in nature. Some cultures have attributed these feelings to the presence of magical beings—fairies and such. But even without turning to magic for an explanation, we can say that nature awakens feelings of peace and contentment that already exist within us.

What the human race is not very good at is exploring and extending these feelings. We do not yet know how to amplify them or produce them at will. The undines have a lot to say on this point. They embody states of peace and serenity that are well beyond anything we encounter in our daily lives. But there is a way of focusing and a level of concentration that can allow us to pass through the gates of our senses and feel and perceive as undines. This section is a step in that direction.

THE MENTAL BODY

The mental body is again in the form of the physical body but is more refined or subtler than the astral body. It relates to ideas, thinking, and analyzing. Unlike the astral body with its sensitivity and response to concrete images and situations, the mental body works with abstractions. We size up situations and solve problems with our minds. The mental body is rooted in concentration and attention. Here we choose when and how we focus our attention. Forming plans, setting priorities, and determining time frames and means for fulfilling our purposes are mental-plane activities.

Experiences with the astral body are more personal and emotionally engaging. Mental-body experiences are more detached, almost as if we are observing something from a third-person rather than a first-person perspective. If there is too much mental emphasis, an individual may be excessively detached and aloof. Too little mental emphasis, and an individual loses clarity and perspective.

If I imagine my mental body to be filled with water, I find myself exploring the deeper aspects of serenity, stillness, and clearness. There are also magical forms of perception. The mental body filled with water can act like a magic mirror or crystal ball. You can feel reflected in yourself the life within any other being.

AKASHIC OR SPIRITUAL BODY

The spiritual body is an intuitive level of awareness that operates independent of thought, feeling, or physical forms though it may express itself through any of these. In other words, it is consciousness that does not identify or define itself through any specific form. It can also penetrate through space and time with its awareness or intuition.

On this level, we experience universal aspects of water such as cosmic or all-embracing love. There is a sense of presiding over the ideals that guide and inspire all beings. We sense the one life that flows through all of us. On this level, we feel one with all beings and also an inner peace so deep we feel one with the universe.

THE MAGNETIC FLUID

Within water is also a subtler presence called the magnetic fluid. It is similar to the way the flow of blood produces a magnetic field in and around the body. If you can sense or feel auras, you can probably pick this up as well.

One way of sensing the magnetic fluid is by placing your mind within water. Then you focus on the bonding, attracting, and contracting qualities of the water. Remove the sensation of water and focus on these qualities alone, and you may be able to sense a magnetic field of energy.

The magnetic fluid is cool, soothing, contracting, and attracting. It is nurturing and supportive. It contains within itself so as to shelter and to protect. Instead of being intense and explosive, it is rhythmic, gentle, and receptive. It possesses healing power.

In psychological terms, it is empathic, sensitive, and responsive. It is kind and tender. It draws together, bonds, joins, and unites.

On a mental level, it can place itself within or make itself a part of another person to the extent that it can sense the entirety of the other's life within itself. It seeks to heal, complete, and make whole whatever it touches or influences.

In this sense, it is nearly incomprehensibly receptive—it is utterly open and empty while at the same time giving life to others. It is so encompassing that it can embrace, shelter, and protect anything.

In spiritual terms, then, it reaches toward embracing, all-encompassing love. It presents us with feelings of wonder, ecstasy, and beauty. This feminine awareness reveals the deepest mysteries at the core of the self.

We could say that peace, happiness, contentment, serenity, well-being, delight, affection, tenderness, sensuality, pleasure, bliss, ecstasy, compassion, and love are qualities that are present when the magnetic fluid is operating successfully. This magnetic fluid is present in men and women, though women tend to have a much higher and more natural charge of it. Becoming aware of it directly strengthens it and allows us to make it an active part of our consciousness.

Obviously, if a person's mind is influenced by the magnetic fluid, it is easy to try to bring out the best in other people. Instead of viewing others from a position of competition and insecurity, a person's mind is empathic, sensitive, and caring.

Though largely unknown in our world, the feminine essence or magnetic fluid is so receptive and so giving that it has power over everything because it is the source that gives birth to all of life. The magnetic or feminine essence also controls its opposite—the electric fluid. In geopolitical terms, those who master the feminine mysteries are able to take responsibility for the unfolding of the world—they have the capacity to guide, inspire, and also set boundaries on all acts of executive power.

Almost all of Western civilization is focused on acting on and producing results in the external world. We have an extroverted civilization. The magnetic fluid holds a different vision. It has a direct, inner connection to anything that exists. It is able to feel and be a part of anyone simply by extending its magnetic field into and around another person anywhere on earth.

The electric fluid has the power to destroy the world, such as through nuclear weapons. The electric in itself does not know how to recreate the world through love. The magnetic has this specific power: it can join and unite, not through propaganda, beliefs, or ideology, but rather though a heart-to-heart connection between people. Just as there are no limits on the yield of a hydrogen bomb, there are no limits on the influence of the magnetic fluid to create peace and love.

A Simple Exercise for the Magnetic Fluid

Imagine a blue or blue-green ball of water six feet in diameter in front of you. It is cool, magnetic, and contracting. It is attractive, soothing, and calming. It shelters, protects, and heals. It is receptive in the sense that it is utterly empty of form and completely open—able to receive and contain the soul of any being within itself, nurturing, inspiring, and empowering it to attain completion and fulfillment.

Now imagine that this ball changes into an exact replica of yourself. It is you standing or sitting there in front of you. Sense how this person is different from yourself. What qualities and powers does this person have that you do not?

Next imagine that you are this person who embodies the spirit and primal energy of the feminine. What is this like for you? Consider ways in which the person you imagine could become part of your life and also how that might change you and those around you.

THE ESSENCE OF THE FEMININE SPIRIT

When I imagine water surrounding myself and also inside of my body, I can also sense a magnetic field of energy. The magnetic fluid is similar to magnetism in a magnet or in nature, but it is subtler. If you place your hands in water, you can feel the water touching the skin. From the pressure and cooler temperature, it is not so difficult to imagine sensing the water nearby that does not touch the skin. Again, if you focus on the binding, contracting, and attracting qualities in the water but remove the physical sensations of water, you have a sense of the magnetic fluid.

Though the magnetic fluid can be treated purely as an energy, it also has many psychological, cultural, and spiritual implications. For example, we might attempt to bring these into focus by asking, what is the magnetic energy that balances the world at this time? Also, what is the essence of the feminine spirit? What feminine power can balance, harmonize, transform, and inspire the extroverted, electrical energy in our world?

I pursue the answer to these questions on five levels. On the *physical level,* this energy is already present in nature. It is the entire world in its wintery, watery, nurturing, and preserving aspects. Its imagery and presence are in an arctic bay, a frozen lake, ice melting at the beginning of a small stream, a snow-covered field, and so on.

On a physical level, water can extend our perception the way the body is an extension of our conscious awareness. If I imagine, for example, Sacred Falls here on Oahu, it does not start as an image in my mind. I feel I am right there in the pool. I can feel the entire surface of the pool and how its edge touches the cliffs. I can feel ripples contacting the stones, the currents beneath the water, and the temperature change from sunlight producing warmer water near the surface.

If you can sense the magnetic fluid, you can actually extend your awareness beyond your body. The magnetic fluid automatically enhances feelings and perceptions. With it, I can perceive in and through the element of water without the need for human thoughts. With a slight shift in focus, I can become the entire stream beginning with the raindrops falling at the summit of the mountains and ending as the stream flows into the sea.

To put it simply, you perceive that the water is a part of your nervous system. You can sense directional aspects of water involving changes in temperature, fluidity, movement, and magnetism. You touch something with your finger, and you feel it in your fingertip and also in your brain. But with the help of the magnetic fluid, water becomes your fingertips and your body and your skin.

What is most remarkable is how this awareness contrasts to normal perception. We are land-based mammals. We experience space and separation in extremely distinct ways—spatial orientation, territories, body shape, and personal space. But awareness expanded into and through a magnetic field is altogether different.

On an *etheric level,* it enables one to sense the vital force in all beings. You feel a part of the vitality in others. A hospital does CAT scans and MRIs. The magnetic fluid is a similar mode of perception without the need for instruments.

On an *astral level,* the magnetic fluid enhances a psychic ability to immediately connect with and sense another's inner life, nurturing and inspiring the other as well. When I am sitting close to a person* who has strong magnetic energy in their aura, my psychic abilities are enhanced. Without effort, I can sense personality traits of someone that person is talking about, whom I have not met and who is not present.

I could meet and interview someone for several hours and in this way get to know the person. When the magnetic fluid is strong, I can know the other from within in ways that no interview could ever reveal—without even meeting them. The magnetic fluid enhances soul connections.

If I focus on another individual, it is as if that person is in front of me now. The connection feels completely real, almost as if you could reach out and touch, communicate with, and sense the other's feelings from within. This is another reason why the realm of the undines has been closed off to our civilization and to the human race. Undines use their abilities for the sake of empathy, beauty, and sensuality. Human beings, however, could easily abuse such powers for selfish reasons.

In a sense, then, a great cultural and spiritual war has been going on in Western civilization to conceal this knowledge of the feminine. Abuse of this feminine power would immediately undermine the development of will and also of science. The qualities of intellectual

---

*In regard to questions about gender neutrality, I have never experienced this enhancement of psychic abilities by being around a man, even mermen in human form. The female anatomy with its estrogen has magical capacities perhaps unique to that gender which, to say the least, Western civilization has a vested interests in suppressing.

Even in the very yin water principle, the "male" mermen still have a yang quality of wanting to take charge compared to the female mermaid who is simply more receptive and giving. It is a spiritual way of perceiving—if someone is more receptive, giving, and uniting/embracing, we could call it feminine. If someone is more take charge, asserts some sort of order, and obsesses on acquiring power, we could call it masculine.

You can ask a mermaid to change into the male form of a merman and she can do so instantly. But that suppresses her receptivity to some degree. The astral plane spirit has the capacity to "if I self-identify as something, then that is what I am."

objectivity and also of freedom of volition, the individualism in our world, would rapidly deteriorate.

The task of the masculine, among other things, is to set and to defend boundaries for the sake of ego identity and productive capacity. The feminine, by contrast, overcomes all boundaries—it alone has the power to unite opposites. Working together, the masculine and feminine are responsible for human and divine creativity. Opposed, they destroy human beings, culture, and the world.

The bottom line is that the proper use of the magnetic fluid depends on one's heart: does an individual or a society have the commitment to seek and then to use power for the sake of love? The feminine spirit is no less powerful than the masculine. All our war machines and political and military hierarchies mean absolutely nothing before the magnetic fluid. This is because our world depends on external power and might. It has no defenses against those who can easily extend their awareness anywhere or inside of anyone on earth.

For this reason, our stories and fairy tales about undines reveal almost nothing about these beings. Our theologies, metaphysics, and science are ignorant about both the spiritual universe and the many roles magnetism has yet to play in technology and industry. In the past,

---

(cont. from page 220) In our world, we are working with evolutionary biology where 150 million years ago xx and xy chromosomes separated. Now, in perhaps twenty or more years we will be able to take a pill on Friday and on Monday we will start changing physically into another gender including hermaphrodite if so desired.

For a magician, there is an "inner" ideal of uniting opposites within oneself—full masculine and full feminine as in becoming androgynous. But this is a spiritual, an inner plane thing. The intricacies of male–female social and biological identity, however, do not influence the universe itself: stars remain hot, intense, radiant, emitting light to the ends of the universe. They are yang. Space itself, the ultimate feminine presence, is so receptive it contains and shapes all those stars and galaxies. The masculine and feminine in cosmic terms not only balance each other. They are always perfectly one with each other while retaining their own form and formlessness. The magician seeks to find this image and creativity of the universe within himself. By contrast, gender identity involves how individuals perceive themselves in relation to other people and society.

in spite of the suffering that has resulted, it is possible that this has been for the best. But you cannot put off the deepest issues within the heart forever. There comes a time when the choice has to be made as to whether we are committed to love or to fear and to hate.

On the *mental level,* the magnetic fluid is inspired and compassionate. It is motivated to set up the learning conditions and environment in which each person can develop in the best way. It finds the optimum influences and circumstances for growth. It senses what others need and seeks to fulfill those needs.

On the *akashic level,* it establishes a feeling of oneness with all beings and a feeling that all beings are one with each other. It heals, shelters, and protects your inner life.

If you put all five levels together, the magnetic fluid in its positive aspect is everything that nurtures, enhances, amplifies, brings to completion, satisfies, and inspires. It is the image of the mother, daughter, sister, maiden, lover, muse, and divine guardian all at once. It is one with you forever, continuously, and it is there to bless you and establish wholeness within.

Such energy annihilates loneliness and separation because you feel and perceive your connection to others from within. A woman, or man for that matter, who embodies the magnetic fluid does not play the role of a mother or a caregiver for a limited number of years—for example, until a child reaches adolescence and leaves the home. The power to nurture and to be connected to others, inspiring and guiding them, never ends. The physical function of being a caregiver makes a natural and powerful transition into becoming a spiritual function. Similarly, responsibility and involvement in one's individual family gradually extends out to encompass the entire world.

We have at present a global community based on external modes of communication and relationships. But the religions of earth do not at this time provide us with a global inner community, a direct heart-to-heart connection to others anywhere on earth. The magnetic fluid, as an expression of the essence of the feminine spirit, offers this.

SUMMARY

The magnetic fluid is so empty, so utterly receptive, so giving, so free of identifying itself with form that it has power over everything because it is the source that gives birth to all of life. It is the power to shelter, contain, nourish, and transform the life and soul of any being. As such, the feminine spirit is and always will be the guardian of the deepest mysteries within the self.

If you went on a quest for the Holy Grail and found it, the Grail would still be an external thing. The quest, the search and journey, might lead you to test and to establish qualities of nobility, courage, compassion, and justice within yourself. This is a great accomplishment.

Finding the essence of the feminine spirit, the magnetic fluid, within yourself is far more than a Grail quest. It is actually joining with your opposite. It is internalizing within oneself one of the most powerful forces in creation. Our world knows nothing about this journey and this quest.

If you want to be creative and to see your vision through to its realization, then you need to do these things—to bring together and unite the full power of the feminine with the full power of the masculine. If you consider one of these components to be of lesser value or significance than the other, then you inevitably produce an inferior product.

This is how the electric and magnetic fluids operate in the universe. The masculine in its essence foresees what it wishes to accomplish. It puts up the energy to do this. It envisions, plans, and acquires the skills necessary for success. But this is a total waste and an absolute failure without the feminine. The masculine is inspired by and empowered by the feminine. The feminine brings the vision to life through love and feeling. It provides the soul, the heart, and the nurturing.

The feminine never stands in an absolute void and creates from out of nothing. This is precisely the skill of the masculine. It is the envisioning side of the process. The masculine never unites itself in its total being and through love to everything that exists. It does not have a clue as to how to do this. But if you want to be creative and see your purposes fulfilled, then to some degree you will learn to do both. Otherwise, you accomplish less. Your work will eventually waste away because it lacks one or the other: the strength and courage to begin and to oversee, or else the love and the heart that inspire and bring to fruition what is conceived.

12

A Study of
Well-Being

The word *peace* has different meanings. Some people might use *peace* to describe an abstract ideal or the result of faith or emotional stability. It is also used as a goal when settling interpersonal or international conflicts. So instead of peace, we can use the word *well-being* to describe the feeling that gives us our greatest ability to respond with appreciation to the physical world in which we live.

We have a fundamental need to feel safe and secure. When we feel sufficiently secure, well-being develops. In a state of deep well-being, a person is able to completely accept the world as it is. There is a sense of belonging to and participating in an unfolding process of life that is completely natural and nurturing. In this state, a person senses that everyone and everything are within and carried along by this flow of life.

However, this feeling is not a product of a consciously held belief. Rather, it is spontaneous. This kind of appreciation of life occurs on a level much deeper than that of the conscious mind. It comes from the depths of the psyche, and it arises out of the physical sensations of the body. From these two sources comes the feeling that life in essence is protective, sheltering, and fulfilling.

With well-being, we view the world from an emotional perspective that is larger than the narrow limits of our identity and personal desires. Although the strength or weakness of our coping skills and ego are important, with strong well-being our primary focus is not on our performance or self, but on the world. Responses such as reacting with fear and defending preconceived ideas play a minimal role next to this more fundamental interest—seeing, accepting, and appreciating our surroundings.

With strong well-being there is no discomfort when someone does not agree with our point of view, and there is no individual isolation or loneliness to overcome. From a state of well-being, the world appears to be full of interesting things. Each situation is appreciated on its own terms.

COMMON EXPERIENCES WITH WELL-BEING

We can review the experiences of those with strong well-being as a way of seeking to develop this feeling in ourselves. For example, such individuals perceive the world as a place that is richly satisfying and fulfilling. And yet this evaluation is not based on the extent to which their own personal needs are being satisfied. They are not greedy. They are not driven to possess whatever they can in order to ensure their own security. They intuitively experience themselves as already part of the richness of life. They experience the abundant energies of life flowing directly through their own bodies.

One factor contributing to this outlook is that they usually have excellent childhood memories. They can frequently recall childhood dreams, which still influence them as they consider their goals in life. They often have had spiritual experiences when they were very young, but they do not view these dreams and experiences as somehow removed from the adult they have become. Rather, they see them as seeds that are in the process of growing into fruition.

Many of these individuals once belonged to small but richly diverse communities. They knew everything about the life of that community—its history, its ethnic groups, its social institutions. They were acquainted with many people and had a number of close friends. At some point in time, however, they typically left these communities because they felt the need to move on in order to grow.

Another experience common to those with high well-being is that they feel an unusual sense of peace in particular places. This place may be simple or spectacular. It may be a church or temple. It may be an ancient place of pilgrimage, or it may be a particular location in which the déjà vu is too overpowering to be something merely personal.

There are also many places in nature that evoke a profound feeling of well-being. Sedona, Arizona; White Sands, New Mexico; Mount Desert Island, Maine; and Yosemite, California, are examples. Another such place is the tiny island of Iona, off the coast of Scotland. Guidebooks mention that tourists with no previous experience of Iona disembark from the ferry and immediately notice the isle's spiritual, timeless quality.

ETHNOGRAPHY: HOW INDIVIDUALS TALK ABOUT WELL-BEING

If you were to meet someone with a strong sense of well-being, you might ask them to tell you about their ability to accept life. For example, ask them to describe themself when dealing with major decisions or problems. Ask them to identify the most important resource that they draw on at such times. And later, ask them to describe the inner flow of their life.

I have found many similarities in the answers to these questions by individuals with strong well-being. Here are some of the phrases they often use:

Things in life happen naturally when they are ready to happen.
Everything good that is coming my way in life will happen to me.
I feel that I am part of the flow of life.

This flow of life feels like being in a river and moving along with it. On some level, I only have to accept the flow to be a part of it. No exertion is required.

The present does not proceed from the past and move into the future. Rather, the past, present, and future are simultaneously together within the same landscape of time. And in this landscape, the events of my life are already interconnected and interwoven.

There is a continuity and naturalness to life.

Life unfolds from an inexhaustible, inner source.

If I lose something important to me at one point in my life, it can be found again later during another stage.

Another person put it this way: Well-being, for me, is a sense of timelessness—no outside goals or explanations are needed to justify how I experience things in the present. Nothing needs to be connected to the present moment of perception. I am absolutely in my own timeless space when I paint, garden, or hang out with my partner. This comes through to me as a feeling. I do not have to think when I am just doing and experiencing things.

For these individuals, even relationships do not really end. What is begun in one relationship can be carried on and fulfilled in another relationship. They frequently say that they enjoy many people and that it is hard to choose someone to marry; they find it naturally interesting to be around all kinds of people.

When they do marry, they do not worry about their partner. They are not possessive or jealous. They bring a spirit of cooperation and flexibility to the relationship. Their relationships are gentle and relaxed rather than intense. If the relationship comes to an end, they are often very generous and compassionate in talking about their former partner.

In summary, for these individuals everything in life is where it is supposed to be. Life can be completely accepted just as it is. Who they are is not defined by the goals they pursue or what they accomplish. If asked who they are, they might say that they are someone who is part of the ongoing flow of life.

Individuals who describe their experiences in these ways are rather rare. Nonetheless, we are dealing with a very primal feeling. This well-being gives us our greatest capacity to appreciate and to feel part of the physical world.

The first time I met someone who had this very strong sense of well-being, I felt totally accepted. In fact, I suspected that there was a catch. To my surprise, the individual was not trying to sell me something. She had no belief system she wanted to pass on to me. She did not want to get something from me or need me to confirm who she was.

She just accepted me as I was. There were no conditions, no expectations. I was amazed at how receptive and appreciative she was of me. She was interested in everything about me. It seemed to me that the whole world of nature was alive within her. Because she saw the world as being radiant with life and full of wonder, it was apparently natural for her to look for that same radiant life in others.

BODY SENSATIONS

I once counseled a woman who had recently completed graduate school. She was struggling with her career choices. She characterized herself as being preoccupied with schedules and the need for commitment. She pointed out, however, that her preoccupations interfered with her ability to pursue relationships in a warm and natural manner. She felt off balance and frustrated in relationships. She missed the warm, safe feeling she had had when she was very young. At the same time, she said that she had always had a very strong sense of destiny in regard to her career. She felt an inner sense of being pulled along in her vocation, like her work would be important and always very exciting.

At this point I used the focusing techniques developed by Eugene Gendlin. In brief, I asked her what it would feel like if she imagined she were experiencing her sense of destiny right now rather than as something she hoped to attain in the future. She closed her eyes. Her eyes moved quite rapidly under her eyelids; her lips became fuller; and her breathing slowed.

After a minute, she described what she was feeling within her body, which Gendlin calls the "felt sense." She said, "I feel like I am in a river, flowing, and accepted. I don't have to do anything. I can just be. Things just happen." I then asked her what her inner, critical voice said about this way of experiencing things. Her response was that she had not been allowing unplanned things to happen.

I described the difference in the quality of her voice, her facial appearance, and her degree of relaxation. Together we explored her single-minded pursuit of career and destiny and this new resource that might help her—this degree of calmness, relaxation, and feeling part of the flow of life.

I give this example to suggest that perhaps we all have a remarkable sense of well-being within ourselves. It may not be easy to discover, however, for there can be much that obscures it, and it may be that it has a slightly different feeling for each of us.

DREAMTIME

We can discuss well-being in different ways—as a feeling or as a way of perceiving and interacting with people. We can refer to it through visual images. However, we may understand well-being even more if we approach it in terms of dreamtime. This term is used by the Aborigines of Australia, who have lived in the Australian deserts for fifty thousand years.

In dreamtime the events of the physical world somehow overlap and blend with such things as mythical time, a spiritual dimension, or the world of dream and intuition. In this personal and collective perspective on time, experience deepens, and opportunities once lost can be found again.

A fundamental aspect of dreamtime is its vast landscape. This landscape does not have coordinates such as past, present, and future. Rather, this landscape is a world to be experienced and explored, a world that is timeless in dimension and inexhaustible in conception. In it there is no end to what can be discovered, felt, and experienced.

In contrast to looking at the world in a very literal, pragmatic fashion, Carl Jung and others have sought a broader framework for understanding human experience. Jung spoke of what I would refer to as the dreamtime that belongs to the whole of the human race. Each culture has a particular assembly of archetypal or transpersonal images that summarizes its particular sources of inspiration. These images are transformers of motivation; they step up and down the forces that drive us forward in our lives.

However, well-being can be so dramatically pronounced in some individuals and so seemingly inaccessible in others that we might well imagine that those with strong well-being have learned to tap an archetypal, mythical dimension of awareness. On the other hand, as tempting as this may be as a mode of explanation, there remains a simple quality that belongs to those with strong well-being.

They have a sense of time that is completely open. They are not running out of time. They are not rushing through time to get someplace. They may comment, "Time for me is not like it is for other people who say that they have only so many hours and have to get so much done."

These individuals do not think of themselves as using time. They just go and do things. Often it is coincidental or accidental events that have led them to their life work. This is not so hard to understand. These people are unusually receptive to things that come their way, and they are sufficiently free from insecurity that they can make room in their lives for something completely new. Looking back on their experience, they see that the course of their lives was in no way predictable, and yet they also feel that whatever has happened to them has happened for a reason.

This openness to life's vicissitudes follows from their feeling that the most wonderful experiences in life already surround them. Everything and everyone are interconnected. Life unfolds as a whole. Feeling part of the unfolding of life, they take delight in fulfilling their basic needs for home, family, friends, companionship, and work. They are not complacent because of their acceptance. They are not resigned or stagnant.

Instead, they delight in whatever they are doing at the moment. And when they do find that they have become bogged down in some stage of life, they have a remarkable capacity to renew themselves. They connect again to their original sources of inspiration in life, whether these are from childhood experiences and dreams, nature, or spiritual resources. For them, what is most special about life is always near to them. They can find it within themselves, touch it as bodily sensations, and feel its closeness and support.

Frank Waters, author of *The Book of the Hopi,* summed up this sense of well-being and time in *Pumpkin Seed Point,* a recounting of his experience in New Oraibi, Arizona, where he went to do research. Living in isolation from his friends and enduring a long, cold winter, he wrote:

> Yet sometimes I awake in the silence of the night with an intuitive feeling of its mysterious context. It is as if I am no longer caught in a moving flow but becalmed in a placid sea that has depth and content, a life and meaning all of its own. At these moments of utter peace I feel absolved from the necessity of hurrying through space to reach a point in time . . . for time seems then a living, organic element that mysteriously helps to fashion our own shape and growth.*

Waters, *Pumpkin Seed Point,* p. 100.

The undines possess an astonishing quality of well-being and peace. It derives from feeling a part of all the waters of the earth. Their senses extend outward through the oceans and rivers. And, like the undine queen Isaphil, the other undines perceive the world with a feeling of lunar serenity.

13
How to Meet Undines

For the first ten years, I did not talk to anyone about my experiences with undines. I simply did not know anyone who saw them. Consequently, my experiences were private. Now I know individuals whose experiences are somewhat similar to my own.

One woman can channel an undine the moment I speak the undine's name. Another woman sees undines whenever she goes to the beach. A third woman describes undines with words and poetry similar to my own when we sit down together and meditate.

A fourth woman uses undines to assist her in her career and in making friends. One man wrote to say that an undine appeared to him and gave him her name. Another man told me he meets undines in his dreams. And then there are those like me who seek women who can express the beauty of undines through art.

But any contact with the inner planes and archetypal energies that undines embody can carry with it a sense of disorientation or confusion. Whether as a medium or a magician, when powerful feelings flow through you, it helps to process them. You find a place for them in your life. You establish a perspective so that you can say, "Here is the natural world with its enchanting beauty and overpowering feeling of peace, and here is my personality. Here is where the two overlap and interact, and here is where they go their separate ways."

One woman wanted me to channel a specific undine only with her and never to meditate on the undine with anyone else. This is like saying the angel Gabriel is the possession of a specific group or religion and no one else should be allowed to interact with him. I want to share my experiences with everyone. There is nothing I would hold back.

Earlier I described a few methods for working with the imagery of water. These methods were focusing, contemplation, dialoguing, invocation, evocation, meditation, poetry, and path working. In the following I expand on some of these and present a few other ways for connecting to undines.

FIRST METHOD: AN ACADEMIC APPROACH

Some might prefer an *academic* approach for gaining rapport with an undine. For example, we could try studying oceanography. Then we proceed from science to literature, in which we explore our imagination. We could write a story as if we are the thing we are studying—become various marine organisms known and unknown, the ecosystems and their dynamics.

Become waves, the tides, the currents; drop down off the continental shelves into the ocean depths; send your mind out among the reefs and atolls; become an archipelago or the North Atlantic current; become the North or South Pole or an ice age as it comes and goes.

In a similar literary vein, try writing a journal as if you are an undine. Make an entry each day for what you—the undine or merman—did to occupy your time. Talk about your dreams, your hopes, your innermost secrets, your desires, your actions, and your plans. Talk about the things you love, what you notice about other undines and about any human beings who have caught your attention.

If you develop your empathy for the sea in this way, then daydreaming and imagination are ready for that magical shift in consciousness. This occurs when you say, "I would like an undine to come and express herself through my voice or share with me her feelings and dreams, to talk to me about herself."

What I have just written is absolute nonsense for a great many people. But like I say, and I will assert my own experience on this point, there is no greater power than the power of love. If you open your heart and reach out, you are free to join with anything in the universe. The divine world has placed no restrictions on this activity.

You do not need to be an initiate of a magical order. You do not need a robe, wand, magic mirror, or magic circle. You only need to love. Stick with it. Play with it. Let your imagination be as free, vast, and deep as the sea, and undines will find your spirit similar to their own.

Shall we give it a try? I wrote the following words when I imagined I was an undine who had entered the body of a woman. It is not perfectly clear to me if I was writing these words or if an undine was writing them through me. In any case, you can see how exploring undine sensuality might increase our perceptual abilities.

The undine says, "I am found in the ten thousand different sounds of waves breaking on the shores of the world. I am sounds of laughing and lovemaking. I am joy overflowing. I am the sea's own breath rising from the depths, exhaling in a sigh and with passion as she tastes with her tongue salt and spray of waves' crests dancing free in curling drops of rain."

SECOND METHOD: DIALOGUING

Another use of imagination is dialoguing, or active imagination. Perhaps first mentioned by Carl Jung, you take a strong affect or feeling toward something and imaginatively change that feeling into the image of a person with whom you can speak. For example, spend some time meditating on the sea and the life within it. Get a feeling for the waves, the currents, the depths, the temperature changes, and the varieties of fish and sea life. Recall your experiences with the sea.

Next, feel that the only thing that exists within your consciousness in this moment is the presence of the sea. At this point, you can probably notice some sensations and feelings that arise in your body due to this contemplation. Take those feelings and your sense of the sea and change them into the image of a person, in this case an undine who embodies what you feel and sense.

Play with your imagination until your visual image of the undine feels right. Sometimes you have to work at this, and sometimes an image of an undine appears whose presence is fairly powerful, even overwhelming. This feeling of presence or connection is common when using active imagination. Now talk to the undine. You can be casual or serious, playful, flirtatious, or intense. It all depends on your mood and personality.

This process involves two things. You ask interesting questions and make comments that feel appropriate to the situation. And you allow the undine, who embodies your subconscious connections to the sea, to reply and interact with you in an independent manner. This is a creative interaction because the image represents a part of yourself that is otherwise not directly available to your consciousness. A dialogue with the image of an undine is a dialogue, then, with the depths of your self and with the archetype of the sea.

You can also imagine that you are within the undine and identical with her. I will often project my mind into an undine so I can look back and see myself through her eyes. This gives me an undine's perspective and a feeling for what it is like to interact with a human being. After you are familiar with assuming the imagined form of an undine, you can also attempt to do the same with a real undine. You scan with your mind for an undine's presence, and then you attempt to sense what she is feeling.

There is a dog barking next door as I write. It takes little effort for me to imagine how the dog's consciousness works. There is a dove outside cooing. It is pretty easy for me to imagine I am that dove. The ocean is two miles from my house. If I place my mind out among the waves and the sea, it does not take me long to perceive through the mind of an undine. The world takes on an entirely different perspective when I do this.

Projecting into another person and imagining you are that person is a basic, straightforward, and simple exercise in psychology. It can be used to develop empathy. Projection also relates to role-playing, in which you act like another person to get a feeling for what that person is like. I would recommend that everyone become acquainted with this act of transferring your mind at least into an image of another person.

Earlier, I wrote about the difference between an imagined and a real undine. The discussion I had with the imagined undine illustrates the method of dialoguing. It was not actual contact with an undine. Dialoguing is similar to visualizing yourself acting in the way you want when participating in a sport or interviewing for a job. Or you can imagine talking to someone about a certain topic and then compare that to an actual conversation.

Later on, through deeper concentration and patient meditation, when you desire to speak with an undine, you are in a position to notice the difference between what you imagine and what occurs with an actual contact. We all possess intuition. Through a focused mind and a strong desire, intuition becomes psychic. There comes a moment when what you sense is more than imagination or the imagery of a waking dream or contemplation.

THIRD METHOD: PROJECTION

This third method uses a higher level of concentration. In this method, you project your mental or astral body into the undine's domain on the astral plane. In this case, you are not first sensing and then connecting to the undine. You are rather entering a spiritual domain within nature and then sensing the undine from that location.

Some individuals are born with this ability, and for some it is a blessing while for others it is a curse. One such blessed individual is the head of a large magical order. Another individual has the same ease in connecting to the inner planes, but has been diagnosed as schizophrenic.

In the first case, the individual's consciousness is sufficiently integrated to utilize their experiences creatively. In the second, the individual's consciousness has been overwhelmed by the disorienting influences of the inner planes to the extent that their behavior is not acceptable to society. The inner plane contacts have done serious harm to the connection between the individual's mind and emotions.

Projecting your consciousness outside of your body is usually a fairly challenging endeavor for most individuals. Again, it helps to complete some basic training. In the CIA's covert operations involving remote viewing, the military screened millions of soldiers and then chose a few who had the highest potential for psychic abilities. Some of these individuals had little difficulty performing remote viewing and afterward returned again to an everyday mode of experience.

Some, however, brought back from their journeys to the inner planes terrible nightmares and acute vulnerabilities—they felt they were subject to psychic attack at unexpected moments. The military is designed to accomplish missions. It is not designed for helping individuals to recover from traumatic experiences. The goal of the CIA is national defense and not individual development. It has no interest in attaining harmony with the universe. For individuals exploring the elemental planes, it is good to keep harmony in mind.

Here are a few comments on the spiritual resources you need for projecting your mind into the domain of undines. First, train your consciousness so the link between your mind and your physical senses is very strong. When you use psychic abilities, you basically are turning a sense of perception away from the physical world and using that sense on the inner planes. You need, then, to be able to bring your sensory perception back to the physical world without suffering any distorting effects.

If, for example, you are upset, then your senses usually do not work as well. If you have the feeling that something unknown is attacking you, then you may look at even your best friends and see enemies. The feelings (that is, the astral energy) overwhelm your mind-body connection, thereby distorting your interpretation of what is happening to you.

One way to strengthen the mind-body connection is to practice concentrating on each of your five senses. Though it may take years to develop, you visualize something and hold that image in your mind for a minute up to a half hour without other thoughts disturbing you. You work in this way with all five senses. This practice enables you to give your full attention to the present moment and to disregard any inner plane influences or disturbances.

Second, it is always helpful to practice with the akasha, or the spiritual source of the element you are working on. The divine aspect of the water element involves omnipresent, all-embracing love. This divine aspect gives a sense of being one with the universe or one with anything that exists.

If this level of consciousness is strong in you, then the extreme magnetic, attractive energies you may encounter in the domain of undines will feel natural and right. Undines are a form of divine consciousness being expressed in a specific, concrete way. The undine who vibrates within your astral body the feeling of perfect love, absolute peace, or oneness with her or with the sea will not overwhelm you. She will not be able to possess you, enchant you, or leave you feeling lost and desolate when you return to your daily life.

This is because you can see her as someone you can learn from and get to know better. You see her magical powers as serving a purpose. They do not turn you away from your involvement in your own life activities. Instead, you can see that the undine's mode of love and bonding are something that can be shared between human beings.

Third, studying oceanography or being a marine biologist may help you intellectually understand the sea, but it is not going to help you understand undines' emotional makeup or magic. To work with undines, it helps to love the water element—rivers, lakes, the sea, and so on. If you have a profound love of nature, then an undine will perceive you as having a magical authority like her own, if not greater.

The nature of love is that it is free to join with and become one with anything.

Finally, it is very beneficial to be able to convert your contact with undines into some useful activity—to express it through art, healing, singing, poetry, writing, sculpture, painting, and so on. In this way, your creativity enables you to ground your inner-plane contacts in our world so they can be shared with others.

Without some form of sharing, an individual may suffer from acute isolation. But when you express or share yourself, you expand your consciousness. This helps integrate your personality. In other words, you discover the value and applications of your inner-plane experiences.

FOURTH METHOD: PSYCHIC PERCEPTION

Another way of interacting with undines is to be psychic, that is, clairvoyant, clairsentient, or telepathic. You can develop these higher levels of perceptions in yourself, or you can work with a medium. I use these three forms of perception though I am better at clair-feeling—I can feel what others feel, and I am good at describing auras (the nature and qualities of any spiritual being).

Some individuals just have these abilities. They can see energy and spirits. But there are preferences individuals have and different inclinations. Some individuals have amazing psychic abilities, but they choose never to use them.

If you spend time studying the water element, lakes, seas, rivers, and the watery vibration on the inner planes, then you will notice the slightest change in your perceptions, feelings, thoughts, and sensations when an undine is present. If you don't pursue these things, then an undine can be sitting next to you at the beach and you may not notice anything.

Undines are nature spirits who occupy the inner planes. They have a great affinity for the water element and a close tie to the etheric or subtle vibration of water. When the undine is mature, she can influence our physical world through the power of magic that resides in the water element.

In some cases, however, the undine can in fact materialize. If you find gold or a diamond on the ground, you are free to pick it up and use it as you will. If an undine finds a lot of free energy available, she is free to use it to materialize, to take on physical being and corporeality. A medium, for example, offers a lot of free energy to a spirit. The spirit can then inhabit to some degree or speak through the medium's body or in some cases materialize in the same room outside of the medium's body.

I make this point because the physical world, unlike the astral plane, has a lot of energy stored in physical matter. Matter is very restricted and limited. It has a history. There are stones lying around that are billions of years old. They assume a specific form and stay with it. But if you split enough atoms at once, you have a nuclear explosion.

Franz Bardon mentions that it is possible for an undine to take over the body of a human woman and to live a life as a human being. She retains all her magical powers and her own personality as she does this. Bardon says this may occur when a magical pact is made between a magician and an undine.

In this case, the undine may find a young woman who is dying. At the moment of the woman's death, the undine takes the body and revives it, placing her own undine astral body within the human's physical body. Bardon says he once warned one of his students not to perform this magical action with an undine. But the student went ahead and did it anyway—and this within the twentieth century! (See "An Undine Possession" in chapter 8 for an example of this kind of magical action.)

On the other hand, sometimes individuals allow themselves to be strongly influenced by a spirit to such an extent that they almost share the same consciousness. The elemental or nature spirit has the memories and thoughts of the human being, and the human being has the intuition and magic of the elemental. This can be done in positive and negative ways. It can also be done through ritual or occur naturally during moments of inspiration. For example, a dancer, singer, poet, or artist can fall into a natural trance and share or channel the elemental while performing or producing a work of art.

I know another woman who is not a medium. She is strong and flexible enough with her will that she can simply focus through herself an undine's presence. To a significant degree, her body temporarily becomes the body of an undine. But I would still not call her a medium. What she does is completely effortless. One moment I am touching her body, and the next moment I am touching the body of an undine without having moved my hand.

In this case, I experience an undine as if the undine had taken possession of the woman's body. Using telepathy, I can ask the undine questions, and the undine responds to me as if she is within the woman. When she is linked to the undine, different parts of the girl's body have the feeling of different aspects of water in nature: a waterfall, an ocean, a lake, the North Atlantic current, and so on.

As I have mentioned elsewhere, the undine tells me that many other undines want to cross over. They want to play a greater part in influencing humanity. If mankind's actions are changing the biosphere and the oceans, then they feel it is time for them to have an impact on mankind.

There is always a degree of creativity or interpretation involved in using mediums or in interacting with nature spirits. It can be difficult to determine exactly what part is telepathic interaction and what part is imagination. You can, for example, hire a skilled medium, mention the name of an undine, and in the next moment have the undine answering your questions. Even in this case, it is not always clear if the medium is reading your mind and responding to your imagination or whether she is actually connecting to the undine.

Of course, on religious grounds some people would never use mediums. And there is a lot of room for deception. I mention using mediums, however, because I can look at anyone and sense the spirits that are close to them or the powers that are hidden within them. The spiritual worlds have their own rules, and these rules rarely have anything to do with our religions.

There is also a simple form of telepathy that can be used to contact undines. You ask a question while directing your attention to a specific undine or to any undine who might care to respond. You put some concentration, feeling, and energy into your question. In other words, think about why you are asking it and why an undine would respond. You ask, and then you just wait in a completely open and receptive state of mind.

The impressions that come to you in response may take any number of forms. You may feel a physical sensation in your body. You may get a feeling. You may receive a visual image or hear a sound or song. You can practice this since discerning faint impressions requires an effort on your part. And then you learn to interpret your impressions, amplifying and clarifying them.

From my point of view, the human brain is so powerful that it instantly connects on some level to anything in the universe toward which you direct your consciousness. Thinking about something creates a connection. It is up to you to develop the connection so it conveys the information you are seeking.

One simple method for practicing telepathy is to imagine a small ball of light or water. The ball contains a thought or a question. You imagine the ball leaving your forehead and moving along a thin string of light that extends from your head to the person or spirit you wish to communicate with. Again, you wait with an empty mind for a response.

It is not as if the other person or spirit is consciously responding to you. It is more like the ball bounces off the other person's aura or mind and then returns to you. But in this case, the returning ball of energy configures itself so as to answer your question.

It is similar to radar or sonar. A pulse is sent out, and what returns may indicate distance, size, and type. In this case, it is more like question and answer. Telepathy has a great many variations and applications. This method is a simple way of beginning.

FIFTH METHOD: CONTEMPLATION

This method is an advanced form of contemplation. It is similar to the previous method involving telepathy, but it uses a higher level of concentration.

You empty your mind so there are no distractions. You also put aside your ego and your identity. You do not refer back to yourself. With this empty mind, you concentrate on something. Before you try this with an undine, you might like to try it with various people you know or even people you have not met.

You focus on the person. You hold the picture of this person before your mind. And now you sense the vibration that appears. The only thing that exists at this point in your awareness is the image and vibration of what you are concentrating on.

This is somewhat similar to imagining a huge room or a stadium. At the center is a picture or the thought of a person or spirit. Now the lights grow dim until the only light that remains illuminates what you are focusing on. In this pure receptivity of mind, there is no longer a building. There is only empty and dark space around what you are concentrating on.

There is no subject or object. There is no you sitting in the room somewhere else looking down. Your awareness is the emptiness and the form within it.

In this state, you become the vibration of what you are concentrating on. Under the discussion of magical empathy, I gave the example of imagining you are another person. That method involved working with form. By contrast, this is a formless meditation. We are after the vibration or energy that is underneath the form or image.

Sometimes people can be very confusing for us. It is hard to work with them. They shift from warm to cold, from engaging to withdrawing, from being attentive to being terribly distracted. In cases such as this, it can be helpful to sense the other person's underlying energy or vibration. The other person may operate as if there is no center that integrates who he or she is.

But if you sense the other's vibration, then who the other is will always be clear to you. Then it is easier to accept and work with the person without being confused or worn out. All of the other person's changes are still consistent with what you perceive to be true about this individual.

I try this method on a merman. From an empty state of mind, I concentrate on his name, Ermot. I immediately see images of rivers and streams. But if I persist in sensing the energy rather than the form or images, I sense a passionate love of the purifying, healing, renewing, and uniting power within flowing water.

I do not need to rely on a form or image to feel this passionate love. It is a pure state of energy. As I persist in contemplating, I become this energy. It is the only thing now existing within my awareness. In sensing this energy within this nature spirit, my aura begins to change into his. With just a slight effort or shift in consciousness, Ermot and I are now aware of each other's presence.

If Beethoven had sensed Ermot's aura as I am now doing, he would have written a tenth symphony. The "Ode to Joy" would expand and include the feelings of being fully alive. The beauty of Ermot is astonishing.

SIXTH METHOD: WATERY ENERGY

In this method, you create through your imagination a charge of watery energy in a specific location. For example, you imagine that the room you are in contains a dense vibration of cold, watery energy. Blue green is a good color for water.

In other words, you imagine that part of the sea and the vibration of the undine's own domain or aura are surrounding you. Make it cold, thick, and wet. Then add to the physical sensation a love that feels a part of all the oceans of the world; this love is one with anything that draws near to it. Then if you call out to an undine, the undine will feel comfortable coming to associate with you.

You can also combine these methods in varying degrees at the same time. I often will project my mind into an undine's domain so I am right in front of an undine. I will sense and tune into her world and her aura. And then I will reproduce that watery astral vibration in my room and invite her to come back with me.

In the first instance, my senses do not see my room at all. They are focused inward away from the physical world even though my eyes are open. In this example, I imagine my body is hollow and filled with water as if I have become an undine. When the undine is in my room, my senses are focused on her and are not so clairvoyant because she has a denser vibration and is almost visible.

SEVENTH METHOD: A SIGIL

There are many methods for interacting with undines that involve traditional magic. With the undines and mermen mentioned in this book, it is possible to use a sigil. A sigil is a magical diagram that operates like a phone number. It offers a direct link to the spirit it represents.

The sigils for the spirits I mention are found in Franz Bardon's book *The Practice of Magical Evocation*. One way to use a sigil is simply to visualize it in front of you or draw it with your finger in the air. The stronger your visualization, the more effective it is. For example, you hold the picture of the sigil in your mind for a period of time, however long is comfortable for you.

This is similar to meditation or contemplation. You focus on something and then notice what impressions come to you while you do this. A sigil can be so effective that it is like an evocation. By concentrating intensely, the spirit moves from whatever it is to being directly in front of you.

It helps also to imagine the feelings and ideas that are appropriate for the spirit you are working with. If I concentrate on Istiphul, I can imagine that the lines of her sigil have her vibration or energy in them. For example, there would be a sense of her intense beauty, love, and empathy.

You can also add to your visualization the idea that the lines are on three different planes at the same time. The lines you visualize are meant to be physical to represent her physical body. You also imagine the same lines occurring on the astral plane to represent her astral body and on the mental plane to represent her mind.

In other words, you visualize the exact same lines. But you imagine them to possess different vibrations—on one level they contain a physical vibration; on another level the vibration is emotional in nature; and a third set has vibrations that belong to the mind. This multilevel concentration is like opening a gate to the inner planes and the realm of the undine.

When you are on the phone, you hear another person's voice with its intonation, pitch, and volume. There is more feeling and connection than occurs, for example, with an email. In a similar way, the sigil comes alive as you put more feeling into it.

EIGHTH METHOD: ART

This method involves art. This is the same as the first method, but it extends over years. If you create a poem, story, song, or painting about an undine, you are changing the vibration of your aura to some extent to match that of an undine. If you employ empathy and imagination, you are learning to think and feel like an undine. It is then possible for an undine to contact you using inspiration, feelings, intuitions, dream images, or other methods.

On the other hand, if you do something that captures the undines' attention, that engages their interests and the things they love, you have a better chance of working with them. In this case, you are acting as their agent on earth. Being somewhat narcissistic, they love to be represented in art and written about. If you write a story or screenplay or work on an art project involving undines that is meaningful to them, they will notice. (For more on art projects, see appendix A, "Incarnated Mermaids.")

SUMMARY

If you wish to interact with undines, it is important to develop your empathy and imagination. Know your experiences with water and the feelings and moods that accompany them. Explore your imagination and test the extent to which you can sense what an undine might feel and how she might perceive. Then you have a basic repertoire of sensations, feelings, and perceptions that you can draw upon to understand any new and original experiences you might have in interacting with them.

If you have never thought about what love or friendship is, then when you have an intimate relationship with another person, you may not be very quick to insist that the interactions be fair. You have not thought about the need to be assertive and the possibilities of warm, supportive, but clear communication. And it may not occur to you that you need to use your imagination and make an effort if you are going to discover what is in your partner's heart. The same is true of undines. You have to make an effort and search the other's heart and spirit if you want a creative and meaningful interaction.

14

EXERCISES AND REVIEW

There are many different ways of internalizing a feeling, a spiritual presence, or an inner truth.

You can use the method of *focusing*—notice the feelings that arise in you as you verbalize a description of an experience. Open to the feelings and let them transform as they vibrate, echo, and expand within you.

You can use *contemplation*—let the words or phrases that describe an experience sink into your mind and lead you to a place of dream and vision beyond the limitations of thought and reason.

You can use *dialoguing*—let the feeling within the words appear to you as a person with whom you can speak and who speaks as you listen. Discuss your different perspectives and ask the tough questions.

You can use *invocation*—let the words that describe an experience raise your awareness to a higher level so that you feel closer to something that is greater than yourself and that now has greater access to you.

You can use *evocation*—speak the words describing a spiritual realization as if your voice first spoke them so that what they mean rises from the core of your being.

You can use *meditation*—open your mind with care and concentration so that the vibration of the words (their essence, the light and life within them) becomes a part of your mind, your body, and your soul.

ESSAYS

You can use *poetry* (as poetry and words of power existed in ancient times)—let the sounds and imagery speak to your heart and imagination of and with the primordial powers of creation. How? Similar to meditation, you become very still like a mirror. And then with more feeling than is typical of meditation you let what is in front of you appear within you so that you overcome the separation.

You can use *path working*—somewhere between daydreaming and waking up within a dream, begin an imaginative journey that moves between who and where you are to what you wish the world to be.

Or, to sum it all up, you just become the thing on which you are concentrating. Become a lake, a river, or a sea as if you are identical to it.

UNDINE INSPIRATION

Which of the following descriptions of water and undines can you make your own?

From the undines to humanity: The universe is on fire with wonder, beauty, and ecstasy.

> *Peace like a river*
> *Peace like the sea of stars on fire*
> *Peace like a heart that loves forever*

—AMUE

If we understand that water is itself a sacrament, sensation, and symbol given to us that bears witness to omnipresent love, then we shall know a peace that flows like a stream from the dawn of time to the ends of eternity.

—THE STORY OF AHMED

There is a peace as vast as the sky, as deep as the sea, as still and clear as a mirror, and flowing like water.

—A MERMAN

The Sidhe possess an absolute contentment—an awareness in which the inner self is at peace with the universe.

—ISTIPHUL

The gate to the astral plane of the undines opens the moment your body feels the vastness of the sea flowing through it.

—ISTIPHUL

At night I dream that I have become a silver chalice. And within this chalice is gathered the purest essence of all the stars. When I dream this dream, though I am but the sea, I feel I have become one with the universe.

—ISAPHIL

Imagine what this would be like: imagine taking all the sensations, feelings, and moods that the seas create; imagine binding that beauty and wild passion into one light, one dream, or one vision of completion; and then being able to transmit this to another through your eyes, the touch of your skin, or a kiss.

—ISTIPHUL

Place your hand in water and feel it connecting you to all the seas on the earth. Become a billion waves dancing to a thousand separate winds. To know me is to learn to perceive as I do. For a moment, let go and be as me—the soul of the sea.

—ISTIPHUL

This is the first key and the gateway to all the mysteries of your soul—to relax, to be calm, to open from within, to be so still you reflect easily within yourself the being and the life of all that exists.

—ISAPHIL

In your soul, waves roll five thousand miles, and magnetism flows between the poles.

—ISTIPHUL

Where can an undine go
To share these things with a human soul?
The dark depths of the ocean trench,
The slippery touch of the jellyfish and the nautilus,
The caress of arctic cold,
Or the warmth of curling up on a tropical beach,
Of a woman walking out of the sea naked and free,
Drops of water anointing her skin.

—ISTIPHUL

In water are love and sharing—the experience of life giving birth to life and of flowing in and through another. In water is the absolute destruction of loneliness, separation, and isolation. For undines, each moment is a magnetic sea containing the dreams and the taste of ecstasy—each moment arises from and resonates with the love sustaining all life on earth.

You taste our inner essence—a love that flows without ever being lost and gives all of itself in every moment.

—AMUE

Her touch annihilates loneliness.

—ISTIPHUL

Love is a pilgrim journeying through a land of ancient shame, unbearable pain, and yet never-ending wonder—because it will never be satisfied until it is one with another.

—OSIPEH

What an absolutely terrible and yet wondrous gift of unspeakable beauty human beings possess—to be so lonely, so far away from sharing heart-to-heart. And yet to be so proud—knowing there is nothing you cannot endure because one day you will become radiant like the sun and magnificent like the stars.

—ISTIPHUL

The female form embodies a way of thinking that men cannot imagine. It is receptive, open, nurturing, offering, and giving of itself. Affection extends everywhere and into everything.

—OSIPEH

Zen koan: What lies hidden within the moment?
Answer: A stillness that embraces the universe.

Afterword

Here, at the end of this book, I can now define the genre of the modern fairy tale. There are seven points. First, the spirits in modern fairy tales do not belong to a specific ethnic or national group. Instead, they have a global outlook. Their sphere of action is the entire biosphere.

Second, the kings and queens of the four elements are not creatures of imagination. They are not inferior to us or of less significance. By interacting with them, we discover that they are more knowledgeable about nature than are our scientists. Furthermore, they possess abilities and powers that we have yet to acquire in the near or far future. In this sense, they are our teachers. In terms of the elements in which they specialize, their actions and responses indicate that they are not less but more human than we are.

Third, unlike past writers who simply gathered existing folktales into collections, I have had to travel at least halfway to the Otherworld to get the best stories. It is possible to enter the realm of fairies (in this case the realm of undines) and learn to act, perceive, feel, and think as one of these beings. Modern fairy tales, then, include firsthand reports and recount the details of journeying between the realms.

Fourth, traditional fairy tales often take place "once upon a time." By contrast, mythical time and history interact in modern fairy tales. Consequently, it is possible to find living human beings who have powerful connections and extensive experience with the fairy realms. For example, some individuals are simultaneously active in both human and undine evolutions. Though they appear in human form, they possess the full powers and psychic abilities they either acquired or previously possessed when they sojourned in these other spiritual realms. Through interviews and careful listening, it is possible to observe through their experience wonder, awe, and beauty rising to the level of the sacred and divine.

Fifth, the genre of the modern fairy tale is genuine mythology. It asks these questions: Why are we here? What are the deepest purposes of life? What are our options? The writer of a fairy tale, like the writer of mythology, finds themself in a position of repeatedly encountering experiences that no previous systems of explanation can comprehend. So they tell a new story that in essence declares, "Our conflicts can be resolved; in spite of the horrors and suffering, it is possible to walk the path of life in harmony and beauty." For example, I ask an undine queen to share her secret desires and innermost dreams. If you ask this question to the right spirit in a magical realm, the answer inevitably produces a profound change in yourself. The story that results may offer a new definition of human nature.

Sixth, the fairy tale is a study of how human consciousness can be expanded. At present, we extend our perception of the world by using physical objects such as microscopes, telescopes, and telephones. We enhance our movements by using cars, trains, ships, and planes. To be more productive, we use laboratories, factories, mines, and refineries.

From the point of view of the kings and queens of the elements, there is nothing wrong with human science. The problem is that our consciousness operates within a narrow band of awareness. Our nervous system ends at the surface of our bodies. Our five senses are dependent on physical organs.

By contrast, nature spirits utilize energy fields to extend their perception and to interact with the physical world. For example, the undine queens identify their consciousness with the magnetic fields of the oceans and all the waters of the earth. Anything that water touches, they can touch also.

Since undines specialize in love, empathy, and ecstasy, they see the human race as still asleep—or as one undine put it, "Human beings are part dead." She was not being sarcastic. She was describing the difference between how she feels in human form as compared to when she is an undine in the sea. By definition, then, fairy tales communicate new forms of perception in an effective and persuasive manner.

Seventh, fairy tales not only outline new destinies for mankind, but they also warn us of possible dangers. For conscience to operate effectively, the five elements of earth, air, fire, water, and akasha must be equally developed and in balance. However, water, which supports love, feeling, and empathy, is profoundly weak in our civilization. What is perfectly natural for an undine or a woman with undine empathy—to sense instantly what anyone else on earth feels in this moment—is almost unheard of in our civilization.

One result is that when a scientist makes a breakthrough, offering mankind some new power, the technology inevitably falls into the hands of malicious dictators and dominating political regimes. This is a collective failure of conscience. It is an indictment of the human race.

Undine empathy enables individuals to discern immediately whether another person is healthy, loving, and harmonious or the opposite. For undines, we are all equally part of the magnetic field that encircles this planet. In the modern fairy tale, the myth of separation is overcome. We all share a collective responsibility for each other and for the planet as well.

In summary, in a traditional fairy tale, the elements of the story are treated as if the story is real, even though the tale is considered to be fiction. The writer makes up their own rules, and the reader suspends belief in order to enjoy the story. In a modern fairy tale, you can observe these things for yourself and draw your own conclusions.

In a modern fairy tale, belief is never the issue. Though some individuals report these stories as firsthand experience, the heart of the story involves encounters with wonder, awe, bliss, and ecstasy. Along the way, we are offered suggestions on how to extend our perception and expand our consciousness.

In a nutshell, the undine queens are not less human. They are our teachers. All their powers and abilities are latent within us. The modern fairy tale tells us that nature still waits for us to discover its mystery and beauty.

APPENDIX A

Incarnated Mermaids

In 1996, I studied the auras of four mermaid queens and interacted with them in a variety of ways. In 2009, while editing the first edition of this book, several quotes by two mermaid queens caught my attention.

Istiphul said to me, "You wish to know our deepest secrets. In the near future, we will find a way to share these things with you. You will meet mermaids in the flesh, and then you shall understand our nature."

And Isaphil, "I assure you that one day you will meet women who have worked with me and who have mastered all that I am. But first you must complete your journey."

It was not easy for me to grasp what these mermaid queens were saying. There are very few references in occult or world literature that described in detail a mermaid incarnating in human form and living among us as if she was one of us. Such a woman would face huge challenges. There are staggering differences between the mermaid realm with its vibration of pure love and human civilization where we compete and fight with each other over scarce resources. And an incarnated mermaid would experience startling realizations as she grows up. There is no user's manual lying next to a crib when a child like this is born that explains to her the rules by which human society operates. She is on her own.

If you think about it, if a mermaid wants to have "a human experience," it would serve no purpose for her to know in advance that she is not human. Otherwise, when she has to deal with a difficult situation, it would be easy for her to say, "The choices I make here do not matter. I am a mermaid. I do not have to take this life seriously."

Among the fifty or so masters I have studied with from many traditions, none of them embody the vibration of water in their auras. Add to this that Franz Bardon, whose methods I was practicing, pointed out how easy it is to become enchanted by the beauty of these women. The idea of a mermaid in human form was intriguing, but I had nothing to go on.

Nonetheless, in an attempt to meet incarnated mermaids, I put out a global casting call on a model website for women who could portray through the performing arts—singing, dance, modeling, and the like—what a mermaid in human form would be like. To my surprise, I received immediate responses from several women who embodied the water element.

One woman was a model from Australia. Within two weeks, I flew her to Oahu, Hawaii. We did photo shoots for six days on the North and South Shores. And I did videotape interviews with her on what it was like for her to grow up, reviewing her entire biography and any unusual experiences she had had. I even wrote a "fairy tale" as a back-story about her called, *The Double Changeling*.

Slowly over the next few years, I was able to do extensive interviews with a number of these women. This led to my posting an essay on the internet called "Traits of Mermaid Women." Now, about every two months over the last twelve years, a woman writes to me from some part of the world. These women say to me things such as,

> "I googled *mermaid* and *women* and found your essay. You are the first person to understand who I am. It is like you are inside my head reading my mind."

"I read your essay, 'Traits of Mermaid Women,' and I am shocked because it is so much about me. Like the part on innocence fits me."

"Everything makes sense to me when I read your stories in *Mermaid Tales*. Even specific details that I've never shared with anyone. The way I feel about relationships, about nature, about love, about being alive. I feel joy, so deeply I cry sometimes out of beauty. I don't know how to thank you enough. I feel so much gratitude for being able to share all of this with you. You seem to understand me better than I understand myself."

"I have just finished reading your book *Undines* and it is the most profound, wonderful book I have ever read. When I read your book, I didn't just read the words. I felt it the way I feel music. It is a physical energy that goes up and down in my body. I have been doing that with music forever but this is the first book that I have read where the energy manifests that way."

One of these mermaid women in her sixties had given up on trying to reveal to others what she felt inside. She had never met anyone who understood her. She asked me, "How do you know I am a mermaid?"

I lifted up my hand and felt her aura and replied, "Because you have the one element of water in your aura." A few hours later she texted me and said, "When you felt the water in my aura, I could feel exactly what you were feeling with your hand."

She had also been part of a group that believed the astral plane was an inferior state of being. I held up my hand again and said, "This is the astral plane." She said, again sensing directly what I sensed, "That is what I call spirit."

As they grow up, they observe that they are not like other people. Several times I flew a small group of six merwomen to Hawaii who had never met anyone like themselves. One of them recounted how when she was little she asked her mother, "Mother, I am not like other people. Is there something you are not telling me?" And her mother replied, "You are of water. You are a mermaid." In her country she is well known, an "influencer" in social media. And yet, if she discussed openly that she is a mermaid, she would be in danger. In her nation, they kill women who they suspect to be mermaids.

There are other things about mermaids I could only discover through interviewing them and observing them firsthand. For example, they produce what I call a cocaine effect. When you are in their physical presence, the dense water in their auras flows through you with its soothing, calming, healing, and renewing vibration. You feel released and at peace as if you had just spent a month out of doors sailing around the world or camping by an ocean bay or a lake high in the mountains. Like taking cocaine, you feel larger than life, complete in yourself, and at peace.

But when you move thirty to sixty feet away from her, this benevolent influence vanishes. Outside of the influence of her aura, you return to your normal self. But that is not how it feels. Instead, you may feel acute withdrawal symptoms—nervousness, unease, anxiety, or a strange sense of loss.

To overcome this cocaine effect, one would need to learn how to produce the watery aura of mermaids in themself. But this is extremely difficult because there are no teachings by any religion on meditating effectively on water. I pointed out to one Taoist master that he was teaching earth, air, fire, and akasha to his students but not the water element. He replied, "It is impossible to teach Westerners about the water element."

Even when an individual can internalize the vibration of water, there is still a serious problem. As a song says, "There's no sorrow, toil, or danger in that bright land to which I go."

The water element suppresses one's survival instinct. If you feel bliss overflowing from inside of you, it is hard to remain vigilant and alert. The fire element emphasizes willpower. The earth element is solid and hardworking. The air element is keen and perceptive. But those elements have difficulty operating if you feel you can just "go with the flow." Mermaid love has no tough love. And it does not demand accountability. Yet in our world, we have to remain vigilant if we are going to survive.

These women often look just like any other woman. They talk to you in a normal way though they are remarkably receptive and vivacious. So it is hard to imagine that they do not have a human soul but rather are immortal beings from the astral plane in human form. But then I give some of them an electric thermometer. They can hold it in their hands and drop the temperature between five and thirty degrees in a few minutes.

These women also have huge problems with stalkers. If they ride a bus, a complete stranger may get off at their stop and follow them home. Since they have close ties to water, which has an average temperature in nature of a few degrees above freezing, I sometimes suggest they imagine ice-cold water around themselves or an iceberg next to them.

This can stop someone from following them. One woman thanked me because she can now ride the bus in peace. But people on the bus may then say, "It is freezing in here. Someone should turn off the air conditioner." I have seen people walk near them and start to shiver before they put on a coat or sweater.

When our culture is more familiar with the psychology of the water element, we will regard these women as teachers. They can show us new things, such as, "Here is what it feels like to never have a mean thought, to never be jealous, and to never lose your innocence." Or, "Here is what it is like to feel a flowing stream of water moving through yourself that cleanses you of negative thoughts. Here is what it is like to dissolve any feelings of separation or isolation from others." Or, even as Jesus once said of his future disciples, "From out of their bellies shall flow streams of living water." Those who teach such things already dwell among us.

TRAITS OF MERMAID WOMEN
(A BRIEF SUMMARY)

Relation to Water

As children, these women may spend many hours a day in water (sometime ten hours or more)—either in a bathtub, a swimming pool, a lake, or the sea. As adults, they prefer to be around large bodies of water. Some of them send healing energy to other people while they are in the bathtub.

A Series of Quotes by Different Women

"For me, being in water feels better than being anywhere else."

"As a kid, there were times when I needed to get away from my family, out of society, and being in the water was the only peaceful place."

"Whenever I would get upset about something and couldn't get near the ocean, I would fill up the tub and get in and just float around until I was all wrinkled."

"I mentioned having to get into the water five or six times a day to keep myself feeling okay. I only feel comfortable when I am in water. I can only do energy work on others when I am fully immersed in water."

"As a teenager, I would sneak out and swim in the pool in the backyard every night."

"I spent a lot of time near water when I was a child. They had to pull me out of the sea. I never wanted to get out."

"I went to the ocean today. No human words could describe the experience."

"The ocean is my mother."

"I need to be near water. I don't need to get into it, just be near it. I don't think a stream or river would quite do it for me. Because it is not deep enough. It doesn't have the depth that my spirit needs to have. I draw energy from the water. I think I would start to feel like I was drinking too much coffee if I lived near only a stream or a river."

"When I am in water it is like nothing else exists. Ten minutes are like six months. But when I come out of the water, I am stuck again with human consciousness. But I am making little advances. I allow my brain to feel like it is full of water, and then there is no difference between being human and being a mermaid. My body takes on a water vibration."

"I just remembered, my grandma said [that] when I was young I would not get out of the water. The family used to joke about it. I had a pool most of my life and would spend weekends when not in school in the pool for at least ten hours a day."

"I always knew I was a part of the ocean, and I feel wholly me in it."

"Everyone jokes that I have a pre-swim personality and a post-swim personality. By swimming, I wash away the day. Most days I swim 2 kilometers or more. Water is my happy place. It's where I regenerate, meditate, heal, recharge, refresh, relax, and rebuild. It is my home and my sanctuary. I'm much more free in the water. Walking is heavy. Swimming is freedom."

"I have always felt certain things were lacking from my life. I never lived near water until my early twenties, and this is when I began to feel really alive. I was so happy. And then I moved back to the Midwest and lost that feeling until I returned to Hawaii. I can only get that feeling if I get in a pool or bath. I feed off the magnetism that the water brings me. The water enhances all my senses. If I am sick or in pain, I get in the water as it is what comforts me. Sometimes you hear people say they are married to god. I sometimes feel I am married to the ocean."

"When I was a kid, whenever I got into the sea, I always thought that she was hugging me like my mom."

"I have a different connection to water than what I have with people. It is as if I can merge my soul with water. Within water I feel loved unconditionally, revitalized, refreshed, renewed, happy, pure, cleansed, and euphoric. All these words do not fully describe the feelings that water brings."

A man shared with me, "Our child adores water. From the time she was born she has begged to take baths and showers and would stay in for hours upon hours if we would let her. I think she probably just has an affinity for water, but it would be odd if she were a child of the water spirits."

I wrote back, "I consulted with another mermaid woman. Her advice is to let your daughter spend as much time in water as she wants to. The thing you can do for her is to make sure she has other happy and healthy children to be around and to learn from since at that age she is very impressionable."

Quotes on Innocence (and Being Uninhibited)

"Speaking of being sexually uninhibited, that is how I have always been. I don't understand or feel the emotion 'shame' that so many others speak of. I don't understand the guilt that goes with sex. I am a very free, loving, and a wild spirit when it comes to sex."

"I am perfectly capable of being 100 percent uninhibited with sex. I can have sex with someone without feeling any attachment; I can be attracted, but it doesn't go beyond that. I would never use the word *special* to describe having sex with my lover, even though it is special in the social sense of not having it with any-one else."

"Hearing the sound of the waves and feeling the silky currents on my skin can easily bring me to climax in every sense of the word."

"I still to this day do not understand the whole love and sex thing. For me, the two are separate. No wonder humans get so confused in relationships."

"I love sex. But for me love and sex are not bound together. Sex is a natural bodily function. Love is of the heart—it is a soul-to-soul connection. Love does not require physical consummation in order to be fully expressed. Love is what I am."

"I can get off when a man looks me in the eyes. It is as physically exciting as actual penetration. If the right man looks into my eyes, I will come. . . . I may do it silently. I may do it discreetly. I may do it in the middle of a busy downtown sidewalk. On the days I wear nothing under my skirt, the wetness runs down my legs after a man truly penetrates my vision with his own."

"When I was young, I used to get confused because no one knew how to think in an unselfish way. I couldn't understand why people were selfish. Even now, I see it, but I still do not understand it."

"I have never had a mean thought in my life, even when someone intentionally hurts me."

"Being mean is beyond my comprehension because I don't understand how to feel that I would want to hurt somebody. I have never felt that."

"Something that came so natural to me seemed to be difficult for others. I never understood why love always had a cost or repercussions. For me, I love with my entire being. I don't understand why humans must try or work at loving each other. You love someone for the good, the bad, and the ugly; and if you can't forgive, then you really don't know how to love at all."

Quotes on Contact with the Astral Plane

"For me, the astral plane is more real than this world. It is a different reality. Astral colors are amplified. Green is the most brilliant. You could take everything that is beautiful here and magnify it by a thousand times. But eating an orange there is not as real as here. Taste and smell are more real in this world. But in the astral, colors are far more beautiful and intense."

"The realm of mermaids is beautiful, magical, and there is so much love. It is beyond euphoric. And there it is so much easier to help others since we work in unity. There is happiness and comfort and no conflict."

"When I go to sleep at night, I wake up on the astral plane. I am then able to interact with spirits or visit people in this world."

Quotes on Death and the Departed

"Sometimes someone who has passed on can give me the experience that they went through. This can occur in seconds or minutes. For example, I touched the helmet of a man who had been to Iraq and all of a sudden I was in Iraq in my head, seeing a tank overturned in water. I felt crushed, and I could not breathe. . . . I see the men who died and they show me things like their baby being born and that they wore funny hats. I was able to relay a message to the man who tried but was unable to save them. He was not able to deal with it."

"I had a friend who at age twenty-five died in a car accident. A few years later I could feel his energy around me. For two years I saw him in dreams and near my bed, or I would hear him call my name in the early morning. One time, in no more than a few seconds, he showed me his car wreck, the hospital where he died, how his mom felt, how he felt, how his friends felt—I saw it all. I even heard the doctors talking to his mom while he was standing there watching, invisible to their eyes. He showed me the operating room and what the doctors were saying."

"We do not die. We just use these bodies as vessels for our human experience."

"I do not fear death; I am happy to be here and to learn, but I am also excited about moving on."

"I don't believe in death. It is just leaving the body and I am moving on."

"Death is not to be feared or even of major importance. It is merely a transition."

"I am trying to make my husband understand some things. He is upset about a friend who will die soon of cancer. And he just does not understand that when his friend dies, he will then actually be more alive than ever."

"I never understood the attachment humans have with their bodies. I sense the soul that has left the body. I try to encourage them and help them in adapting to their new situation."

"I was thinking today about funerals. You know in my entire life I have only been to one. Why do people mourn when they should be celebrating the new journey the departed are taking?"

"I used to give ghost tours in Prague. Funny because I could actually see and talk to the ghosts. I got to know the seventeenth-century executioner of Prague. He shared with me details about his life that are not in the history books. He also warned me about taking the ghost tour into places where it was not safe to enter."

Quotes on Psychic Empathy

"I can walk into a room and tell what everyone is feeling inside."

"I can walk up to a stranger and feel what the other person is feeling every time, good, bad, ugly feelings, it doesn't matter."

"I can feel others' pain. By flowing my energy through someone, I can calm that person down. It is like taking them off to the side and giving them a breather. This kind of direct connection can help when words do not."

"When I meet people, I will see flashes of their lives and feel their pain and joy."

"An example of my empathy is when my daughter gets her feelings hurt at school over something most adults would think is silly. I can zoom to when a similar experience happened to me as a child and relate on that level. At the same time my empathy skills feel her pain as if I am living in that very moment that she experienced."

"If I let my guard down, in an instant I can be inside of someone else and feel their pain."

"I read a friend's letter to her boyfriend that she had written nine years before. Not only did I feel what she thought and how she felt when she wrote the letter, but I also felt how the man felt whom the letter was written to. She was breaking up with him. I could feel his pain. I even got sick to my stomach because of the mental/physical anguish this man went through. It was as if we had become one."

"If you speak of someone, I can instantly tell you about that person. I can feel what other's feel and read their minds."

"My intuition works like this: I see the full potential of someone's soul and I feel like I should help this person to connect with that essence. And I trust that they want to become this version of themselves."

Quotes on Time

"Schedules do not matter. They are just something I know I have to do with my conscious mind. But I can be in my sense of timelessness and still do the things that I have to do. Though I plan and schedule, I remain in a timeless space."

"By flowing in each moment, time becomes timeless."

"I was just thinking today how I can tap into a memory and it is as intense and powerful as the moment it happened. The same energy is there. Time and space do not exist within my mind."

"I am playing a part as a human being. Obviously, to act human is to do what they do, which is having goals and striving to attain them. But I do not like being asked, 'What are your plans?' I simply try new things to see if they feel right and are comfortable."

"I try to act human. But I have no purposes or goals. I just go with the flow."

"When I was four, I did not feel any different than I do now. You could put me into that little four-year-old body and it is still me. And I know that I will feel the same when I am older." Another woman responds: "Thank you for putting this into words for me—I've been struggling to explain that one to myself and others for a long time. Especially the part of not feeling any different now from when I was a child."

"I am the same person now that I was as a child. Events in the outer world do not change who I am inside."

APPENDIX B

MESSAGES FROM SYLPHS, GNOMES, AND SALAMANDERS

Some of the characteristics of these entities are discussed in Franz Bardon's book, *The Practice of Magical Evocation,* and it is to this work that I refer when mentioning his descriptions.

SYLPHS

The Sylph Cargoste

All winds fall within the scope of Cargoste's mastery—the trade winds, the storm winds, the tornado, and the hurricane—he has absolute command over them.

When Cargoste is over the Pacific Ocean, he senses the winds of the North and South Poles. He is aware of the remnants of a hurricane off Baja, the effects caused by El Niño, the jet stream, and the ozone layer. He is aware of the temperature, humidity, and pressure in the clouds for thousands of miles.

He can sense the arrangement of electrical charges in clouds anywhere over the Pacific or the Atlantic. He is aware of the weather patterns on the other side of the planet since the atmosphere, for him, is one fabric and one matrix. And he is aware of these many aspects of the atmosphere all at once without relying on thought or having to change his mental focus from one thing to another.

I ask Cargoste, "From where do you come, and what is your commission?"

Cargoste replies:

The voice that would create must have breath to speak; the heart that would soar free must have wings to fly; the mind that would be enlightened must be as clear as the sky.

You ask what it is like to be me. I will tell you. I am the movement of winds without beginning or end. When I lay my head down to sleep, the total configuration of the Earth's atmosphere is in my dreams—the waves of the sea and the clouds that roam free, winter's cold breath and summer's heat, spring's newness and fall's release—I keep them all in harmony.

But I rarely think about myself. Though the name Cargoste refers to me, you will have a hard time defining my identity. I have no more personality than frost when it coats a leaf with white or rain changing into tiny crystals of snow. Is there excitement in the heat released as ice forms on ponds? Is there desire in the gust that carries the milkweed seeds above the ground?

My longing is to sail beneath the stars at night at eighty thousand feet. The bubble of air locked inside ice as countless ages roll by, the calm eye of the hurricane so still the leaves of trees are undisturbed, and the eyes of a bird searching the reaches of eternity for the chords of forgotten songs—all of these are within my mind.

I am my work. The tides in the sky and the streams of wind, the weather conditions, and the cloud formations—these capture my imagination. The sky of the earth is the circumference of my passion.

Do I recall my beginning and how I came into being? The sky was not always blue. It was redder with a purplish hue, and great fiery wastes were the earth's face. I was placed here to clear the sky so the stars could shine. My task is obvious. My commission is to preserve light and life and to maintain balance between fire and ice. What makes me different from other sylphs, as you can see, is that the entire planet and every living being, every wind, every season, and every weather condition flow through my dreams.

The Sylph Parahim

Parahim is a beautiful sylph of high rank who dwells in the sky above the clouds. She has a profound sense of harmony. For Parahim, music and tones are magical. Being in her presence is like sitting beside a harpist whose songs are of passion and peace.

Parahim also has an unusual empathy for certain kinds of human beings. Sylphs by nature are aloof and distant from humanity. They desire neither to possess nor to be possessed. They cherish independence and freedom above the need to conform or connect.

But Parahim has a sensitivity that extends beyond atmospheric conditions. She is acutely aware of those whose minds are like the sky. This interest of hers is unmistakable. When you concentrate on her, she notices and turns her attention on you. She immediately scrutinizes the strength of your brain waves. Because the air element fosters telepathy, it is easy for sylphs to attune themselves to the vibration of others' thoughts. This is something Parahim does very well.

Parahim enters my room. Walls, windows, and doors do not limit her freedom of movement. She smiles at me in a way no woman has ever done. Her smile reflects the willingness of her soul to stand naked so nothing is hidden. Her openness is part of her creativity—she has many magical songs that penetrate the heart. They are subtler than wind, breath, or a lover's caress.

The gaze of her eyes is most remarkable. She can see the haunting desire that arises in an unknown place within your soul, and in the same moment she can sing a note of freedom and release so that you let go into a serenity that satisfies every need. I see clearly how these qualities and abilities exist within her as I touch her aura with my mind.

My mind enters her body. I am astonished and amazed as I enter the astral realm of the sylph. It is like leaping from a high diving board, but there is no pool in which to fall, and no movement at all. Perhaps this is what the astronauts feel when they are outside the space shuttle—just drifting weightless with the vastness of the Earth suspended in space beneath them. But to be in this sylph's body is to be completely still, silent, and quiet. There is no drifting. The weightlessness is a relaxation so great it is a challenge to try to comprehend it.

I am aware of Parahim's mind as well. For her, the forces shaping and determining the course of our lives seem like images appearing in a mirror. We cling to them or flee from them, delighting in them one moment and then hating them the next as if they have the power to shape our feelings and to bless or curse our lives. But for Parahim the mind is both the mirror and the light appearing within it. The mind of a sylph does not lose its spacious openness though storms appear and whirlwinds rage nearby.

The Sylph Capisi

Sylphs have an extraordinary hypersensitivity. The airy substance that composes their bodies makes it most uncomfortable for them to drop down to the earth for anything more than a few moments. Normally, they would feel uneasy and put off being near to the ground—unless they have a very good reason for their visit.

I can feel Capisi's aura here with my hands: She is buoyant, weightless, and floating. Her body exudes subtle rays of whitish-blue light that connect her to wind currents and to the thunderstorms far in the distance over the horizon.

She is very aloof, but it is easy to see why. She is vulnerable and sensitive. Yet freedom and harmony are her essence. She strives to balance the natural elements while she herself remains completely at ease. She blends contrary impulses, mutually exclusive desires, and a whole hierarchy of purposes striving to gain an edge one over the other.

I have seen her set a cloud rolling upon itself like a mouse on a treadmill running round and round but remaining in one place. I have seen her raise her hands with her palms facing each other, wave her fingers, and cause a cloud to dissolve before her in moments.

With a gesture of one hand, she can change air pressure and temperature over the Grand Canyon so clouds drop down within it while the sky is clear overhead. And with her other hand guiding a gust of wind she can knock the hat off a state trooper hundreds of miles away in Albuquerque. And this she can do without even rustling a leaf in a tree nearby. Such is her command and ability.

Today Capisi is wearing a transparent cape with a ribbon of a scarf fluttering around her neck. Her body too is almost transparent. It appears to be made out of pure light, though I dare say you would not want to offend her. I should also mention that in a gesture with the back of her hand she could knock the roof off a house a hundred miles away.

Though her capacity for rapport is profound, Capisi resists forming bonds. Yet in spite of her aloofness, she knows an entire spectrum of pleasures. To the human who can see her, to the one who is acquainted with how to enter her domain, her touch is pure bliss. Her touch suspends another within a sweetness so vast it banishes everything that burdens or weighs the soul down.

I glance at her hair and see images of tornadoes whirling and storm clouds forming. When her hair swings about her neck, I see lovers stealing away into groves of pine and birch trees to have their bliss. Somewhere on earth perhaps there is a harpist with fingers so nimble, so magical, that her songs could echo the play of Capisi's hair in the wind—each hair is a separate song about a place where the heart has found true happiness.

But Capisi is also serious. Her aptitude is for air pressure—for perceiving where there are highs and lows and where air currents collide and disappear. She senses the shifts between moving fronts. Adjusting them just so, she creates a harmonious pattern within the atmosphere, setting boundaries in which weather patterns move.

GNOMES

There are gnomes who specialize in raising the vibration of matter. Not too long ago we called this alchemy. There are gnomes who work with gemstones. It would appear to us that they are merely cutting stones, but in fact they are engaged in a spiritual endeavor. They invest the stones with magical powers. Diamonds, rubies, amethysts, and so forth not only take in and break light into beautiful reflections; they also serve to preserve and amplify consciousness. A gnome can place some of his own spirit into a stone that then can be used to benefit others.

Some gnomes work with trees and forests, with topsoil, herbs, healing, and fertility. They know about roots, bark, leaves, and seeds and the active chemical ingredients within these. For gnomes, trees have consciousness. Gnomes play a role in observing and increasing this.

Some gnomes are interested in mineral deposits, rock formations, and mountains. As humans, we may discuss physical matter in terms of chemistry, molecular bonds, or geological formations. A gnome, by contrast, perceives not physical matter but waves of electromagnetic vibrations. For mermaids, the ocean is a living being. For gnomes also, physical matter itself is alive; it stores and releases energy, has memory, and to some degree, conscious purpose—for gnomes, the physical universe is evolving.

The Gnome Mentifil

Mentifil's aura shines with a brownish-black light. It is as if silence has taken on a color that glows in the air. This light embodies endurance and patience. When you look at Mentifil's face, he looks academic like a scholar. He looks shrewd and clever like an inventor. He is detached and questioning like a scientist engaged in an endless series of experiments. But still, the aura remains.

It is as if you could take the essence of a mountain chain and boil it down, distill, and refine it so that the result is a silence enduring through the ages. Mentifil's aura is a magical space. If you get close enough, you see the events of thousands of years flickering before your eyes, passing by in a few moments of time.

Franz Bardon says that Mentifil is a powerful gnome with many qualities and powers. These include a knowledge of medicinal herbs and the secrets of alchemy. Mentifil can change the molecular structure of an element and control natural processes within the mineral kingdom.

Though there is a timeless quality about him, Mentifil is also robust, friendly, and entertaining. Meeting him is like encountering the soul of a forest walking down the road toward you. You smell the trees. You see leaves on the ground, branches rustling in the breeze, the roots, the soil, and the ages through which the trees have been growing. Mentifil has a deep sense of peace and an animating zest.

I imagine a gnome like this never gets lonely. His interest and curiosity never die. Sights and sounds from other ages are still fresh in his memory as if ancient events happened a few hours before. But Mentifil does not mourn or feel attached to the past. He is always very busy; you can see it in the way he stands—he looks like he has a lot to attend to and is ready to get back to it the instant we are through. Still, he is, always was, and always will be captivated by what is happening in the present moment. His concentration is that complete.

Mentifil is an embodiment of the great treasures and mysteries of the earth. As I sit here next to Mentifil, his aura begins to blend with mine. In a strange way, I feel at home. And like certain stone circles that have visions hidden within them, Mentifil is waiting for that time when a race of beings on this planet will come forth. And saying the right words, comprehending his mind, and seeing through his eyes, they will share and celebrate an ancient and unknown wisdom throughout the world.

The Gnome Musar

Franz Bardon says of Musar, "In the kingdom of the element earth, Musar is one of the most respected of spirits. He may be called a genuine magician of the earth."* As a specialist in the magic of the earth, Musar studies the electromagnetic drifts moving through the ground. These energy movements are caused by storms, geologic formations, and the orbiting moon. Musar knows how to attune himself to these energies and to direct them to practical ends.

Musar feels that the fault lines and mountains talk to him and answer his questions about their origins. He perceives the history of a mountain, its internal stresses, its erosion patterns, and the forces that have shaped it and that will wear it down. Musar can dip his finger into a subterranean stream and instantly identify the minerals present, their concentration, and the sources of the stream. He senses forests and the evolution of trees and plants and how they affect the earth. You could say that Musar is a master of feng shui, the Chinese art of understanding how space and energy interrelate.

Musar's hearing is as sensitive as high-tech equipment. Analogous to a bat or dolphin, Musar emits something like a sonar pulse. But no echo is reflected back. Rather, Musar feels vibrations in the far distance as though his aura is capable of scanning and determining what exists many miles away. What he senses translates into visual images that define for him the structure, quality, and composition of geologic formations.

Musar can sit watching the stars moving through the sky from dusk to dawn and feel no more than a moment of time has gone. He can gaze into past ages and epochs of time and not feel in the least old or weary. For Musar, everything that has shape, form, and weight is fascinating and full of wonder.

Unlike a mountain or a plateau, Musar never grows old. He is constantly full of enthusiasm. For Musar, there is no need to hurry; there is no need to worry—each moment is satisfying; each moment is a treasure of the heart. The silence in which he dwells is a magic well from which he sips and drinks the beauty of the earth.

---

*Bardon, *The Practice of Magical Evocation*, p. 127.

I ask Musar to appear. Musar stands in my room six feet in front of me. He looks like a middle-aged man who is robust and active. He is about five feet tall, sturdy, and strong. His muscles seem to be made of steel though they are not at all bulky.

There is also something about Musar's presence that is reminiscent of a Nordic king. His poise is that of royalty. You can sense a power present that is hard to identify. He is one of those gnomes who can be absolutely still as well as completely engaging. His personality is warm and friendly, yet he radiates dignity and virtue.

Musar's voice is deep and resonant as if the rocks of a mountain were given a voice with which to speak. I have the distinct feeling that Musar spends a great deal of time walking down ancient pathways on the inner planes or through subterranean caverns. When Musar speaks it is like he has a speech already prepared—a speech he has developed and delivered to other magicians with whom he has spoken in other ages.

Musar explains that he has studied human societies since their beginning. He likes to form close ties to humans who like to experiment. Human beings are fascinating to him, though he has not yet figured them out. They keep redefining what they are and what they want.

Whenever I meet with Musar, he continues telling me a long tale about an ancient kingdom that existed after the end of Lemuria and before the beginning of Atlantis. His themes are familiar. He talks about when true love first appeared on earth. He talks about love as being the highest magic. And he talks about the human heart—of the mystery of desire that takes hold, makes new, and also knows when to let go.

The Gnome Erami

Franz Bardon describes Erami as a "powerful gnome-magician." Erami teaches the magic of sympathy and how to prepare a magic mirror. He teaches practical applications of earth magic and how to gain protection from various dangers.

Similar to Musar, Erami is aware of the energy within the earth over a wide area. Erami perceives earth energies as having a fluid quality.

When we look at ice, we have no difficulty thinking of it as frozen water. We realize the same substance falls as rain and flows as rivers into seas.

For Erami, physical matter has a light glowing within it. This light or vibration can be released and move about. It is freed by gravity waves, magnetic tides, thunderstorms, and changes in temperature. The way we can feel a static charge of electricity when we place our hand in front of a computer monitor, Erami can feel the energy or electronic vibrations being emitted by physical matter.

When you work with gnomes, you get used to the incredible persistence and endurance they bring to anything they do. They place their minds within something physical and then very slowly raise its vibration. Since many gnomes have existed for millions of years and since they love precious stones, it is natural for them to spend thousands of hours or days meditating inside of a gemstone or whatever captures their attention.

Erami says, "Transformation and change are everywhere in nature. It is natural to ask, 'From what source do these transformations arise, and what is their perfected course? And in what way can they all be brought into harmony and unity?' I have asked and pursued these questions for countless ages. I am free to share the knowledge I have found with humanity."

SALAMANDERS

The Salamander Itumo

Franz Bardon says that Itumo is a male spirit of fire who likes to be near the surface of the earth. His specialty is creating and controlling thunderstorms. He has knowledge of all aspects of thunderstorms. He is able to control lightning and electricity at will both as forces of nature and as subtler energies on the inner planes.

Itumo appears in my room. He is not here in a physical form. I do not think anyone else would see him except a psychic or clairvoyant. But to me his presence is a brilliant, sparkling light. As a result of his presence, I feel an immense increase of energy in my throat.

Itumo's aura is a declaration in and of itself. It says, "If there is something you need to get done, I am the conviction and the power to manifest it." As I meditate on his presence a few moments more, it becomes clear what he is all about. He says, "You can find anything if it is what you require to accomplish your work in life. To do this, you only need to comprehend my mind."

I spend a few more moments attuning my mind to his. Itumo's presence stimulates the imagination. His aura reflects thunderstorms and lightning within it. Itumo says, "What you see around you—the flashes and explosions of lightning—all this power is found within you. When you join yourself to a stillness so complete that opposites are united within you, then you shall attain all that you seek. Make no mistake—I exist to remind the human race that there are will and power enough to alter any fate and to attain any destiny."

Meditating with Itumo, it is easy to see how the most difficult problems can be solved and the greatest obstacles overcome. To bring this insight into the physical world so it actually changes something takes a lot of work. It requires that you learn how to amplify and sustain electric and magnetic energies within yourself.

The Salamander Pyrhum

Pyrhum is a powerful salamander who is extremely dynamic and quite difficult to engage in conversation. Within the sphere of the element of fire, Pyrhum has the rank of a mighty sovereign with innumerable fire spirits under his control. Pyrhum can teach about every aspect of fire as it exists within nature or as it relates to magical practices.

Pyrhum says to me,

I oversee all fire on earth, and I care not much for your race. I am not arrogant. I just have no respect for human beings because they have not sought to discover the power hidden in their hearts. They think power is external to the self, that it is found in the ability to bind matter or to subject other living beings to their will.

If I close my eyes and concentrate, I can sense all the seas, lakes, and streams of magma that exist within the earth. Oh, I have tried to share my wonder and the inferno of my exuberance with those who dwell on the surface of the world. But it is useless. Their minds are too narrow. Their hearts are too closed.

The great bards will not speak of me in a song lest they risk being drowned in an abyss without entrance or exit. And so even at night when your race falls asleep, I am unable to appear in your dreams. Even the tongues of flame with which dragons speak in your fairy tales and myths neither hint at nor reveal a trace of my existence. I dwell within a realm well-hidden beyond human reach or belief.

The essence of my being is fire turning within and upon itself, becoming hotter, denser, more intense, growing in power, expanding and reaching out, striving to cross every boundary, seeking to create a flame more refined and pure, more full of might than any other that exists. Shifting, twisting, pulsating, and throbbing with an implacable hunger, burning with an unquenchable thirst, I have mastered fires as old as the earth. They contain powers so ancient no god or goddess has ever sought to explore or command them.

The ancient domes of flame where I dwell and the seas of fire I watch over, thrust up mountains and move continents. Yet this fire within the earth also exists to forge the will of those who follow the path of spirit. Those who would explore beyond this planet and taste the mysteries of the cosmos can first sojourn here, take nourishment, and be replenished by the powers that have shaped the earth before continuing on their journey.

Consider the reactor in a nuclear submarine. With the same ease as in contemplating a candle, I stand within that invisible intensity flaring between the rods of uranium or plutonium. But here is the distinction. The physicist and engineer use mathematical calculations, tolerance of alloys, coolants, and turbines to convert fire into electrical power.

But my approach is more experiential. I become the pleasure the vision contains as I taste the naked flames—for here is the heat that causes atoms to split and to break. Gathering itself, the fire builds a will capable of melting steel and any molecular bonds man or nature can fashion. When your desire for power as a race is greater and more pure, you will discover far more mysteries that are hidden within radiation. I say this because the power the atom conceals is one of the wands of power I wield.

Consider lightning, another natural phenomenon as ordinary as rainbows and clouds. The crash of the lightning striking, the thunder echoing, the flash dazzling—your nervous system notes their passing and you may react by saying, "Oh, look at that!" But my response is more artistic. I am as a great painter who will not be satisfied until he has captured on his canvas the mysterious beauty of the woman whom he gazes upon. In rapt contemplation, I explore every nuance, quality, and property of the craving that electricity reveals as opposites reach to clasp each other's essence in their grasp.

And so as one entranced—my mind within both the earth and the sky—I concentrate until my own body is magnetized and electrified. The valleys and ravines, the trees and streams, and the electrical charges flowing through hills become part of my being. And in the cloud—soft, yielding, flowing, whirling—particles of charged energy full of yearning passion respond to the earth until it is ready to burst and its voice speaks with the lightning's flame. My soul is the home of the thunderstorm. Passion has led me to fathom the secret desires that move nature from within.

When you have existed for countless ages as I have and studied every natural phenomenon in which fire plays a hand, you master what you study. I tell you I can point my finger on a clear day and cause lightning to strike where I command. Such is the power of those who hear the call of love and hold nothing back when they respond.

But fire, in its essence, is not selfish, jealous, or self-possessed. And the dream of destruction is not found within it. Quite the contrary.

Fire testifies to the power of spirit to give birth to light, to create without limit, and to make the world beautiful—this is the source of its inspiration and the will it conceals within.

There is a wonder so great, a bliss so magnificent, and a love so mysterious that the physical universe has been created to cloak and shroud its existence. Were we to enter this gate too soon, we would find ourselves consumed by a presence and a light unimaginably bright. Nonetheless, I am free to speak of what I have witnessed—the secret treasure hidden in the core of the Earth is a song that resonates in harmony with the universe.

For each of us there comes a time when we are invited to give breath and voice to this song: when all fear is gone, when power means nothing at all—when it is merely a cloak we put on or take off like the mantle a king wears who has no cares of his own, no desire for a throne. We are ready when our will has tested itself by striving to cross every boundary separating nature and spirit.

And when the joy within us is so great we are ready to explode—because we discover within our hearts that no separation or limitation or enclosure can contain or shape who we are—then this song is free to sound its chords within us. And we, in turn, become part of the power unfolding the universe.

The Salamander Tapheth

The salamander Tapheth has a remarkable affinity for the explosive, raw force of fire in nature. If he could, he would master the plasma exploding from the surface of the sun. He loves electricity and magma breaking free.

If you lit a candle and asked Pyrhum and Tapheth to expound on the magic of that flame, you would get a different emphasis from each one. The basics would be the same, but at a certain point their perspectives diverge. Working with Pyrhum results in discovering the power hidden deep within you. With Tapheth, your enthusiasm and your desire to act and change the world are vastly expanded.

I pursue the relation of the external world to the internal—to what extent fire, which symbolizes light and will, is an actual energy we possess and can develop within ourselves. I ask about how matter and spirit interact and how desire can be transformed into the power of spirit.

Tapheth says to me:

I can see from your aura that you were an alchemist before, you are now, and you will be evermore. Every fiber of your being hungers and thirsts for the power to create something from nothing and to celebrate the birth of light that shines forever. In this way you are like me. There is no end to your curiosity or your tenacity in searching out the mystery of matter and energy transforming.

Fire is used to shape and refine matter into the forms and substances that you need. But if you are after power, then fire itself becomes the object of your investigation. We can search for the highest essence within fire. I seek the one fire so pure and refined in its power that matter and spirit are joined in its presence. I would master this fire within myself so that my will is freed of all limitations. This desire is in the hearts of salamanders the way the thirst for wisdom and love is in the hearts of human beings.

The power to purify, to heal, to rejuvenate, and to transform is part of this art. There is a fire that takes matter and refines it so that its substance and outer form shine with its inner spirit. This fire is so original and commanding that it makes all things new by the quality of its light and by the intensity of the spirit it exudes—this I pursue, the same as you.

The Salamander Orudu

Orudu is a king among salamanders. Many other salamanders are his subjects. He controls the eruptions of volcanoes; he can cause them to happen or stop them from happening.

His work encompasses the planet. He is a coordinator, mediator, and architect of shifting continents. He acts on his own initiative according to his own insight. He builds according to his own designs. He strives to perfect his work and to accomplish all that he plans.

There is no fire on the surface of the earth or under the earth that cannot be influenced by Orudu's will. And though his plans are his own, he is neither arbitrary nor capricious. He has a profound and intricate understanding of how his actions influence the rest of the planet.

Orudu adds this about himself:

A blacksmith heats metal, hammers it on an anvil, and shapes it according to his needs. A master fashions a sword by intricately weaving the metal into a more perfect form. A steel mill blasts molten iron with oxygen to burn up the carbon so the metal can be hard and endure. Even so I lay hold of the world, bending mountains and moving continents to comply with my will.

I take into account the erosion of winds and rains. I consider the cooling effect of water as my volcanoes rise from the seas. I take into account gravity, ice ages, and the shifting poles. I study the resiliency of rocks, their cracks, and fault lines. I foresee and initiate earthquakes with my mind. Vegetation, rivers, water tables, and deserts—these too I oversee. I am a craftsman, and my work encompasses both the depths and the surface of this planet.

Orudu is nearly seven feet tall and of massive build. Red colors radiate about him like lakes of fire alongside a lava flow. He has a very strong forehead and a square chin. His back contains incredible power. There is a sea of fire within his strength. There is a terrible and fierce will present, a will that both destroys and creates.

When Orudu speaks, his voice echoes in loud and thunderous words. I imagine I could hear him easily twenty miles away. His very breath carries a force like magma under great pressure breaking free.

His eyes are a cross between a blowtorch and a welding torch. They are dazzling, and their power is a great reminder, as if you needed any, that this is a being from another realm—looking into his eyes is like looking into the mind and heart of a volcano.

It is easy enough to imagine that if you ran into Orudu in a dream or vision, you might be afraid. You might feel you were facing the mouth of chaos opening to reveal an abyss of flames. But there is no need for us to overreact or to be melodramatic. Orudu renders a service to the earth. He is one of her assistants. He is responsible for a small part of the biosphere.

CONCLUSION

When I watch the weather report and see the satellite radar and computer-generated animation of weather systems, I think to myself that this is an approximation of the knowledge sylphs possess of the atmosphere. The images on TV show three-dimensional, real-time, accelerated movements of weather systems. They show images in color and infrared. Computer models look into the future with real ingenuity. Our knowledge of meteorology is invading the sylphs' fairy realm and the sylphs' knowledge of what moves the winds.

In a similar way, when it comes to salamanders, I watch numerous documentaries on volcanoes. Some of the scientists are not just seeking a better understanding of tectonic plate movement and volcanic activity with the intent of advancing knowledge and warning others about eruptions. There are a few scientists whose fascination with fire borders on obsession. They enter craters to gather samples of lava in tin cans while hot lava is splashing down on the ground around them. One volcanologist, before he was killed in an eruption, spoke of his plan one day to ride a metal canoe down a stream of molten lava. These men act like they are apprenticed to salamanders like Pyrhum or Tapheth.

In regard to gnomes, there is an overlap between our science and a gnome's approach to chemistry and physics. Clearly, it is our intent to know all there is to know about physical matter and its components. We know more than gnomes about the origins of the universe and the subatomic particles that originated with the big bang, although I am sure some gnomes can sense even these things.

I do not think gnomes are aware that a trillion neutrinos pass through their bodies in every second. We set up procedures for measuring these things. I do not think gnomes experiment with creating antimatter as do we. Renowned physicist, the late Stephen Hawking, for example, had a holographic picture of the universe inside his mind. He probed the insides of black holes and quasars with his imagination. His mental images resonate with the universe. Gnomes have no advantage over us when it comes to astrophysics.

Of the four elemental beings, we are perhaps weakest when it comes to undines. When you touch the body of an undine, you can sense all the oceans of the earth, the silent calmness of the ocean trench, and the thrilling trill of ice cracking inside a glacier at the North Pole. But this is not all. The undines' love is an introduction to divine omnipresence. Their love reveals the longings of our hearts and visions of how our deepest needs may be fulfilled. Though oceanography has become a major scientific endeavor, the study of the empathy and sensitivity that undines possess is still in its infancy. Undines barely have a presence in the literatures and mythologies of our world.

And yet the question remains, is the human race ready for a full disclosure of the magical wisdom possessed by elemental beings? This question is no longer irrelevant. The entire biosphere of the Earth is now within our power to study and to influence, to protect or to destroy. Our fate depends on the extent to which we take responsibility for our actions.

My stories are not an attempt to turn us away from the choices we must make. To survive, we must guard and manage the planet Earth not only with science and ecology, but with love as well. My purpose, therefore, is not only to create a new psychology of nature and to infuse ecology with a spiritual dimension. My goal is the responsibility that leads to the enlightenment of the world. To do this, body, soul, mind, and spirit must be in alignment.

If the beauty of the sky, oceans, mountains, and volcanoes can be reflected within our hearts, then we can understand any human being on earth. If we can taste the ecstasy of the four elements in nature, then we will seek to be of service to humanity. If we can find in ourselves the powers of creation that have shaped and that sustain life on our planet, then we will also create works of beauty, wonder, and art. Every society and age has the task of unfolding its own vision of the union of nature, human, and spirit. This book is my contribution.

APPENDIX C

Poems

A Mermaid's Secret Desire

A man met a mermaid one day
Within the sea where she does play
He says to her,
Share with me your secret desires
And your innermost dreams
For I am most keen
To explore the invisible and the unseen.
She replies,
If I assume the form of a woman
To become your lover
Renouncing all others
I would a human soul acquire.
But if our love is betrayed
I will cease and be no more than the foam on the waves.
And you will die like me
But the greater loss will be to humanity:
Were my soul a human being to embrace
There would be a dawning of a new age,
Peace would fill the earth
The broken heart would mend
And your race would retain

Youth and beauty into old age.
The man replies as he looks into her eyes,
I cannot say if you speak truth or lies
But this I know:
I fear what I cannot control;
Perhaps in another age
When men love beauty far more than me
These mysteries shall unfold.
Woe to humanity!
For these words were spoken
Ten thousand years ago.
And so we still await the day
When men are no longer afraid
To taste the beauty hidden in their lover's eyes,
Hidden from the beginning
When the stars first began to shine.

Double Changeling

The tale is told
How fairies from the Other Side
A child exchange, a trade is made
But I speak with ease
Of greater mysteries than these:
She addressed the undine queens
With words never before heard
Was not her love of water the same as theirs?
The lakes, the rivers, the streams, the seas—
One taste, one embrace?
Was not her love everywhere in every moment
Their own reflection, their own perfection?
Did she not know how to let go and flow:
There is no past or future
No wisdom or destiny

The sea shall encompass each with ecstasy.
Council was taken, all problems debated,
A decision rendered:
If she would step aside from mankind
All privileges and gifts of the undines
Would be granted
For as long as she wished to remain
Until that day the divine
Sets before her another way
And so for a thousand years
In a group of three she did play
Among the waves, as pure delight,
A song unlike any other
The sea did sing and dream at night
But now she returns
The divine intervenes
For what purpose am I called?
My peace disturbed?
What service am I to render to mankind
That the realms of bliss I must leave behind?
Child, human child, turn away
From the sea so wild, so free, so filled with beauty
Walk again among mankind
Think not that humans
Are selfish and greedy
Vulnerable and needy
Blind to the beauty that shines
In the sky, the earth, the trees, the seas,
Rather, imagine what they shall be
Once freed of all need
If they were but to taste the love you feel
They would be healed
As once before you did implore another realm to open its door

Persuade mankind with your receptive grace
Every moment boundless love does embrace
Return again, Oh human child
From the sacred and the wild
Walk again among humanity
For what purpose do you ask?
Fulfill this task:
Set them free.

For Jessamyn

I love your eyes
So quiet and peaceful—
A place to let go and forget who I am
Until I awaken to the sound
Of waves breaking on the shore
And the scent of the sea
I see the man I was meant to be
Walking toward me
Your eyes dream him into being.

●

POEMS BY THE MERMAN ERMOT

The Stream

The girl and the stream
Are the same dream
Letting go into the flow
To know love .
As water knows
It curls and turns
Swirls and yearns
Lying beside you
She dreams your dreams

Love Is Drama

In Act One
The suspense is intense
It begins in the inciting incident:
Something happens you did not expect
The ordinary is interrupted
The accepted is broken
Something is lost
Something is missing
The tension in the air is electric.
In Act Two,
Love has a hold on you
Whether you want it or not
Love declares,
I will find you
It does not matter your loss
Your despair, your fear
Or the obstacles far or near
This is the arch of the plot
The climax of the story is always the same
You must choose
To wager all
Or else you lose.
In Act Three,
What else could it be?
You are set free,
The lover is in your dreams
The Great Mystery, the epiphany,
The wonder of flesh, heartbeat, and breath,
In your heart you and another
Will never be separate.
My story is lightning in the dark
It is the unknown, the forgotten, and the "to be"

Captured, led captive,
Or set free as desire seeks
To satisfy its needs.
My story blends despair and rapture
Into one drink
It is the taste
Of hunger and delight mixed together
To remake your life.
My story is told again and again
In you and in everyone around you
It is life unfolding
It is the gate of joy
Opening and closing.

Further Reading

Bardon, Franz.* *Initiation into Hermetics.* Salt Lake City, UT: Merkur Publishing, 1999.

———. *The Key to the True Kabbalah.* Wuppertal, Germany: Dieter Ruggeberg, 1986.

———. *The Practice of Magical Evocation.* Wuppertal, Germany: Dieter Ruggeberg, 1984.

Mistele, William R. *The Four Elements.* Saint Neots, England: Falcon Books Publishing, 2019.

———. *The Hermetic Tree of Life: Elemental Magic and Spiritual Initiation.* Rochester, VT: Destiny Books, 2024.

———. *Mermaid Tales.* Saint Neots, England: Falcon Books Publishing, 2018.

———. *Mermaids, Sylphs, Gnomes, and Salamanders: Dialogues with the Kings and Queens of Nature.* Berkeley, CA: North Atlantic Books, 2012.

Waters, Frank. *Pumpkin Seed Point.* Chicago: Sage Books, 1969.

Yeats, W. B. *Fairy and Folk Tales of Ireland.* New York, New York: Touchstone Books, 1998.

---

*Bardon's books are readily available from online vendors as well as from the Merkur Publishing website.

INDEX